ML

G000098380

International Socialism 1

Spring 2009

Contributors

Kieran Allen is the author of *The Celtic Tiger?: The Myth of Social Partnership in Ireland*.

John Baxter is a regional academic at the Open University and co-author of the books *The Right Chemistry* and *Genetic Manipulation*.

Alex Callinicos is the author of *An Anti-capitalist Manifesto*, *The Resources of Critique* and a forthcoming work on *Imperialism and Global Political Economy*.

Eddie Cimorelli is an engineer and senior Unite union rep.

John Cooper is a postgraduate student and activist at King's College London.

Terry Eagleton is the author of *Literary Theory: An Introduction*, *After Theory* and *Trouble with Strangers: A Study of Ethics*.

Neil Faulkner is an archaeologist and author of *Rome: Empire of the Eagles*.

Iain Ferguson is a co-founder of the Social Work Action Network and author of *Reclaiming Social Work: Challenging Neoliberalism and Promoting Social Justice*.

Panos Garganas is the editor of the Greek newspaper *Workers Solidarity*.

Elaine Graham-Leigh is the author of *The Southern French Nobility and the Albigensian Crusade*.

Jane Hardy is Professor of Political Economy at the University of Hertfordshire and author of a forthcoming book on *Poland's New Capitalism*.

Penny Howard is a postgraduate student in anthropology at the University of Aberdeen.

Charlie Kimber is a leading member of the Socialist Workers Party.

Michael Lavalette is a socialist councillor in Preston and a co-founder of the Social Work Action Network.

Jonathan Maunder works at Bookmarks, the socialist bookshop, in London.

Ken Muller is a school teacher in north London.

John Newsinger is the author of a forthcoming book on the IWW, *The Flames of Discontent: The Wobblies and Class War America*.

Richard Seymour runs the Lenin's Tomb blog (http://leninology.blogspot.com) and is the author of *The Liberal Defence of Murder*.

Megan Trudell is currently researching Italy in the wake of the First World War.

Desperate debates over desperate measures

The United States is witnessing the "worst downturn in post-war history";[1] German engineering's foreign orders are down 50 percent on a year ago, Japanese Industrial production down 30.8 percent;[2] world trade has fallen 31 percent; 20 million Chinese workers have returned unemployed to their villages;[3] 392 million Africans living on less than $1 a day face a 20 percent cut in living standards.[4] The global economy "has fallen off the cliff", laments Warren Buffet, reputed to be the richest man in the US.[5]

The financial tremor of August 2007 has turned into an earthquake that has brought down the world's mightiest banks and now threatens some of its mightiest industrial corporations. We wrote a month before the tremor that "things will seem to be going very well until overnight it is discovered they are going badly. And, as they say, when the US gets a cold, the UK can easily catch influenza".[6] We were right, except that it is the US that has got influenza, of a particularly virulent variety, and Britain is in danger of getting double pneumonia.

There is complete confusion as to what do about the earthquake at its American epicentre. The Troubled Asset Relief Programme (Tarp), the mega bank bail-out of six months ago, failed to prevent CitiBank and Bank of

1: *Financial Times*, 28 February 2009.
2: *Financial Times*, 27 February 2009.
3: *Financial Times*, 9 March 2009.
4: Unesco's figures, cited in *Financial Times*, 11 March 2009.
5: Quoted in *Financial Times*, 10 March 2009.
6: Harman, 2007, p158.

America from coming close to collapse within weeks. Its successor, Tarp II, has been no more successful. One indication of the scale of the problem is the lack of effectiveness of rocketing federal spending, which has reached an unprecedented peacetime level of 27.7 percent of GDP (compared to revenues of just 15.4 percent).[7] During the New Deal of the 1930s the high point was 8 percent of GDP.

The situation is no better in other major parts of the system. Successive stimulus packages in Britain, Germany, France, Italy and Japan have not stopped the slide in their economies, while China, seen as the saviour of the world system only a year ago, has been hit by collapsing exports and the deflating of its own real estate bubble. It has undertaken "one of the world's largest fiscal stimulus packages (roughly double America's as a percentage of gross domestic product, taken at face value)".[8]

Thieves fall out

The desperation of those who would manage the system grows by the day. Back in September they believed that a turn to limited Keynesian measures would be enough to deal with the crisis. Now full nationalisation of the banking system to get credit moving again has moved from the fringes to the centre of debate. This is producing strange political alignments. In the US, "Lindsey Graham, the Republican senator, Alan Greenspan, the former chairman of the US Federal Reserve, and James Baker, Ronald Reagan's second Treasury Secretary, are in favour. Bernanke, current Fed chairman, and an administration of liberal Democrats are against".[9]

The issues are in part ideological. The Democrats do not want to be seen as in any way "anti-capitalist", while the Republicans run no such risk. But there is a more profound division over the perceived depth of the crisis. The prevalent view until recently was that there was a liquidity crisis in the banking system—that is, the banks have made misjudgments and lost lots of money but they would be able to survive if only they trusted each other sufficiently to start lending again. The problem, according to this view, is essentially a monetary one and can be solved by monetary solutions—first by lowering interest rates to near zero and then by "quantitative easing", the equivalent of "printing money" to hand over to the banks to lend.[10]

7: *Financial Times*, 28 February 2009.
8: *Financial Times*, 5 March 2009.
9: Martin Wolf, "To Nationalise Or Not To Nationalise Is The Question", *Financial Times*, 4 March 2009.
10: In Britian the most forceful argument for quantitative easing has come from left wing commentator Graham Turner, although he is critical of the way it is taking place.

The more pessimistic view is that the problem is not liquidity but "solvency": the banks have lost so much that were all the figures to come to light most would go out of business immediately. The far from radical *Financial Times* columnists John Kay and Martin Wolf (see Alex Callinicos's review of Wolf's recent book in this journal) have been edging towards this position—along with an important part of the US establishment. James Baker, who was in both Ronald Reagan and George Bush Senior's cabinets, argues:

> The US may be repeating Japan's mistake by viewing our current banking crisis as one of liquidity and not solvency. Most proposals advanced thus far assume that, once confidence in financial markets is restored, banks will recover. But if their assumption is wrong, we risk perpetuating US zombie banks and suffering a lost American decade.[11]

This viewpoint is put well in a recent book recommended by Wolf, *The Holy Grail of Macroeconomics* by the economist Richard Koo.[12] Koo argues that depressions like of that of the 1930s and of Japan in the 1990s differ from ordinary recessions because they arise after big firms have lost money but dare not admit it. As a result instead of investing they hoard money until they have restored their financial situation—which can take years—and managements try to keep the scale of their indebtedness secret right up to the moment they go bust. Citibank's claim that it made $19 billion in the first two months of this year, achieved through the simple expedient of excluding from its calculations write-downs of unrecoverable loans, suggests he is correct on this score.[13]

Koo wrote his book as the present crisis was just starting to unfold. But the implications are clear. If the crisis arose from the banks (and firms such as Ford, General Motors and General Electric that relied on finance for much of their profits in recent years) owing more than they could pay back, it will not be solved by central banks giving them more to lend.

The money being poured in by quantitative easing will simply disappear into a huge hole. While it does so, investment will dry up; more firms will cut production, sack workers and sometimes go out of business; the recession will deepen and the banks' balance sheets will deteriorate further. The only way to get out of the crisis would, according to this argument, be

---

11: *Financial Times*, 1 March 2009.
12: Koo, 2008. The title echoes Ben Bernanke's description of the explanation for the great slump of the 1930s as the "Holy Grail of economics".
13: *Financial Times*, 11 March 2009.

massive state intervention involving both the nationalisation of the banks and huge budget deficits as governments undertake the investment that private firms will not and give money, directly or indirectly, to consumers to spend.

Immediate political problems for those presiding over the system will flow from their economic troubles. Not all capitals suffer equally from the crisis. Those that suffer least object to the state intervening, and threatening to tax them for doing so, in order to help the capitals suffering most. So sections of the Republican establishment in the US may accept bank nationalisation and huge fiscal packages, but not the party's congressmen. And even those who are beginning to see nationalisation as the only way out are doing so reluctantly. Their great fear is that once the state has control of major chunks of the economy it will face pressures to run the economy in the interests of the mass of people.

States and tensions

There is an even more fundamental problem. For more than 30 years capitalist expansion and restructuring have taken place across national boundaries, even if this has not gone as far as some theorists of globalisation claim. But the states that must try to deal with the crisis are, by definition, geographically limited entities. They are trying to apply national remedies to multinational problems. Nationalisation is one such national solution, but it immediately raises the question of what happens to the foreign holdings of multinationals. Does the national state bail out foreigners or buy up their stakes? If it does so, it is opening itself and its national tax base to massively greater bills. If it does not, it might keep one part of a multinational enterprise going, while forcing the rest to sink—as seems possible with General Motors and its European subsidiaries Opel and Vauxhall.

This goes back to another argument we have long made in this journal. The units of capital worldwide have reached such a size and become so interconnected that the old capitalist solutions to crisis cannot fully work. Letting some firms go bust so that "creating destruction" gives new life to the survivors risks opening up a black hole as healthy firms are pulled down by the unhealthy ones—as happened when the bankruptcy of Lehman Brothers on 15 September 2008 tore holes in the balance sheets of banks thousands of miles ways. But Keynesian remedies of state capitalist intervention are just as problematic. For instance, White House officials are "concerned that the US stimulus spending will leak out of the economy to support growth elsewhere".[14] In other words, the point is being reached where the giant

---

14: *Financial Times*, 4 March 2009.

corporations are not only too big to fail, but are also too big to save without disrupting the networks of trade and investment on which profit making increasingly depends. That leaves governments and capitalists alike wandering around in the dark as they try one scheme after another in the hope that somehow they will stumble upon economic revival. Some commentators even dread that revival, were it to come quickly, would merely take the form of another bubble and then another horrific crash.[15]

These problems are bound to increase tensions between states. It is not just a question of capitals trying to exploit domestic stimulus programmes through "buy American" (or French, or British, etc) clauses. It is built into the fact that national states are the agencies for attempting to limit the impact of the crisis. This is the key to explaining the sudden flare ups between governments over alleged protectionism. The fine words of national political leaders calling for common solutions to the crisis do not translate into a single coherent project for dealing with the problems of the world economy as a whole. That has already been shown by the polemics between Chinese and American officials, by the wrangling of the different states that make up the EU, and by US complaints that European stimulus packages are too miserly. It will almost certainly be shown by the outcome of the G20 meeting in London, set to take place while this journal was being printed, whatever is said in its official statements.

The weaker states

The problems with the Keynesian attempts to deal with the crisis are bad enough for the big economies. They are devastating for the smaller ones. Within the Eurozone those most affected are the group sometimes referred to as the PIGS—Portugal, Ireland, Italy, Greece and Spain. Doubts about their capacity to afford stimulus packages are raising the level of interest to be paid on state debt, and producing speculation that they will break with the euro so they can devalue their currency to make their exports more competitive.

Even worse hit are the former Communist states of Eastern Europe. Their economies were boosted in the first half of the current decade by euro loans for mortgages to a total value of $1,500 billion—and now the fall in the value of local currencies means people cannot afford to repay these debts. Commentators are comparing the crisis they face to that of the East Asian tigers in 1997-8 and Argentina in 2001-2.[16]

15: Stephen Roach, one of the handful of mainstream commentators to foresee the present crisis, warns of this in a column in the *Financial Times*, 10 March 2009.

16: *Financial Times*, 18 February 2009.

The terms attached to loans offered to Eastern Europe by the IMF and the EU do not make provision for any stimulus at all but are just like the deflationary packages imposed on Latin America in the 1980s and East Asia in the late 1990s. Just 20 years ago the people of Eastern Europe were told they could find a way out of the terminal crisis of the old Soviet bloc through military integration with the US and economic integration with the EU. Now the hollowness of such promises is laid bare as they are left to sink or swim in the new crisis.

But there are worries even closer to the centre of Europe. "American officials worry that many European countries, such as Switzerland and the Netherlands, are host to banks that have assets larger than their home country gross domestic product. Iceland, in other words, may only be the thin end".[17] Meanwhile in Britain "something close to desperation is starting to develop inside government", according to one well-placed commentator. "After watching the slide in bank shares, one cabinet minister did not altogether joke when he said, 'The banks are fucked, we're fucked, the country's fucked'."[18]

The politics of bitterness

The result of the economic crisis everywhere is bitterness mixed with fear. The bitterness is palpable in demonstrations in Greece, the Baltic states and Ireland, in the one-day strikes in France and in the media interviews with those suddenly sent back to the countryside in China. It has already brought down the government in Iceland and is shaking the one in Ireland (see Kieran Allen's article in this issue).

Governmental circles elsewhere dread that what is happening can open up the way for political forces outside the comfortable consensus of establishment politics. The Chinese government is frightened that the mass sackings of workers in its export industries can lead to unrest. In Russia one government adviser is "warning of a 'remake' of the street protests that helped to bring down the Soviet Union" 20 years ago.[19] In Britain, Howard Davies, now director of the London School of Economics, but previously head of the employers' organisation the CBI and of the Financial Services Authority, writes, "Our politics, for now, is being played out in an ideological vacuum. That could be dangerous: it is an invitation to the far left and right to peddle their beguiling certainties".[20]

17: *Financial Times*, 4 March 2009.
18: "Labour Stakes Its Reputation On Second Gamble", *Guardian*, 19 January 2009.
19: *Irish Times*, 10 March 2009.
20: *Financial Times*, 4 March 2009.

Who fills the vacuum will not be determined by the course of the crisis alone. There is a vivid contrast in Europe between the role of the left in channelling discontent in, say, Greece (see our interview with Panos Garganas) and the way the right have had a clear field in Hungary[21] and are making the running in Italy (see Megan Trudell's article). Traditions from past struggles play a role but so too does the presence of a left able and willing to take a lead in directing the bitterness.

Britain's vacuum on the left

The record of most of the British left since the collapse of Lehman Brothers is very poor indeed. As we wrote in our previous issue, left leaning commentators, such as Polly Toynbee, Seamus Milne or Ken Livingstone, and the leaders of the big manual unions all told people to rely on Gordon Brown. At Labour's conference in September Derek Simpson, joint general secretary of the biggest union, Unite, described Brown's speech as "a welcome warm up after 30 years of inaction and neoliberal economics".

For a few weeks it did seem that, even if Brown had no solution to the crisis, he could fill the ideological vacuum by appearing to have one. That was until the onslaught of redundancies and closures began. When Woolworths shut, closing hundreds of stores and destroying 30,000 jobs, the unions and established left had nothing to say to those suffering as a result. In the following weeks a third of manufacturing firms made redundancies, nearly a quarter introduced short-time working and a 7 percent cut in wages[22]—and the main union leaders did nothing but beg the government to provide handouts to the employers, while negotiating pay cuts and lamenting that they were not consulted enough before the sackings.

Discontent abhors a vacuum. There was always the danger that without a lead from the left it would be filled by the right. A *Socialist Worker* pamphlet published in October warned:

> Supporters of the existing system believe they can survive any crisis through a mixture of lies, minuscule bribes and threats. The lies will be that someone other than capitalism is responsible for the loss of jobs—the worker in a Chinese sweatshop, the Polish plumber, and the refugees from a war instigated by the US.[23]

21: Tamás, 2009.
22: *Financial Times*, 9 March 2009.
23: Harman, 2008.

Sometimes one wishes one's prophesies were wrong. We certainly did as we watched videos of construction workers marching through the streets of Staythorpe, Nottinghamshire, chanting "Foreigners out" as part of a series of strikes around the slogan "British jobs for British workers".[24]

A minority of British workers have always digested wholesale the racist and nationalist ideas pumped out by the gutter press—a third have historically voted Tory. What we saw at Staythorpe and elsewhere was this minority providing an ideological lead to many others who wanted to express their discontent, something which the Nazi British National Party (BNP) were hoping to take advantage of in June's European elections.

But in this case the nationalist xenophobia did not originate on the right. It was Gordon Brown who raised the slogan "British jobs for British workers" at the TUC two years ago—with the only dissenting voice that of Mark Serwotka, leader of the PCS civil service union. A key role in carrying the slogan into construction was played by the same Derek Simpson who praised Brown in September, assisted by another Unite official, Charlie Whelan, who happens to be Brown's former press secretary. Simpson went so far as to pose with a Union Jack and a poster that read "British jobs for British workers" between two models from the *Daily Star* newspaper—a publication that runs articles attacking immigrants and asylum seekers day after day.

Sections of the left seemed incapable of distinguishing between workers' legitimate bitterness at what the crisis is doing to them and the reactionary direction in which they were being led. Seamus Milne quoted approvingly Simpson's view of what was happening: "In reality, as Derek Simpson...said, the campaign of strikes 'is not about race or immigration, it's about class'... The strikers haven't scapegoated the non-union Italian, Portuguese, Spanish and Polish workers".[25]

Supposedly further to the left, the Socialist Party was enthusiastic about what was happening, boasting of its role in the first strike at the Lindsey oil refinery, denouncing those supposedly "taken in by the headlines in the capitalist press which highlighted the 'British jobs for British workers' element in the struggle", and urging support for the Staythorpe protest.[26]

It is true that the workers who took part in the strike and protests had reason to be bitter. The big construction firms have for decades used contractors and subcontractors to try to divide the workforce. It is also true that the solidity of the workers' action pointed to the possibility of a class

24: The video in available on the Lenin's Tomb blog, http://leninology.blogspot.com
25: *Guardian*, 5 February 2009.
26: *The Socialist*, 11 February 2009.

response to the crisis. But that does not make what actually happened into such a response. The slogan of the strike was not against subcontracting in general or for jobs for all workers wherever they were born. It *was* "British jobs for British workers". It did easily transmute into "Foreigners out". It *has* given a boost to the BNP. They *have* seized on the slogan to advance their own position in a number of council by-elections and hoped to gain from it in European elections in June.

Fortunately, there are many thousands of militant trade unionists with better instincts than Seamus Milne or the Socialist Party, who see the need for a struggle with the potential to unite all workers. This is shown by the 1,800 trade unionist activists, ranging from ordinary shop stewards to union executive members and even general secretaries, who signed the statement denouncing the "British jobs" slogan.

The problem remains, however, of filling the industrial and political vacuum. Faced with an avalanche of redundancies it is no good waiting to act since once redundancy takes effect the collective spirit built by years of trade union struggle can be very quickly dissipated as workers find themselves queuing at the job centres. The example to follow, as Charlie Kimber argues in this journal, is that of the Waterford Glass workers in Ireland, who rushed to occupy their factory the moment they heard it was going to close. The urgent need in Britain is to pull together the networks of militants prepared to take such initiatives in each locality around a politics that is socialist and internationalist.

Anger over Gaza

The wave of protests against Israel's onslaught on Gaza in January made the creation of such networks at least a little easier. They had fourfold significance. First, they showed how much Israel's actions have shifted the popular perception of the state. Acceptance of attempts to justify its actions in terms of self-defence has waned and so has the liberal assumption that the Israelis and Palestinians are equally to blame. Even the mainstream media are having difficult maintaining their crude equation of anti-Zionism with anti-Semitism. The new Israeli government's dependence for its parliamentary majority on a party led by a Russian immigrant who wants to drive all Arabs out of the state will add to such difficulties.

Second, in Britain at least, the large numbers of workers and students involved in the demonstrations, the 30 university occupations and the scores of public meetings showed the persistence of a strand of anti-imperialist consciousness created by the movement against the Iraq war. This feeling can explode onto the streets—as it did during the Israeli attack on

Lebanon two and half years ago—even if, in between explosions, demonstrations and meetings are relatively low key.

Third, large numbers of Muslims took to the streets for the first time in four years. This is welcome evidence of a decline in the intimidatory impact of the wave of Islamophobia and police repression—although, unfortunately, not of the wave itself. Fourth, the mood in the demonstrations and occupations was often not just anti-Zionist and anti-imperialist, but also anti-capitalist—reflecting the fact that the movement this time erupted with the global system in crisis and much of its ideological justification discredited.

All these points are important for the future. It is possible to take up old arguments about the character of the Israeli settler state, and its connections with imperialism's drive to control Middle Eastern oil, with much wider audiences than in the past. This is the key to breaking apart the Zionist argument that equates attacks on Israel with attacks on Jews generally. It is also the key for dealing with the view, encouraged by the Western media, that Palestine is a religious question. Unsurprisingly, this view can be widespread among young Muslims who have just become involved again in protests alongside non-Muslims. Challenging it means pointing out that the same US interests backing Israel, and the wars in Iraq and Afghanistan, have in the past sponsored death squads in non-Muslim countries such as those of Latin America. It should be added that this argument will never be won by those on the left who have anti-Islamic prejudices of their own, over issues such as women wearing headscarves or veils.

The anti-capitalist element to the protests is incredibly important. It represents one way of drawing together forces that can begin to fill the vacuum on the left, just as the forces produced by the wave of student and anti-Vietnam war protests did in the late 1960s.

Finally, it must be stressed that the economic crisis and the replacement of George Bush by Barack Obama do not mean the "war on terror" has gone away. The Obama victory, as we pointed out in our previous issue, represents a coincidence of two completely different sets of forces. There are those who made up the rank and file of the election campaign and want some sort of deep seated change in society. But there is also a section of the US ruling class that sees the Bush years as disastrous for US capitalism. The two groups are by no means ideologically distinct. The term "liberalism" in the US covers both, harking back to the notion from the 1930s that policies for rescuing US capitalism can provide positive reforms for the mass of people.

This was not even true in the 1930s, as John Newsinger shows in this journal with his account of workers' struggles in 1934, and it is certainly not true today. On certain specifics there can be a degree of coincidence: tens of millions of workers want a state organised health service, and so do firms weighed down by the cost of heath insurance; Ford, General Motors and Chrysler want government aid and their workers want to keep their jobs; a big chunk of the political establishment want to put Iraq behind them, and the anti-war protesters want the troops home. But when it comes to implementing the policies a gulf opens. So one aim of health reform for US capitalism is to cut the cost of provision to those who already have coverage, and the schemes to rescue Detroit have involved the demand that the workers accept lower wages and reduced health provision for retirees.

The divide is shown most clearly in foreign policy. The Iraq withdrawal schedule leaves 135,000 troops in place until later this year and another 50,000 supposedly non-combat troops "to train the Iraqi security forces and conduct anti-terrorism missions" even after the end of next year. Meanwhile troops withdrawn from Iraq are to go to Afghanistan and military spending will continue to rise over the next year.

All wings of US capitalism, the liberal Democrats as much as the neocons, are agreed on one thing. They have to limit as much as possible the impact on US global standing of the retreat from Iraq. That means showing that the US still has the military might to lay down the parameters within which politics operates in the region from the Nile to the Indus, even if this now involves negotiations with Iran or with sections of the Taliban.

Just as the death of half a million Iraqis from sanctions was a "price worth paying" for the Democrat Madeleine Albright a decade ago, so the bombing of Afghan and Pakistani villages is a price worth paying for her successors in Obama's administration. They will exact an even higher, and even more gruesome, price if that does not achieve their goal. The focus of the "war on terror" may have changed but the war goes on. And so must the campaign against it.

References
Harman, Chris, 2007, "The Rate of Profit and the World Today", *International Socialism* 115 (summer 2007), www.isj.org.uk/?id=340
Harman, Chris, 2008, *Capitalism's New Crisis: What do Socialists Say?* (SWP).
Koo, Richard, 2008, *The Holy Grail of Macroeconomics: Lessons from Japan's Great Recession* (Wiley).
Tamás, G M, 2009, "Letter From Hungary", *Socialist Review*, March 2009, www.socialistreview.org.uk/article.php?articlenumber=10743

Greece after the explosion

Panos Garganas, editor of the Greek newspaper Workers Solidarity, *spoke to* International Socialism *about the latest developments in a country that has witnessed the emergence of powerful movements from below.*[1]

In December 2008 Greece was at the centre of media attention with the protests that followed the killing of a school student by the police. How has the situation developed since then?
The movement that exploded in December has died down. Exams have caused a lull in the student and school student mobilisations. Politically, the government survived the explosion in December but is in real trouble and has had to go soft in order to avoid new explosions.

What was the background to the December explosion?
The background was the government attempt to privatise education. This has been going on for the past two years and has met with fierce resistance with occupations in the colleges and schools.

The media were predicting in December that the government would fall or that there would be an election. Why did that not happen?
The Conservative government only won the election in 2007 with a majority of one. It has been a weak government from the start. When the explosion happened, with a dramatic night with riots in the centre of Athens, there were widespread reports that a cabinet meeting was discussing

---

1:    Previous interviews and articles on this subject are available in *International Socialism 119* (www.isj.org.uk/?id=453) and *International Socialism 112* (www.isj.org.uk/?id=244).

a state of emergency—which would have meant suspension of the constitution, arrests and so on. It backed off from this and instead decided on a different approach. This involved a reshuffle and putting forward the line that all the political forces in parliament must get together to deal with the economic crisis and the tensions from the riots. This change of tune is the real reason the government is still there.

The parliamentary opposition, Pasok (the equivalent of Labour in Britain), is calling for an election but at the same time is very open to working with the government to deal with the crisis.

So were Pasok able to act to cool down the movement?
Their influence among young people is limited. They could not do much about students occupying their faculties and even less about school children occupying the schools. What they could do was use the trade union bureaucracy to prevent workers coming out on the streets, and that has been a factor.

The worst example of this came in the middle of the explosion after the unions called a day of action for 10 December 2008 with a demonstration in the middle of Athens. The government made an appeal for the unions to call this off because of the riots and the bureaucrats responded. The demonstration did take place because the rank and file revolted, aided by the far left. But it was a key moment, with Pasok showing they have a lot of strength in the trade unions and they could use it to defuse the situation. There would normally be all sorts of struggles at this time of year but the union leaderships have been holding them back. However, they are under pressure from below all the time and already they have had to call a 24-hour strike for 2 April.

How can the union leaders do this? Does Pasok still have support in the working class?
It is the main force in the leadership of the unions, and when it comes to holding the movement back it gets support from a right wing inside the trade unions—together they control the TUC and the main union federations. To start a fightback you need a rank and file revolt.

Pasok are leading in opinion polls and so their leadership is arguing there is no need for to escalate the action because sooner or later elections will get rid of this government.

They have support, even though a succession of Pasok governments have carried through neoliberal attacks.
That is true, and the experience of so many years of Pasok governments

means that there is not much enthusiasm for them. They lead by 4 or 5 percent, which is very little considering the anger and the hatred that exist for this government.

You have two main parliamentary oppositions to the left of Pasok—the Communist Party and the left alliance Synaspismos—and then you have the far left. How have these different forces related to the movement?
The response of the parliamentary left has been disappointing. The Communist Party has had the attitude that it is adventurist to organise occupations and all-out strikes. They have a very conservative attitude and explain it by saying the balance of forces is not favourable to the workers' movement since the collapse of the Communist bloc, and so we should rebuild slowly and steadily without going for advanced forms of struggle. In reality they have been very much against the explosion. They were against students occupying their colleges. They even tried to physically block student assemblies taking place in some cases. And they split demonstrations and marched in the opposite direction to avoid clashes with the police.

In a climate where there is a lot of radicalisation to the left, the Communist Party is holding on to its position in opinion polls but it is not making any advances.

Synaspismos, which emerged from the Eurocommunist section of the Communist Party, had a vacillating attitude. They supported the explosion after the killing but they soon came under pressure from the government to denounce violence, and they were equivocal on this. And there is a lot of pressure on Synaspismos to come out in favour of a coalition government with Pasok. They have knocked that back, saying there is not enough ground for a common programme involving Pasok and Synaspismos, but even this position is not very clear. There is a social democratic right wing in Synaspismos which is saying the left must take a "responsible" attitude towards joining a progressive government.

Throughout 2008 Synaspismos was the rising force on the left and had reached something like 18 percent in opinion polls. Nowadays it is somewhere between 7 and 8 percent. That is the result of taking such a timid position during the explosion.

Last summer people said the Synaspismos leader, Alexis Tsipras, was seen very much as a sort of folk hero leading the protests. You say that has changed.
At that time there was a lot of talk saying that Synaspismos were going to overtake Pasok in opinion polls. They were riding a wave. But they were too cautious in exploiting this shift by coming out with clear left wing

policies and supporting the struggles. Instead they became more moderate because the leadership believed that was the way to get more votes. So, for example, the government tried to implement a new law that is privatising colleges by holding elections in the universities for new college authorities. The students opposed this, organising occupations, spoiling the elections and so on. There was an attack on this in the press and by right wing forces, claiming the students were irresponsible and against democracy. The leadership of Synaspismos vacillated. They could have come out in support of the students the way they had done earlier on. But this time round they were much more moderate, and that cost them support among young people.

The explosions mean that things have become polarised, so the parliamentary left have had to make a choice. Either they go along with the polarisation and step up the fight or they vacillate because the stakes are higher. That is where they have gone wrong in the last few months.

When we interviewed you last year you made some analogies between Synaspismos and Rifondazione Comunista in Italy.
Synaspismos do not talk much about Rifondazione these days. They used to be very close allies in the European Left Party, but today Synaspismos prefer to talk about Die Linke in Germany. They are ducking the debate over why the Italian experience went wrong. Their social democratic wing argues they should have a coalition with Pasok, similar to the coalition Rifondazione had with Romano Prodi in Italy. These people are quite outspoken. The left in Synaspismos does not want to follow the Italian example but is confused as to what to offer as an alternative.

Do Synaspismos have a mass membership base?
The Communist Party is stronger in terms of a mass base—it has more members and greater strength in the trade unions. It has a daily paper that sells something like 25,000 copies on Sundays, while the Synaspismos paper sells something like 5,000 copies.

Tell us something about the far left.
I should say a few things about the anarchists first. They have been quite active during the riots. They have had an attitude that is openly substitutionist. For example, they occupied colleges despite the students. There was one example where the anarchists were occupying the building and would not let the students have a general meeting to decide whether they would have an occupation.

Anarchist and autonomist ideas are quite widespread. This is understandable in view of how vacillating and negative the official left has been. They have also been built up by commentators from the mainstream press who explain the explosion in terms of what they call the "precariat" instead of the proletariat—young people with precarious jobs. That is the mainstream explanation for the riots. The idea that precariousness has to do with capitalism, with the working class fighting back, with the class struggle, these are issues that are very much contested. This is a debate that has to be had.

The far left acted as a force that tried to turn the explosion into an organised movement. It came out as the most successful section of the left. It supported the students and the school students occupying the colleges, and it supported the rank and file revolt on 10 December when the trade union leadership cancelled the march in the centre of Athens. It has also been prominent in the campaign to defend immigrant workers who are under attack. For instance, there is the case of a woman called Konstantina Kuneva, a cleaner trade unionist from Bulgaria who was attacked by thugs and has become a symbol of the fightback, not just by immigrant workers but by organised workers. Something like 100 trade union bodies are supporting this campaign, despite the Greek TUC doing nothing about it. There is now a new campaign from below demanding a legal ban on redundancies and nationalisation of the firms that violate it.

In the middle of the Greek explosion Israel invaded Gaza and there was massive anger. The far left was very active in the protests over Gaza, which shifted the whole attitude in the country to Israel. For the first time slogans such as "Embargo on Israel, not Gaza" had a mass resonance.

At the same time there has been a step forward in the unity of the far left. We were able to organise an initiative for the unity of the anti–capitalist left. The meeting to launch that initiative was the biggest meeting we have had since the 1970s—something like 3,000 people took part in Athens and big meetings are taking place all over Greece.

The eruption of the economic crisis has been a big factor in Britain in pulling the Labour Party back behind Gordon Brown and encouraging union leaders to call off strikes. How great is the impact of the economic crisis in Greece? And how important a factor is that in explaining the political shift that has taken place?
The Greek government was arguing up until Christmas that the crisis was an external shock, that the Greek economy was doing all right and that the Greek banks were not involved in toxic products. So, they argued, the Greek economy would continue to grow—3 percent was the official

forecast when they presented the budget last autumn. Since then they have been forced to admit that this was a completely false picture.

The latest forecast is that the Greek economy will grow by just 0.2 percent this year. That means 100,000 job losses. The Greek banks are heavily exposed to losses in Eastern Europe because they expanded there and into the Balkans. So the latest stage of the crisis is hitting Greek capitalism really hard. That is a factor affecting the attitude of the government. They are scared of the riots. They are scared of the anger that exists among youth and working people, and they are scared of the crisis. They have had to shift from pretending it was business as usual, and that it was necessary to go ahead with the counter-reforms, to the policy of appealing for consensus politics with the opposition to survive the crisis. In substance this means they want the unions to accept redundancies and cuts but they present this very differently from previously.

It is difficult to forecast what is going to happen in the coming few months. There are the European elections in June and there is a lot of speculation that the government will call a general election at the same time with the aim of reorganising Greek politics—probably through a grand coalition of the Tories and Pasok along the German model.

The financial papers now refer to the "PIGS" (Portugal, Ireland, Italy, Greece and Spain), the European Union countries that are going to be really devastated by the crisis. Is there a sense of that yet?

The Greek economy relies very much on tourism and everybody is saying this is collapsing, even though the tourist season has not started. Construction, which is another mainstay of the economy, has slumped. The third element is shipping—the Greek ship owners are a force on the world market—and that has slumped.

So the prospect is that the crisis will be hitting Greece much harder in the coming months. On top of that, the public debt is 100 percent of GDP and any new borrowing by the Greek government costs 3 percent more than borrowing by the German state. These are elements that are destabilising the situation along with the anger that exists. How far these things will go it is hard to say. But I don't think the December riots are the end of the story.

Ireland: the sick tiger
Kieran Allen

Ireland, once hailed as the success story of neoliberalism, is undergoing a traumatic economic crash. In its wake a political earthquake is brewing that could shape its politics for decades to come.

Formerly known as the "Celtic Tiger", the Irish economy grew by 7 percent a year until recently. The term was coined in 1995 by an economist working with Morgan Stanley, who compared Ireland with the more commonly known "Asian Tigers" of the time. Soon the country was hailed by neoliberals as a model for others to follow. Thomas Friedman, the right wing columnist of the *New York Times*, for example, recommended that "old Europe" change its ways and catch up with the "leapin' leprechaun". Here is a sample of his missionary fervour:

> The Germans and French may want to take a few tips from the Celtic Tiger. One of the first reforms Ireland instituted was to make it easier to fire people, without having to pay years of severance. Sounds brutal, I know. But the easier it is to fire people, the more willing companies are to hire people.[1]

In a similar vein, the right wing think tank the Cato Institute published an article on the Celtic Tiger to prove that its growth came after it fully embraced "economic freedom".[2]

1:   Thomas Friedman, "Follow The Leapin' Leprechaun", *New York Times*, 1 July 2005.
2:   Benjamin Powell, "Economic Freedom and Growth: The Case of the Celtic Tiger", *Cato Journal*, volume 22, number 3.

In fact the Irish economy contained two structural weaknesses which have now come back to haunt it.

First, while the early phase of the boom was fuelled by a spectacular inflow of US investment, this began to dry up. At one stage Ireland attracted 25 percent of US investment in the EU, despite having just 1 percent of the EU's population. In later years, however, US companies sought cheaper labour opportunities in Eastern Europe. The Irish state responded by encouraging a property bubble to prolong the boom. Social housing was cut back and a tight alliance emerged between the Fianna Fail party, big Irish builders and the banks to hype up the property market. The result was an extraordinary transformation of the economy. By 2006 construction accounted for 20 percent of gross national product. The numbers employed in the building industry rose to 14 percent of the workforce—about twice the number normally employed in this sector in other countries. A staggering €110 billion was lent to the builders by Irish banks as a mania of greed overtook the wealthy and they came to believe that they could walk on water.

Second, as part of their growing alliance with US capital, the Irish ruling class emphasised financial services. They assumed that by acting as a slightly shady "back office" for the City of London they could attract highly mobile finance to Dublin. In 2006 alone nearly €500 billion flowed into hedge funds based in the Irish Financial Services Centre. Some 70 percent of these funds were actually domiciled in the Cayman Islands, a notorious tax haven, and simply administered in Dublin. Companies such as Merrill Lynch located a major part of their operations in Dublin to benefit from its lax regime. The state encouraged multinational firms to engage in creative accountancy in order to benefit from taxes set at 12.5 percent. By 2005 the *New York Times* was describing Dublin as "the Wild West of European finance".

While the boom continued, the political elite were able to develop a peculiar form of social partnership with the union leaders. Wage increases were constrained by national deals but workers saw living standards rise through tax cuts. The union leaders claimed that in return for encouraging wage restraint they gained influence in the corridors of power. Yet none of this influence appeared to present any obstacle to the transformation of Ireland into one of the most unequal and neoliberal societies in Europe. Union density fell from 44 percent of the workforce in 1995 to 33 percent today.

The crash

Today the whole edifice has crumbled. This year the Irish economy will shrink by about 6 percent, the largest fall ever recorded. The collapse of the property bubble has had a spectacular effect on state finances, which drew a disproportionate share of revenue from this sector. A few months ago the Irish ruling class felt perfectly safe with the EU Growth and Stability Pact, which limited state borrowing to just 3 percent of GDP. Today they will have to borrow at least 10 percent of GDP just to keep the state functioning. They will also be charged comparatively high interest rates because they are increasingly labelled as an "at risk" country by ratings agencies.

To make matters worse, Ireland faces a banking crisis that is even worse than elsewhere. Six major Irish banks hold bad debts estimated at €40 billion. One of them, the Anglo-Irish Bank, is commonly known as a Fianna Fail bank because so many of its directors and borrowers were tied to the party. When it went into freefall, the government tried to bail it out at huge cost to the taxpayer but was forced to nationalise it. Despite injecting billions of taxpayers' money into the two largest banks, the Allied Irish Bank and Bank of Ireland, it is likely that they will also be nationalised in the coming months. The purpose of such nationalisation is, naturally, to offload the toxic debts of the rich onto the population at large. As a result, according to the government's own figures, the economy faces four more years of horrendous cuts, causing social suffering on a vast scale.

The crisis could not have come at a worse moment for Fianna Fail (FF). The party is one of the great peculiarities of European politics: it has a working class voting base even though it pursues policies that blatantly benefit its rich supporters. It developed its peculiar form of populism by translating the high ideals of Irish Republicanism into the small change of economic nationalism. It argues that if all classes in Ireland "pull together", the nation will advance economically and workers will benefit. This appeal was only successful because of the weakness of the Labour Party, which implicitly accepted the same economic nationalist framework. Yet to convince workers FF also needed some real evidence of economic success. The decade-long Celtic Tiger provided this and, for a period, helped to halt the long-term decline of a party that was linked to the Catholic church and "family values".

In May 2007 FF was returned to office on a promise of maintaining the Celtic Tiger. Despite dramatic revelations of corruption, the anxiety of workers about the possible end of the boom led them to vote FF in the hope that they were the only party that could prolong it. Symbolically, the face of FF in this now almost forgotten era was represented by Bertie Ahern, a political conman who mimicked Ronald Reagan in his ability to talk to the "plain people" of Ireland. The party took office for the third time in a row with the help of the Green Party, which had previously masqueraded as a left of centre party.

FF soon found that its spectacular victory was in fact a poisoned chalice. Ahern was driven from office by mounting revelations about the source of funds that financed his election campaign. He was replaced by Brian Cowen, a surly backroom operator of FF, who also had close connections to the business class. Within months of coming to office he managed to lose the vote on the Lisbon Treaty (the replacement for the rejected EU constitution), mainly because voters rejected the growing militarisation of Europe. Significantly, the referendum indicated a sharp polarisation of voting patterns on class lines that had rarely been seen before.

When the economic crash hit, the party was singularly ill equipped to impose the type of solutions that the ruling class wanted. In October 2008 it introduced an emergency budget to cut back on spending by attacking both the elderly and the young.

Over 70s in Ireland were originally granted free medical treatment as a result of an electoral manoeuvre by right wing politicians to secure their votes. But the FF-Green government launched an attack on the very idea of "universal benefits" and insisted on means-testing for medical care. The result was one of the most spectacular protests ever seen. Starting with an assembly in a church, a social movement emerged that drew on networks created by Ireland's "active retirement" groups. Soon 20,000 people marched on the parliament, making full use of a free travel scheme— another "gift" of an opportunist right wing politician—to ride the trains to Dublin. Government ministers, who thought they would receive some deference from the elderly when they expressed their "understanding and sorrow", were booed off the stage. Within days the government was forced to retreat, making apologies for its "insensitivity".

The young faced savage cutbacks in school funding and this too provoked a wave of protest. In a series of huge mobilisations, teachers joined with parents on a number of larger marches. This time the government fared somewhat better because the teachers' union leaders did not show the same militancy as the over 70s. Nevertheless, the FF-Green government was forced to make some concessions.

Even while these battles were being fought at the end of 2008, the ruling class regrouped. The commentariat of the right wing media lambasted the government for its weakness and a determined media campaign was mounted against "privileged" public sector workers. The instigators of this press campaign were the employers' organisation, IBEC, who set out to divide workers in the public sector, where union density is at 80 percent, from those in the private sector, where density has fallen to 20 percent. This had two main objectives: first, to deflect a rising public anger against the rich by scapegoating public sector workers; second, to re-establish a political agenda around a programme of wage cuts. If wage cuts could be imposed on public sector workers, the way was clear for reductions throughout the economy.

Soon the real agenda of the Irish ruling class emerged to full view. Backed up by a chorus of the same neoliberal economists, who did not utter a word of criticism of the low regulatory regime during the Celtic Tiger, their slogan became "Restore competitiveness". Irish wages, it was argued, had risen too far during the boom and, according to Cowen, living standards had to fall by at least 10 percent. Instead of launching a stimulus package to reflate the economy as other governments had done, wholesale deflation became the order of the day. Unemployment was to be allowed to soar so that the working class could be disciplined and forced to accept lower wage levels. Once headline wage cuts were imposed the aim was to reduce the minimum wage, attack social welfare benefits and impose water taxes on a population already overburdened by regressive indirect taxes.

The new agenda of wage cuts became evident when a "pension levy" was imposed on public sector workers. Most public sector workers employed since 1995 already pay a 6.6 percent contribution to their defined benefit pension. However, in order to impose an effective wage cut—while circumventing certain legal obstacles—the government imposed a further levy of between 4 percent and 9 percent on those same workers. Before doing so, however, they embroiled the union leaders in a discussion on "stabilising the state's finances" and then, at the very last moment, landed the proposal for a pension levy on them.

The response of the grassroots was one of huge anger. On 21 February over 120,000 people came out on the streets of Dublin and many took up the call raised by the left for a one-day national strike. The response from the union leaders was, however, ambiguous. Instead of telling the government that workers would not pay for a crisis that they had not caused, they talked about a fairer sharing of the pain. They hired a Swedish social democrat as a consultant to develop a ten point plan which demanded greater tax concessions from the rich but failed to demand the full withdrawal of the levy. Like old singers who could not learn new tunes, they imagined that the game of threatening action and then calling it off to enter partnership talks was still in play. They hoped that after the display of strength on 21 February the government would invite them back into a national consensus to solve the problem of the Irish economy.

However, in the face of a deepening crisis of Irish capitalism and growing pressure from the grassroots, the union leaders found they were no longer free agents. Within days of the huge march they announced a ballot for a national strike on 30 March.

The escalation in class struggle is already having dramatic political effects. Opinion polls have shown a huge swing to the left and a decline in FF support. For the first time in Irish history the party has been overtaken by its main right wing rival, Fine Gael, and, in one poll, by the Labour Party as well. The same poll indicated that in Dublin the party's support appears to have declined to a mere 13 percent.

The Labour Party has so far been the principal beneficiary of this turn. At the onset of the crisis the party tacked left and publicly denounced a state guarantee scheme for the banks. By contrast, Sinn Fein, in an untimely effort to gain respectability, voted for the guarantee. In one of those great moments of irony, the IRA's political wing had decided that bank robbery had to be replaced by state contributions to the financial elite. However, Labour's shift leftwards is deeply contradictory. Even while it attacks the bail-out of the bankers, the party holds to the idea of a national consensus to solve Ireland's economic woes. Its ultimate aim is to shore up its electoral base by tacking left and then to enter a coalition government with the right.

All of this creates extremely favourable terrain for the emergence of new forces on the radical left. One hopeful sign is the development of the People before Profit Alliance, a new coalition of forces that groups together the Socialist Workers Party, former key figures of the Socialist Party and a host of community activists. The alliance will be running about 15 candidates in upcoming local elections and hopes to gain a cohort of new councillors as part of a strategy to offer a more serious electoral challenge to Labour. The alliance has developed an alternative economic agenda to challenge the priorities of the political establishment and has become prominent in a variety of local campaigns that oppose the cuts.

It is also necessary to build a strong revolutionary socialist organisation alongside the radical left. During the 21 February demonstration off-duty soldiers from their union, PDFORA, took part in the huge demonstration, despite pressure from their officers. So did substantial numbers of police, who turned out a few days later to march against their government. As the crisis escalates it will become clearer that every attempt at serious change to ameliorate the suffering of workers will come up against the strict limits of Irish capitalism. The question of a practical revolutionary approach to solving the Irish and global crisis could soon emerge. We are in a race against time to prepare the ground.

Italy one year on

Megan Trudell

The year since Silvio Berlusconi's election victory over the Democratic Party (PD) in Italy has been one in which the right wing agenda of the ruling coalition has been made brutally clear. In the midst of severe economic crisis—officially Italy's fourth recession in a decade—Berlusconi's government has launched a series of assaults on workers, immigrants and students, has allowed the Vatican to dictate policy[1] and has abandoned parliamentary democracy by pushing through a series of "emergency" decrees.

Italy's recession is deepening, although up until recently the government's response had been to "generally act as if it didn't exist". Giulio Tremonti, the finance minister, said in January this year, "You'll see that we improve our position in this crisis, even if it's because other nations are going backwards faster"[2]—despite the fact that Italy's economy contracted more rapidly in the fourth quarter of 2008 than during any year since 1980, falling by 1.8 percent. Only in March did he grudgingly admit that the country faced "a difficult year".

1:   For example, in the recent case of Eluano Englaro, a young woman left in a persistent vegetative state for 17 years, the Vatican intervened to oppose a supreme court ruling allowing her father to find doctors who would end her life. Berlusconi rushed through yet another emergency decree ordering medical staff to restore feeding to Eluano Englaro, though she died before this could be done. The controversy caused open conflict between President Giorgio Napolitano, who upheld the supreme court decision, and the government.
2:   Gavin Jones, "Italy Is Hardly Noticing Crisis", *Reuters*, 18 February 2009.

That is likely to be a considerable understatement: economists envisage that Italy's crisis will hit in "reverse order", with a slump in production precipitating bank collapses.[3] Unemployment is beginning to rise and workers are feeling the impact of the crisis very sharply. Fiat, the country's largest private sector employer, has halted production at a number of plants, and 48,000 of its workers have been affected by temporary layoffs and short working so far this year. There have been losses at Indesit, Benetton and De Longhi. The total number of workers temporarily unemployed and receiving benefits ("*cassa integrazione*") rose five-fold in 2008. Workers in well unionised industries are eligible for such state benefits, but for the 4.5 million "precarious" workers such protection is not available if their contracts are not renewed.

In Turin, where 70,000 workers, pensioners and students marched in February this year in defence of contracts and for rights at work, one local union leader illustrated the depth of the problem: "Over 200,000 Piedmontese workers have been caught up in the crisis in the last few months—that is the same number of jobs that were lost in the ten years between 1980 and 1990".[4]

The Berlusconi government has meanwhile been focusing its fire on the poorest in Italian society. Its savage anti-immigrant policies include a "security package" imposed by emergency decree, which includes instructing medical staff and landlords to report suspected illegal immigrants. Berlusconi and, crucially, his partners in the Northern League and the "post-fascist" National Alliance have deliberately linked immigration with crime following several high profile rapes allegedly carried out by non-Italians. Responding to these, the government has decreed mandatory life sentences for the rape of minors or attacks in which the victim is killed. It has also set out to criminalise all immigrants, proposing the fingerprinting and documenting of all non-Italians. Most ominously, it has provided for street patrols to be conducted by unarmed and unpaid volunteer squads ("*ronde*"), including retired policemen and soldiers.

These measures are designed to terrorise Italy's immigrant population. In July 2008 a coalition of organisations working on rights for Roma people documented a vast number of human rights violations in Italy including extreme violence, harassment and maltreatment by police and officials as well as by right wing youth encouraged by the state's endorsement of racism. Since Berlusconi's election there has been a steady rise in racist attacks—an

---

3: *Financial Times*, 6 March 2009.
4: Quoted in "Marcia Lavoro A Torino: CGIL, 70.000 In Piazza", www.ansa.it, 28 February 2009.

atmosphere of violence that has been condoned and promoted by government ministers. In May 2008 Minister of the Interior Roberto Maroni of the Northern League stated, "All Roma camps will have to be dismantled right away, and the inhabitants will be either expelled or incarcerated." Two days later a Roma camp in Naples was burned down. Following the attack, Northern League leader Umberto Bossi said, "People do what the state can't manage." Maroni has also been quoted as saying, "That is what happens when Gypsies steal babies, or when Romanians commit sexual violence". [5]

The election of Berlusconi's coalition, and the presence in its ranks of the Northern League and the National Alliance, has given confidence and cohesion to the extreme right and since the election attacks have taken place against immigrants from various countries. In October 2008 a 36 year old Chinese immigrant in Rome was badly beaten, in Parma a young Ghanaian student was assaulted by traffic police and in Milan a 19 year old from Burkina Faso was beaten to death by owners of a bar who suspected him of stealing a packet of biscuits. In February this year unemployed Indian labourer Navtej Singh Sidhu was doused with petrol and paint and set alight as he slept rough in Nettuno, south of Rome.

Fascist groups have instigated and whipped up such attacks. One such group, Forza Nuova, covered Rome in posters showing a woman in a white bloodstained dress with the slogan "Stop immigration". The attacks have not been restricted to foreigners. In May Italian Nicola Tommasoli was beaten and killed by fascists who accused him of "communism" in the city of Verona, which has a Northern League mayor; in November a homeless Italian man was beaten and set alight while sleeping on a park bench in Padua in the Veneto region.

The dominance of the right in Italy at present is a very serious development and one which poses difficult challenges for a fragmented and demoralised left. Rather than despair at the current situation, however, it is important to understand how Italy arrived here. The right has not ascended on the strength of its own attractions. Since the "Clean Hands" campaign in the early 1990s, which aimed at ending political corruption and led to the collapse of the Christian Democratic and Socialist parties that dominated the post-war period, successive "centre-left" administrations under Romano Prodi and Massimo D'Alema have failed to provide an alternative to the misery inflicted on the Italian working class by decades of political corruption.

5: "Security a la Italiana: Fingerprinting, Extreme Violence and Harassment of Roma in Italy", report by the Open Society Institute, ERRC, COHRE, Romani Crisis and the Roma Civic Alliance in Romania, July 2008, www.errc.org/db/03/4D/m0000034D.pdf

Berlusconi has been greatly assisted by the supine nature of his opposition. Not only did the Olive Tree Alliance in the 1990s fail to curtail Berlusconi's escalating empire or to press the many charges against him, but they created a culture of "indulgence and pardon" towards him.[6] Such a culture continued under Prodi's recent Unione government and lives on in the PD, whose previous leader, Walter Veltroni, tried to strike a deal with Berlusconi after losing the election and who, in opposition, has been outspoken against the government's racist legislation but has done nothing to organise resistance to the right's policies. The weakness of the centre politicians on immigration has been disastrous—the first raids on Roma camps and deportations were carried out in Rome under the Prodi government after the wife of a naval captain was allegedly raped and murdered by a Romanian in 2007.

The Clean Hands period also coincided with the onset of economic stagnation. For many ordinary Italians Prodi and the centre are detested for taking Italy into the euro—driving up the cost of living and housing—and presiding over the slowest growth in the EU while the political class has enriched itself in ways that bear a striking similarity to the era before the "clean up". Italian parliamentary deputies and senators are, for example, the highest paid in Western Europe, while average Italian salaries are among the lowest.[7]

Berlusconi is therefore making the running in the absence of any genuine parliamentary opposition. The PD offers no serious alternative: its new leader, Dario Franceschini, stated that the *cassa integrazione* should be extended to precarious workers, but the party does nothing to oppose government threats to curtail the right to strike or to back the main CGL union's protests which are trying to build—alongside the metal workers' Fiom union—a united defence of workers.

The left also, tragically, bears some responsibility for the current situation. In joining the Prodi government, Rifondazione trampled on the principles and spirit of the movement that it had been an important part of. Many of the party's activists remain engaged in the student and anti-racist campaigns, but Rifondazione as an organisation is currently preoccupied by internal disputes to such an extent that it is not offering the kind of responsive

---

6: Ginsborg, 2001, p315.

7: The basic salary of an Italian deputy is €11,703 a month. By comparison, British MPs earn €7,450, German MPs €7,009 and French assembly members €6,953. The best selling books La Casta and La Deriva by two journalists on Corriere della Sera, Sergio Rizzo and Gian Antonio Stella, which detail the many privileges of Italy's politicians, have highlighted the extent of national and regional political corruption.

national leadership over the recession or racism that is needed. And it has lost respect and adherents as a result of its compromises.[8] The retreat of the party which won such significant respect and identification at the 2001 Genoa G8 protests and Florence European Social Forum in 2002 in a "Caporetto of the left", to use Perry Anderson's apt description,[9] has demoralised activists and the Italians who identified with Rifondazione.

However, it is not the case that there is no opposition at all. There has been resistance to the security package from magistrates, doctors (who have produced badges saying "We are not spies") and immigrants' rights groups. Restrictions at the immigrant holding camp at Lampedusa provoked a riot and protest marches on the island in January this year. Racist attacks in local areas have been met with anti-racist marches. Government plans to "reform" the education system, including raising tuition fees and cutting jobs in higher and primary education, were rolled back at the end of last year by a massive student movement—the "anomalous wave"—which brought together parents, students and teachers, and forced Berlusconi to postpone the education bill. Berlusconi's proposals to ban city centre demonstrations and outlaw strikes suggest that he is expecting opposition to come from the streets and the workplaces, and there have been national strikes in December and February as well as local protests against job cuts organised by the CGL and Fiom.

These movements have connected politically with the economic situation, with the student movement in particular raising the slogan "We won't pay for your crisis". The question is which political ideas will dominate. Rifondazione's retreat has meant a degree of disillusionment with left parties as well as the—hopefully temporary—absence of a serious force that can generalise struggles and bring them together as national campaigns. In the vacuum, the prevalent ideas among activists are increasingly those of autonomism which often focus on individual action. In the Veneto region members of social centres have physically attacked the citizen squads, especially in Padua, where police have broken up fights between the *ronde* and the "*contra ronde*". A strategy of individual violence will do nothing to break the complex interconnections of racism with the ideology of protecting

8:    One section of Rifondazione's right (confusingly called "Rifondazione of the Left") around Nichi Vendola, who lost the leadership election to Paolo Ferrero, will stand in the European elections alongside the Greens and separately from the rest of the party. The expectation is that the rest of the right of Rifondazione, around former leader Fausto Bertinotti, is biding its time waiting for the PD to split, at which point a "progressive" Democrat wing under D'Alema may provide them with a home.

9:    Anderson, 2009. Caporetto was the site of an Italian defeat in the First World War.

Italian jobs and opposition to globalisation that characterises the propaganda of the Northern League.

It is, therefore, critical that the left refocuses on building strikes and protests to defend jobs and on forging a unified national strategy against racism. The crisis and the combative stance of the government make it likely that Italy will face serious social conflict in the near future. Berlusconi's agenda is clearly the crushing of the movements that brought him down in the past, and his side is more confident and organised than for some time. However, the situation is far from hopeless—it is, rather, cut through with contradictions that suggest numerous possible trajectories for the massive social anger that exists. For example, in regions where the Northern League does well electorally there are also significant movements opposed to a high speed train link and the extension of the US airfield at Vincenza. In Naples the burning of Roma camps took place alongside popular neighbourhood risings against plans to build incinerators and burn rubbish in working class areas that were referred to by the mayor of one town as "civil war".[10]

There is opposition to the government that can be built upon and shaped. The left, though damaged, is far from finished. The majority at Rifondazione's conference in 2008 backed the position that support for Prodi's government had demobilised the movement and hurt the left, insisting the key task for the party was its re-engagement with the movements and rejecting any future electoral collaboration with the centre. The European elections in June represent an opportunity to propose a political alternative to past compromises and to the present impotence of the PD. For example, Sinistra Critica, which broke from Rifondazione last year, are putting forward an anti-capitalist list under the slogan "Banks and bosses should pay for the crisis, not the workers". Such politics have the potential to gain influence in the current volatile climate if they are matched by consistent action against cuts and racism that involve the broad forces we have seen mobilised in Italy time and again over the past decade.

References

Anderson, Perry, 2009, "An Entire Order Converted into What it was Intended to End", *London Review of Books*, volume 31, number 4, www.lrb.co.uk/v31/n04/ande01_.html

Ginsborg, Paul, 2001, *Italy and its Discontents* (Allen Lane).

10: Phil Rushton, "Class Struggle May Be The Shape Of Things To Come In Italy", *Socialist Worker*, 31 May 2008.

In the balance: the class struggle in Britain

Charlie Kimber

"We found out on TV in late November that we were going to close. We just carried on as normal, and it wasn't until we actually came out and we were all upset when we signed our last bits of paper that we thought, 'Well, why did we go quietly?' Why did 30,000 of us go quietly?"
Jayne Maltman, Woolworths worker, February 2009.[1]

Everybody interested in the potential for workers' resistance to the crisis should view two videos shot by BMW workers at a recent mass meeting at the Mini plant at Cowley, Oxford.[2] Management announced that 850 people were sacked with immediate effect. Some had been there for four or five years, but there was no redundancy pay because they were agency workers. In one video a management representative reads from a prepared statement which is full of the double-speak management love. At first workers listen in silence as the manager tells them that their shift is to be abolished and their jobs with it. The language is so convoluted that it does not sink in for a while that they are on the dole, without a penny. Anger rises only as they are reminded to hand in their uniforms or face a £25 fine. In the second video the union rep faces the wrath of the workforce, who want to know why they have been treated like this and why the union is

---

1:   The *Guardian*, 6 February 2009.
2:   The videos are available on *Socialist Worker*'s website: www.socialistworker.co.uk/ art.php?id=17123 and www.socialistworker.co.uk/art.php?id=17134

so powerless. The union man does not criticise the decision to kill the jobs, only the failure to give three weeks notice. The workers' anger boils over. One takes the microphone and demands all the subscriptions back from the patently useless union. Others hurl fruit at the union rep.

As you watch, you may well end up shouting at the screen, "Why didn't somebody call for an occupation of the plant?" The fact that nobody instantly came up with a plan for resistance shows the need for greater workplace rank and file strength, a bigger left and stronger socialist organisation. Who knows what would have happened if the left had been big enough in the run-up to that Cowley meeting to circulate workers with the news that the Waterford Glass factory in Ireland had been occupied and that management were already making concessions. What if one or two well known and well respected Cowley workers were part of left networks that had prepared for just such a moment? What if their Unite union was leading resistance across Britain to every job cut?

All this underlines the importance of subjective factors and the question of leadership. There are times in history when the weight of the material situation is so great that it almost crushes the message for resistance. At other times the mood from below is so strong that even if there is almost no leadership a fight will burst out. We are in neither of those situations. We are at a moment when what individuals do can makes the difference between resistance and surrender. It is a time of alternatives, of volatility, when history is up for grabs.

Britain is not fundamentally different from France, Greece or Italy, countries which have seen mass strikes against the effect of the crisis and are likely to see more. In fact we have already seen the first signs of revolt. The Israeli assault on Gaza sparked a big protest movement in Britain. Large demonstrations took place not just in London but in a score of other cities and towns. It wasn't just that huge numbers protested; it was also their militancy and readiness to defy the authorities. This movement was focused on the brutal killing in Gaza, and the great powers' support for Israel and their connivance with the slaughter. But the revolt was all the greater because of the economic crisis and drew some of its impact from the fact that the world was falling apart. A "non-economic" event (the murder of a student by police) led to the recent strikes, riots and demonstrations in Greece. The Gaza protests showed a glimpse of the same character here.

Britain is certainly not different to Ireland where some 120,000 people marched in Dublin on 21 February to demand that workers should not pay for the crisis. Consider the sequence of events: 500 Waterford Glass workers refuse to accept closure and mass job losses and they occupy their factory. Their example electrifies others, and the unions are forced to call a protest over an increase in pension contributions for public sector workers. This demonstration becomes a focus for much wider anger and bitterness over the crisis. That's what happened in Ireland, and something like that can happen in Britain. But, as events in Britain and the rest of Europe have powerfully demonstrated, right wing forces and the fascists will also try to benefit from the anger and frustration generated by the crisis. When the dam bursts, the pent-up force can go in many directions.

The economic crisis is a process, not an event, and will be the dominant factor shaping politics for years to come. But will workers fight? The answer requires an examination of the balance of class forces. This is not an exercise in prediction; it is an attempt to sketch the general trends and the basis on which we can build towards effective resistance.

Workers' perception of the need for a fightback is fundamentally shaped by the material conditions they face. That is why the scale of the crisis and the attacks on living standards are so important. Crises never unfold smoothly. They proceed through sudden leaps like the collapse of Lehman Brothers in September 2008. Hundreds or thousands of jobs may go every week, but then comes a day that rams home the message of devastation, tearing up people's perceptions of life and shattering long held assumptions about the system. But ideological, political and organisational factors mediate between economic facts and the possibility of resistance. The history of victory and defeat, the quality of leadership among workers and the ruling class, the level of organisation, the political atmosphere in society generally, international factors, the impact of victory or defeat—these are just some of the factors that matter.

Leon Trotsky wrote of the impact of the crisis that broke out in 1921:

> The bourgeoisie will be compelled to exert stronger and stronger pressure upon the working class. This is already to be seen in the cutting of wages which has started in the full-blooded capitalist countries… This leads to great struggles over wages. Our task is to extend these struggles… We have no automatic guarantees of development… There is no automatic dependence of the proletarian revolutionary movement upon a crisis. There is only a dialectical interaction.[3]

He also insisted on the need to recognise the potential for a rise in struggle, even when it was only in its initial stages:

3: Trotsky, 1924.

You cannot deny a beginning of radicalisation because strikes have not yet embraced the main sections of the workers; what can and must be made is a concrete evaluation of the extent, depth and intensity of this radicalisation... Leaders who wish to begin only when everything is ready are not needed by the working class. One must be able to see the first, even though weak, symptoms of revival... The general nature of our epoch...has proved more than once...that, between the first symptoms of revival and the stormy upsurge that creates a revolutionary situation, not 40 years but perhaps only a fifth or a tenth of that are required.[4]

In Britain today there is a battle in the heart of every worker. On the one hand, fear leads to the feeling, "I can't afford to resist or protest or strike"; on the other hand, sudden hardship leads to the feeling, "I can't afford not to put up resistance." Which wins out is not preordained, and can't be read off from the retail price index or the unemployment figures.

An explosive mix

There are many historical examples showing how objective and subjective factors combine to influence the impact of crises on struggle. The New Unionism of the 1880s and 1890s was one such British example. It emerged from the interplay of several factors. There had been a squeeze on profits as US, French and German firms challenged the British capitalist class's economic predominance. The boom of the 1850s and 1860s had given way to a series of crises in the 1870s and 1880s. Capitalists responded by attacking not just the unorganised workers but the class as a whole, ripping up contracts that had given some protection to skilled workers. The philosophy of "partnership" with a paternalist boss was shattered. The conservative unions that had painstakingly grown in the previous three decades were hopelessly inadequate to defend workers. The way was cleared for a revolt of the unskilled, of migrant and women workers, and for the explosive growth of unions that represented the new energy of the movement. But it also required socialist leadership from activists such as Eleanor Marx and Tom Mann to make that potential into reality. There was an interaction of changes in the economy, changes in capitalist organisation and socialist political leadership.

The source of the revival was wholly unexpected: the Bryant & May match girls' strike of 1888, led by young women with an average age of 13, many of them immigrants from Ireland. Their success rolled on to the

---

4:   Trotsky, 1976, pp37-38.

great dock strike a year later, which virtually closed the Thames to river traffic for a month. That victory in turn inspired a wave of organising the unorganised, a growth of powerful general unions that welcomed women, unskilled and migrant workers—and which often declared the need for a fundamental change in society.

A similar process took place in the years of the Great Unrest (1910-14). Real wages fell from the turn of the century, while profits rose. But by itself this did not explain the stormy struggles such as the 1907 Belfast dock strike, the Cambrian Combine coal strike of 1910 and the rail and Liverpool dock strikes of 1911. As Michael Woodhouse puts it, "The change in consciousness of the working class that produced the 'labour unrest' of the pre-1914 period was a reaction not merely to the decline in real wages, but to deep going changes in the organisation of capitalism, and the capitalists' growing reliance on the state power".[5] The open alliance of big, centralised conglomerates with the police and the courts posed class questions with great sharpness. A battle over wages or jobs could rapidly become a much more generalised struggle. Also crucial was political disillusion with the Labour Party. As early as 1908 an engineers' union member wrote, "The most charitable thing that can be said about political action [ie the Labour Party] is that it is slow, so slow that it breaks men's hearts." All these factors raised the spirit of class unity and the willingness to fight.

The strikes of the early 1970s also showed a combination of economic and political factors. The long decline of British capitalism relative to its competitors was already reaching crisis point. The situation internationally was uncannily similar to today, with the US embroiled in a long, costly and unwinnable war (in Vietnam). And inflation was rising after a long period of relative stability. Edward Heath's Tory government was elected with the most right wing manifesto for 30 years and set out to break workers' organisation by a combination of rising unemployment, a centrally policed "wage norm", and anti-union laws. This fiercely political assault led to a series of militant strikes and workplace occupations: the mass movement around the sit-in at Upper Clyde Shipbuilders in 1971; the mining, docks and builders strikes of 1972; the miners' strike of 1974. More than three million days were "lost" in political protest strikes against the Industrial Relations Act, more than one million against the Industrial Relations Court and 1.5 million against the government's incomes policy. Militant trade unionism smashed the anti-union laws, freed the five Pentonville dockers who had been jailed for defying them and eventually forced Heath out of office.

5:    Woodhouse and Pearce, 1975, p10.

None of this would have happened without a politically crucial ingredient—the fact that some thousands of union activists were members or close supporters of the Communist Party or (a smaller number) the revolutionary left. Together these made up only a small minority of the union activists—perhaps 10,000 to 20,000 out of a total of 200,000 to 300,000. But their independence from the Labour Party meant they could push struggles beyond the limits laid down by the trade union leaders.

The three highpoints of struggle—the 1880s, the run-up to the First World War, and the 1970s—help us understand how economics and politics interact. They also show that revolutionaries need to fight to develop the present struggles much further. What then is the background to the situation today?

The level of class struggle

It is a commonplace to say that the late 1980s and early 1990s saw a dramatic fall in the number of officially recorded stoppages, with each year between registering the lowest number of stoppages since the Second World War. There had been an average of seven million officially recorded strike days per year in the 1970s and early 1980s—that is, 300 per 1,000 employees. By the latter half of the 1990s and early years of this century there were just half a million per annum—20 per 1,000 employees. The decline has been sharpest in the private sector (see table 1).

These facts are real and no serious study can ignore them. But there is also a danger of thinking that today will be the same as yesterday. Class relations are marked by sudden and unexpected turns. And there has been a gradual rise in struggle in recent years, with the number of strike days increasing from 157,000 in 2005 to 754,000 in 2006 and then to over one million in 2007. The last figure is well below the level of the 1970s but compares well with the annual average for the 1990s of only 219,000.

The rise in strikes from 2005 built on a (gradually) growing trend of industrial action in the public sector over the previous six years with one in seven of its workplaces experiencing industrial action in 2004 compared with one in 20 in 1998. The increase in strikes was partly in resistance to New Labour's attacks, as it attempted to impose wage limits, often below the level of inflation, and to implement public sector "reforms". But there was also an undoubted political element—the confidence gained by hundreds of thousands of trade unionists from the anti-capitalist mood after the Seattle revolt of November 1999 and from participation in the millions strong anti-war movement from 2001 onwards.

Table 1: Percentage of workplaces experiencing industrial action
Source: Dix, Forth and Sisson, 2008, p6.

	1980	1984	1990	1998	2004
Private manufacturing					
Strike action	19	9	4	0	⋆
Non-strike action	16	12	7	1	2
Either form of action	26	17	10	1	2
Private services					
Strike action	3	5	2	1	1
Non-strike action	3	3	2	⋆	2
Either form of action	6	7	3	1	2
Public sector					
Strike action	15	31	31	3	9
Non-strike action	19	24	8	2	7
Either form of action	26	38	34	5	14

Based on all establishments with 25 or more employees
⋆ indicates less than 0.5 percent but not zero

The question of organisation

Many people (including some of those on the left) still regard this rise in strike days as based on sand because there has been such a withering of union membership and structures.

Chris Harman pointed out in this journal last year that, "despite the decline, the proportion of workers in a union remains higher than it was just before two of the great upsurges of class struggle in the 20th century: the Great Unrest and the explosion of militancy in 1919-20".[6] For all their weakness, trade unions are still a major force, with eight million members and 6.5 million of those in TUC-affiliated unions. That does not mean there is any room for complacency. Union membership has still fallen from 49 percent to 31 percent of the workforce. The union leaders' failure to fight and the consequent lack of successful struggle does not encourage people to join unions, especially at a time of rising unemployment.

6:    Harman, 2008, p77.

The fall in the number of trade unionists is not because workers are streaming out of the unions. The percentage of workers who were once union members but are now not has remained roughly constant at 20 to 25 percent from 1983 to today. And many of them are, in any case, people who have moved from a unionised to a non-unionised workplace, especially with the decline by two thirds in manufacturing employment, rather than people who have ripped up their membership cards in despair. What has changed is the number of workers who have never been in a union. This rose from 28 percent to 48 percent between 1983 and 2001—and the rise is greatest among workers under 25, who are nearly one third less likely never to have been in unions than older workers.

Figure 1: Workers' relationship to trade unions
Source: Bryson and Gomez, 2003, p16

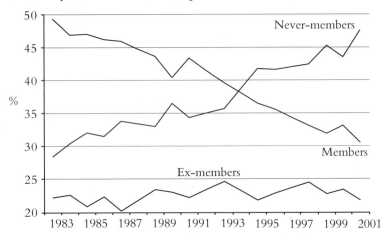

That is a problem and a challenge, but not an insurmountable one. It requires that the unions fight. Where this has happened it has greatly boosted union strength. One well documented example is the local government strike over pensions of 28 March 2006. The Unison union reported, "All regions benefited from the increased activity building up to and during the day of action. March saw the highest monthly recruitment on record." There was "massively increased activity on the Unison website, with more than half a million visitors... The membership form was downloaded 22,232 times in March—more than four times the monthly average... Glasgow City branch secretary David O'Connor was 'totally delighted' to be welcoming close to 1,000 new members to the branch".[7]

Each struggle sees workers stream into unions, giving the lie to the idea that workers join unions simply in order to receive advice or legal support. Some do sign up because they know that they might be facing a disciplinary hearing, but the main reasons are the same as ever: the desire for collective strength and basic representation over pay and conditions and management bullying. And the greatest spur to recruitment is struggle.

What about the level of active members, or workplace reps and shop stewards? Studies show that the number of shop stewards and other lay union representatives in British workplaces expanded considerably in the 1960s and 1970s.[8] One study arrived at an estimate of 175,000 stewards in the mid-1960s, with around two thirds of these in manufacturing plants and the remainder in service sector workplaces. Another arrived at a figure of at least 200,000 for the early 1970s and 300,000 for the end of that decade.

> The total number of stewards grew further in the first half of the 1980s to reach 335,000 stewards by 1984. There were important variations, with a decline of some 30 percentage points in the number of stewards in manufacturing being offset by considerable gains in private services and the public sector…non-manual stewards were nearly as common as manual shop stewards by this point in time.[9]

This expansion in the shop steward network was so great that it outstripped the rise in union membership, the ratio of stewards to union members falling from around 1:50 in the late 1960s to around 1:40 at the end of the 1970s and 1:25 by 1984.[10] The series of defeats suffered by the unions in set-piece battles—especially the miners' strike of 1984-5 and the Wapping dispute of 1986-7—resulted in a sharp decline in organisation at work with a fall in "the overall rate of union recognition, from 66 to 53 percent" by 1990 and in the number of stewards "by almost half" to 178,000.[11] The number of members per steward rose to 37 (although this was only a return to the level

---

7: "Recruitment—Record Success", Unison website, 23 May 2006, www.unison.org.uk/recruitment/pages_view.asp?did=3475
8: Charlwood and Forth 2008, p3.
9: Charlwood and Forth, 2008 pp6-7.
10: The stewards also had more time off for union duties, a process that was not without its problems. In the case of full-time union reps it created in many cases a layer removed from the rank and file.
11: Charlwood and Forth, 2008, p7.

of the 1970s) and full-time officials became correspondingly more influential, taking control further away from the shop floor.

But the workplace union rep has not disappeared. One estimate is that there were 128,000 in workplaces with more than 25 employees in 2004;[12] another suggests there were 160,000.[13] Such figures are fairly similar to those of the mid-1960s. And some 47 percent of all employees in workplaces of more than five people have at least one union rep onsite—77 percent in the public sector, 37 percent in the private sector.

Union representatives tend to be male (56 percent), relatively old (78 percent are 40)[14] and work full-time (92 percent). In addition, black people and ethnic minorities are under-represented. Just 4 percent are non-white.[15] But there have been some interesting changes over time. For example, the proportion of female representatives has increased quite sharply. In 1998 just 35 percent of union representatives were female; by 2004 it was 44 percent. Union representatives have held their position for an average of eight years. About 10 percent do their union work full time, with the rest spending an average of 6.3 hours a week on it,[16] a pretty extraordinary level of commitment from people who are generally unpaid for this work.

Some of the 160,000 union reps are highly bureaucratised. Some are tired and cynical. Some are more a block to struggle than an encouragement. But many are itching for our side to start fighting effectively. They are the sort of people who organised the strikes of recent years, who try to get their workmates to go to protests over Israel's assault on Gaza, who put out leaflets against the British National Party and who feel enthused when they read about the Waterford Glass occupation.

We desperately need a new layer of activists. But we should not think the spine of the working class movement has been broken.

The union leaders, politics, and the rank and file

The existence of unions and of large numbers of shop stewards is not in itself enough to guarantee struggle. And alongside them there is a real force that will always play a contradictory or negative role—the trade union bureaucracy.[17] In the last decade it, and its link with Labour, has been the greatest block to the emergence of struggle.

12: Charlwood and Forth, 2008, p6.
13: Department for Trade and Industry figures, using the WERS, 2004.
14: The Donovan Report of 1968 found a similar age profile.
15: WERS, 2004.
16: WERS, 2004.
17: For a summary of the correct attitude to take towards the bureaucracy, see Kimber, 2002.

In response to the present crisis, the union leaders have sought every means other than struggle. Typical was the attitude of Paul Kenny, general secretary of the GMB union. He told the *Financial Times*, "It is difficult for union officials to stand up in front of members and recommend that they should lose pay. It is much easier just to say 'No, no, no' to employers. But it must be an adult dialogue".[18] The article went on to say that the GMB had already persuaded workers to accept short-time working and cuts in earnings at Hawick Knitwear, JCB and Cosalt Holiday Homes.

This did not save jobs in the long term. After agreeing to the short-time working at Cosalt Holiday Homes the GMB was given 90 days notice of 280 job losses. The bosses pocketed the money from reduced wages and slashed jobs anyway. It was even more gross at JCB. In October JCB workers were blackmailed into a deal which saw a reduction in their hours from 39 to 34 a week in order to reduce production—and with pay cut by around £50 a week. The company, which had already laid off 379 workers in Britain during 2008, said that unless workers accepted their offer, more jobs would go before the end of the year. Keith Hodgkinson, the GMB organiser, said, "I am delighted that we have been able to save 350 jobs. The vote shows the social solidarity of trade union members in action." He spoke far too soon. No sooner had the workers accepted the pay cut than JCB announced that it was going to make job cuts anyway. True, it was not the threatened 350—it was 398. But the matter did not end there. In January 2009 JCB axed almost 700 more jobs. "We are very disappointed at this announcement. Our members have done everything possible, including sharing the misery, to try to avoid further job losses. We will be seeking talks with JCB to minimise the job cuts," said Joe Morgan, regional officer of the GMB union.

These GMB officials were faithfully reflecting the view from the top that struggle was virtually impossible and therefore the only way forward was to plead for the bosses to redistribute the pain between employed and unemployed workers. Instead of demanding that the government take over firms that would not guarantee jobs, the union leaders begged ministers to bail out the employers with billions more cash.

The pressures on bureaucrats affect the left as well as the right—as we have seen with the rise (and in some cases fall) of the new breed of general secretaries. In 1998 a relatively unknown train driver, Mick Rix, won the general secretary election in the train drivers' union Aslef. He was the first in a series of new left wing trade union leaders that became known as the "awkward squad". These included Bob Crow (of the rail and maritime workers' RMT),

---

18: *Financial Times*, 15 December 2008.

Mark Serwotka (civil service workers' PCS), Billy Hayes (postal and telecom workers' CWU), Andy Gilchrist (firefighters' FBU), Derek Simpson (manufacturing, print and finance workers' Amicus) and Tony Woodley (general workers' TGWU). To record the names is to cast doubt on whether many ever deserved to be dubbed "awkward".

In the previous big economic crisis of the mid-1970s the union leaders positively supported the Labour government's attacks on the working class under the cover of the social contract. A central role in this was played by Jack Jones of the TGWU and Hugh Scanlon of the engineering union, both of whom had been elected to their positions as left wingers. Now they were publicly in favour of the package of pay curbs and helped persuade workers to accept falling real wages, mass unemployment and cuts in social services.

None of this means revolutionaries should refuse to engage with union leaders and work with them where possible. The battle between left and right union leaders does matter. If Mark Serwotka were not the leader of the PCS it is absolutely certain that there would not have been the same level of strikes from the union over the past five years. If the right led the union, the ballots for action would never have been held. If more vacillating elements led the union, they would not have mobilised enough people to win the ballot. There can be disagreements with Mark Serwotka over important matters. But only a fool would think he is irrelevant.

The same can be true even when differences between candidates for union positions are less clear cut. For instance, if the choice in the Unite union (formed by the merger of the TGWU and Amicus) was between the two joint general secretaries, Tony Woodley and Derek Simpson, it would be right to back Woodley, for all his faults and despite the fact that he acts as a shield for Labour. He is associated in the minds of workers with a much more militant response to the crisis, has been much more critical of Labour, and has backed key strikes.

There are circumstances in which revolutionaries can and should challenge for national union positions. Having positions on the executives of unions can make a difference when it comes to winning support for resistance. This was shown on a number of occasions last year—for instance in the arguments for the joint teachers', lecturers' and civil servants' strike in late April, in the further education strike on 9 June, and in the resistance to the retreat from action over pay in autumn 2008 put up by Socialist Workers Party members in the teachers' and civil servants' unions, and the health section of Unite.

Revolutionaries have to learn to work with and against the bureaucracy. But the test in doing so is looking at its impact on organisation among rank and file workers. As Duncan Hallas wrote in 1977:

We are for unity in action with all those in the working class movement who are willing to fight, even when the agreement about objectives is only partial and temporary. This includes, of course, unity with whatever sections of the "official leaderships" can be induced to collaborate in particular actions... However, to cooperate with left wing union leaders—and indeed with right wing ones where possible—for particular ends is by no means the same as relying on them. Still less is it the same as believing that "progressive officials" can ever be a substitute for organised rank and file activity... We believe that active and effective rank and file movements are indispensable.[19]

The classic statement of what revolutionaries aim for was provided by the Glasgow Clyde Workers' Committee during a strike wave in 1915. The committee declared, "We will support the officials just so long as they rightly represent the workers, but will act independently immediately they misrepresent them. Being composed of delegates from every shop and untrammelled by obsolete rule or law, we claim to represent the true feelings of the workers. We can act immediately according to the merits of the case and the desire of the rank and file." Easy to say, not so easy to achieve.

Rank and file organisation is far weaker now than in the 1970s. Then networks of stewards had some capacity to organise activity independent of the officials, hold national conferences and coordinate solidarity. But the defeats of the 1980s and 1990s, the wave of closures in the most militant industries, the mass redundancies, the very low level of struggle, and the weakening of a socialist culture took a terrible toll on the militants in the factories and the offices. It is no good appealing to mythical rank and file networks that do not exist, but neither does the temporary weakening of the rank and file mean we should abandon the aim.

The alternative to rank and file organisation is some sort of "broad left", a grouping that brings together rank and file workers, reps, executive members and officials around a general left programme. Broad lefts can be useful, and certainly every socialist should take part in them at the moment. But, with the partial exception of education, they have hardly expanded beyond electoral machines that help to get people into various positions while doing very little to build activity and resistance. They can easily end up dominated by bureaucrats (or prospective bureaucrats) hostile to rank and file initiative. The Communication Workers Union (CWU) broad left is a classic case. It has been incredibly successful electorally in the telecom section of the union but has proved utterly useless in raising the level of

19: Hallas, 1977.

struggle and recently split—with half energetically supporting a deal that attacked British Telecom workers' pensions.

The interaction of all these factors is shown by some of the major industrial struggles of recent years.

The postal workers

Postal workers were among the best organised workers in Britain, with a reputation for militant and unofficial action throughout the 1990s. Wave after wave of unofficial strikes centring on offices such as Milton Keynes, Oxford, much of London, Liverpool, Cardiff and Edinburgh had defended good working conditions and union organisation. Networks of militants could, when necessary, bring much of Britain's post to a halt.

The importance of such networks was underlined in September 2003 after the union lost an official national pay ballot. The management declared that "the world had changed" and that henceforth they would be moving against the union and its militants. The union leaders were left reeling, but the rank and file weren't having it. Within days Oxford postal workers had walked out unofficially—and won. Then London had an official strike speedily followed by an unofficial dispute that spread to large parts of Essex and Kent, with scores of other offices then stopping when they were asked to deal with the mail of offices already on strike. Management had relied on divisions in the union. Now they found they were uniting the workforce in a militant fightback. Instead of the union being crushed by the loss of the pay ballot, it emerged unscathed and in some ways strengthened.

Recalling this success is not just about wallowing in past glories. It is to remind ourselves of the power of the rank and file and the opportunities the union movement has missed to build on gains (however partial and specific) and to revive the movement. The postal workers' victory is not ancient history: it was just six years ago. It came at the height of the anti-war movement, with the anger at Labour growing, with a renewal of confidence after a major local government strike in July 2002, and after left wingers had been elected to top positions in the RMT, Aslef, PCS, FBU, Natfhe, CWU, Amicus and other unions.

But the movement was not carried forward. *Socialist Worker* warned at the time, "The postal workers must build on the networks they have already achieved, strengthen their organisation and prepare for the next time".[20] Instead it was Royal Mail which made the moves, bombarding postal workers and their union with propaganda about the parlous state of

---

20: *Socialist Worker*, 8 November 2003.

the industry, the need for "modernisation", the threat of privatisation and the potential for new technology to reduce the number of ordinary postal workers. Local managers cracked down hard on strikes, removing reps' facility time and withholding overtime after unofficial strikes, and then even after official, entirely legal, strikes. The national union complained, but it did not organise sufficiently hard to reassert the CWU's rights, and such sanctions became the norm. Changes on the national executive resulted in several of those who had been sympathetic to the unofficial movement moving into top positions inside the union machine. At one level this made the bureaucracy more verbally open to rank and file concerns. But it also changed the focus from the organisation of the rank and file to the manoeuvres at head office. The unofficial strikes virtually disappeared, and with them went some of the networks of resistance. The organisation that had won in 2003 was not sufficiently rooted to deal with the new challenges by consistently organising both with and against the bureaucracy, and politically it was narrow, unable to renew itself through immersion in the anti-war movement or to recognise the danger of the union snuggling ever closer to Labour.

This was the background to the national dispute of 2007. In early June some 130,000 workers brushed aside the propaganda from their bosses and voted overwhelmingly for action against pay cuts and 21 changes to working conditions—77 percent voted yes on a 67 percent turnout, with the majority of workers at every Royal Mail branch in the country voting to strike. A series of one-day and sectional strikes eventually forced the bosses and the government to offer talks, but once the strikes were called off, the employers, backed by Gordon Brown, confronted workers with an even more vicious package designed to break the union in order to impose a total transformation of working conditions. There was a further series of official strikes and important unofficial action in parts of London, Scotland and (especially) Liverpool. But the weakness of the rank and file networks meant they were unable to overcome the hesitations of the official union leaders. The union's postal executive (after a major internal struggle) eventually recommended a new deal, pretending it was a victory or at least a "score draw", despite giving away crucial concessions on pensions, "flexibility" and jobs as well as pay. Management have used the agreement to ram through major changes in working conditions and embarked on a slash and burn programme of closures and job losses.

This was not because support for the strikes was half-hearted. Far from crumbling, the strikes became more solid as they proceeded. Scabbing was never significant, and the union leaders' greatest problem was holding back unofficial strikes rather than persuading members to go into battle. Over 5,000 workers joined the CWU and new reps emerged in offices, fresh layers of leadership that could have revived the union. Other trade unionists raised money, came to the picket lines and helped organise joint union meetings. So why didn't this end in victory?

The course of the dispute and the question of rank and file organisation cannot be understood without looking at the wider issues involved. Politics mattered. The postal workers needed allies, and with other unions, particularly the PCS, also in conflict with the government that was a possibility. But in the early days of the strikes most CWU leaders were either indifferent or hostile to the idea of arranging their strikes to coincide with action by other unions, with Labour loyalists such as CWU general secretary Billy Hayes fearful that they would be portrayed as launching a "political" strike. The argument inside the union gradually shifted as delegations from other unions arrived at picket lines and rallies with other unions made strikers begin to feel they were indeed the vanguard of a broader battle. By mid-July a majority of the CWU's postal executive were in favour of seeking serious talks with the PCS over a date for action. But at just that point the majority on the PCS executive drew back, feeling nothing could be done until after consultation with their members. This effectively ended the possibility of a joint strike. Political weakness produced defeat where victory had been possible.

The firefighters

The firefighters' dispute of 2002-3 demonstrated the potential to kickstart resistance to Labour's attacks on workers. But it also showed the lethal consequences of political weakness by the union leadership.

Firefighters' dissatisfaction over pay had been growing for years, and the FBU's "30k" pay campaign delivered one of the best ever strike votes in 2002 and brought the spirit of anti-capitalist protests to trade union demonstrations. The dispute was eventually to see 15 strikes.

As the campaign developed, firefighters' support groups sprang up across Britain, with big meetings attracting key local trade unionists. During the first 48-hour strike 400 drivers and other grades brought large parts of London Underground to a halt as they refused to work without adequate fire cover. The RMT and Aslef rail unions both mailed their members directly saying the union leaderships would back anyone who refused to work normally on a firefighters' strike day. The GMB, Amicus and Unison unions also told their members they were right to raise safety concerns.

The government was in disarray, and public support for the FBU was high during the second eight-day long strike, despite a government propaganda blitz. This was a political crisis for the government, just as it was preparing for war in Iraq and facing a rising movement that threatened to remove the then prime minister, Tony Blair.

But what should have been a strength was turned into a weakness by the FBU leaders. A key role in initiating the campaign had been played by the union's general secretary, Andy Gilchrist, elected in 2000 and hailed as part of the "awkward squad". But from the beginning he signalled the limits of the kind of campaign he was prepared to fight. He got the union conference to overturn a decision from the previous year to open up the union's political fund to back socialist candidates even if they were not in the Labour Party, arguing that the union's link with Labour would secure it influence with the government in the coming pay battle.

It became clear that the leadership had no strategy for winning the dispute beyond a token show of force which they hoped would enable them to cut a backroom deal with John Prescott and other supposedly "Old Labour" ministers. As they saw it, this strategy was being undermined by the very success of the strikes. Although the union leaders claimed to be against the war on Iraq, they used the existence of a minority inside the union who were unhappy about undermining "our boys" in Iraq to call off action again and again while they looked to talks and deals. A special conference rejected a first attempt at a compromise but there was no change in tactics, and FBU members eventually accepted a deal which offered a small pay rise, but opened the way to a wholesale attack on conditions.

The FBU leadership had killed the momentum of the dispute and thrown away the chance to combine the biggest political crisis for the government over the Iraq war with its biggest industrial challenge.[21]

Dick Duane, the acting brigade chair of Essex FBU, told *Socialist Worker*:

Firefighters feel sold out, not beaten. We had a nine to one vote for strike action and overwhelming public support. But when the government stepped in, in the form of John Prescott, everything changed. We made a good argument for some change within the system, but then we came up against a government the union leaders supported. Our union leaders used the war on Iraq to dent the confidence of the members. In the end, after so many

---

21: For analysis of the strike see "Why Didn't The Firefighters Get Victory", *Socialist Worker*, 21 June 2003, www.socialistworker.co.uk/art.php?id=3901

suspensions, firefighters just felt there was no leadership capable of winning the dispute in the way they wanted.[22]

There were activists who recognised the need for rank and file action, and they had some rudimentary organisation—the *Red Watch* paper and the "30K" website, for example. But these were too weak to defeat the executive.

Three TGWU/Unite strikes

The examples I have given so far are from the public sector. But the private sector has also seen important battles which demonstrate a willingness to strike and the power workers still have.

In July 2003 500 British Airways (BA) check-in workers, most of them women, walked out on an unofficial 24-hour strike and shut down operations at Heathrow. A worker told *Socialist Worker*:

> This was a rebellion of the rank and file. Hundreds of people walked off the job and stayed in their restrooms. When managers turned up to talk to them, they told them to fuck off. These are the people who spend all day in uniforms smiling at customers and hoping that they 'have a nice day'. They're the last people you would imagine to walk out unofficially and shout at the boss. The workers didn't wait for the unions' official backing. They just walked.[23]

The revolt happened when management introduced new regulations that would have wrecked the childcare arrangements that had been put together by many of the staff. Instead of waiting to go through all the official balloting procedures, the workers took advantage of the summer pressure period and hit BA immediately. That's why they won. The union officials had very little bearing on the dispute, and it was over almost before they knew it was happening.

But this excellent example was not built on in the wider movement. The result was a defeat two years later in another important Heathrow dispute, involving mainly Asian women, at Gate Gourmet, a company that provided in-flight meals to BA. Management had herded the 667 workers into a room and used a megaphone to demand they accept new (and much

---

22: "More Ideas For The Movement", *Socialist Worker*, 19 July 2003, www.socialistworker.co.uk/art.php?id=4025

23: "Spirit Of Defiance Shakes BA Bosses", *Socialist Worker*, 26 July 2003, www.socialistworker.co.uk/art.php?id=4090

worse) conditions. The workers refused and were dismissed. It was a gross assault, but typical of much that workers had endured in the 1990s. What followed was certainly not normal. Hundreds of Heathrow baggage handlers, check-in workers and bus drivers walked out on unofficial solidarity strike, severely disrupting BA's operations and closing most of Heathrow—one of the most important airport hubs internationally. Had the strike been maintained, BA would have forced Gate Gourmet to retreat, and the workers would have won. But, under threats of crippling legal action and damages of tens of millions of pounds, the TGWU union leaders, who had initially encouraged the walkout, reined in the action. The Gate Gourmet workers fought on heroically for months and became the toast of almost every union gathering, including the TUC conference. But without solidarity they were weak and the majority were eventually pressured into accepting a bad deal.

The Gate Gourmet bosses looked to the harshest anti-union laws in the Western world to ban "secondary action" in solidarity with the striking workers. The leaders of the largest trade unions wrote to the government minister Alan Johnson demanding that at least some of these laws be repealed: "It cannot be acceptable in modern day Britain that a ruthless employer can turn on the most vulnerable workers in this way with impunity. We sincerely hope that these workers will receive the backing of this Labour government and that you will do all in your power to ensure that the deficiencies in employment law are addressed so that this darkest episode is not repeated." His response? He was "not inclined", he told the *Financial Times*, to "make it easier for BA baggage handlers to walk out unballoted in industrial action that has nothing to do with their employer".

So defying the law in 2003 won at Heathrow. Half defying the law lost in 2005. Perhaps some of the lessons were learnt by the time of the strike by 650 Shell tanker drivers three years later. Striking workers picketed three oil depots in Scotland—at Grangemouth oil refinery, Aberdeen and Inverness—waving banners saying "Shell, Gallons of Greed" and "Shell Drivers over a Barrel". From the first hours of the strike, tanker drivers from BP and other companies refused to cross picket lines. When Scottish Fuels, a spin-off from BP, tried to discipline drivers for this, they walked out on strike, forcing it to back down.

The government was shocked and horrified by the speed with which many areas of the country ran out of fuel. It instructed the police to break up picket lines, prepared emergency powers to ration petrol and put the army on standby to drive fuel tankers. But ministers and oil executives calculated that such action would provoke even wider escalation by the drivers. And the government would lose. The Shell tanker drivers received a new offer which was three times the government's recommended level for settlements. This victory was achieved by the drivers' own determination and, crucially, the support of other drivers who had not been balloted and were not legally part of the dispute.

Karen Reissmann

The campaign in 2007-9 over the sacking of health worker Karen Reissmann was both indicative of a mood inside the working class and also highlighted a real problem we face—the victimisation of union activists. Sometimes (as in Karen's case) this is by the employer. Sometimes it is by the union or a combination of employer and union, as with Yunus Bakhsh, who has been fighting for over two years against both his sacking and his expulsion from Unison. Such attempted victimisations are to be expected at a time when the workers' movement is slowly recovering but has not yet found real power. Employers and some union bureaucrats seek to remove the individuals who best represent the growing feeling for revolt.

Karen had led a big campaign, including two strikes, against cuts and privatisation in the first half of 2007. She was suspended in June 2007 and then sacked in November by the local health trust after she spoke out against cuts and privatisation in an interview given to a Manchester-based social enterprise magazine. Nearly 700 health workers took part in a series of strikes in her support in August and September, and workers at the trust launched an indefinite strike in November. In some ways the wider solidarity movement was even more impressive. One of the strikers described a solidarity tour: "When you talk to people face to face you get an accurate picture of how strong our support is around Britain. While in London we were constantly at solidarity meetings—from minutes after we got off the train on Monday, until minutes before we were due to go back on Wednesday. And the whole time we were getting more invitations. In the end we couldn't fit everyone in. People were making comparisons between the issues that triggered our dispute and what happens in their own workplaces." One of the great strengths of the campaign was that it brought together workers, service users and a community; it stressed that what was at stake was not an individual's future, not even just a trade unionist's right to organise, but also the defence of the NHS and decent services for the mentally ill.

Unison was formally in support of the campaign, but very few national officials ever gave the impression that they were 100 percent committed to it, cutting off legal support for Karen after she refused to accept a trust offer to settle in advance of an employment tribunal hearing.

Karen was eventually forced to abandon her struggle after the chair of the tribunal made it clear he did not accept she had the right to speak out against what management had been doing. But her campaign played a role in raising the level of resistance nationally. The cuts which were supposed to flow from Karen's sacking were blocked because of the new layer of stewards recruited due to the fightback. And the chief executive who had sacked her departed—claiming unfair dismissal against the trust!

The public sector pay revolt

For more than three years, limiting public sector pay rises to around 2 percent, at a time when inflation has been far higher, has been a central plank in government economic policy. This has been combined with mass job cuts (especially in the civil service) and further privatisation. The resistance this provoked not only led to the gradual rise in the number of strike days, but also raised the possibility of a qualitative as well as quantitative rise in the level of struggle through the potential for united action by public sector unions. Mark Serwotka of the PCS union played an important role in pushing for this. The strength of feeling at the base of the unions was shown by the way almost every union leadership was verbally committed to some version or other of coordinated action by 2007, culminating in a motion going through the TUC.

The highpoint of the campaign was 24 April 2008, "Fightback Thursday", when around 400,000 civil service workers, teachers in the NUT and college lecturers in UCU struck together against pay curbs. The day was notable for its excitement and vibrancy.[24] The demonstration in London was full of young teachers, many of them women, who sang and chanted, and had the sense that they were standing up for themselves, the children they teach and public sector workers in general. Civil service workers, who had struck repeatedly but on their own in the previous two years, suddenly seemed to have powerful allies. The fact that the government was holding down workers' wages while shovelling billions to the bankers (Northern Rock was nationalised two months earlier) focused the sense of class bitterness. The strike, just a week before important local elections, was also a political blow to the government.

But in the aftermath there was a continuous political fight between those who wanted more strikes and protests, and those, with little faith in the union membership, who saw friendly talks with the government as the most fruitful course. The majority on the NUT executive decided against an

---

24: Some of which shines through even in the official news reports. See www.youtube.com/watch?v=I3t8GHCycj8

immediate ballot for further action. College lecturers in London did strike again on 9 June after a strenuous internal battle. But then a UCU conference voted very narrowly to recommend a new, slightly improved, offer.

However, the mood for action did not go away. Soaring inflation was cutting into workers' pay packets, with the privatised gas and electricity companies imposing massive price increases. Politically the Labour government's abolition of the lowest (10p) band of income tax was a symbol of how Brown was prepared to help the rich. There were also some small but very important strikes. Workers at the Grangemouth refinery won a battle over pensions after coming close to causing nationwide petrol shortages. Shell tanker drivers forced the employers to concede after defying the anti-union laws to picket out other drivers. Strikes by cleaners on the London Underground and distribution workers at Argos were successful. Against this background, Unison local government members in England, Wales and Northern Ireland voted narrowly for action (by 55 percent). The union leaders felt sufficient pressure to call action, and half a million local government workers struck in England and Wales on 16 and 17 July, and thousands in Scotland on 20 August and 24 September. And meanwhile the London bus workers were moving towards strikes across the capital.

The feeling was such that the TUC conference voted for coordinated action, a national demonstration and joint days of action—and would have voted for joint days of strike action had the Unite delegation not changed its vote at the last moment. Serwotka told delegates, "We have done a lot of talking about coordinating our industrial action. Now is the time to put those words into action." There was now a chance to recreate the events of 24 April on a much higher plane, through joint action of 1.5 million workers in teaching, the civil service, local government and elsewhere. But there had already been the first moves to squash that chance. Unison and Unite leaders sent the England and Wales dispute to arbitration.[25]

Then the economic crisis came crashing through the door with the collapse of Lehman Brothers on 15 September. Predictions of mass job losses suddenly seemed real. This required a political response from the unions—for them to pose the pay battles as important in themselves but also as the first shots of a wider resistance by the working class against the catastrophic effects of the crisis. Instead there was widespread confusion, with some influential activists arguing that workers would not fight during a recession or that pay was now "the wrong issue". Important union leaders

---

25: As I write the unions have announced the first formal arbitration hearings will take place on 10 February—nearly five months after the decision to stop the strikes!

encouraged these attitudes by saying Brown had ditched the New Labour agenda and would protect people from the crisis.

When the members of the NUT and PCS, nevertheless, voted narrowly for strike action in ballots, their union executives decided in November to abandon the pay fight, with only those members who were in the Socialist Workers Party resisting the retreat. One member of the NUT executive told the *Times Educational Supplement* that "people were 'in awe' of the current economic climate and did not believe it was the right time for strike action".[26] The pay revolt, in the sense of a united public sector campaign involving several unions across different sectors, was dead. Over 1.75 million public sector workers are now on multi-year deals which will be hard to reopen. This retreat did not "clear the decks" and make struggles over jobs or closures easier. It made them harder.

The history of the pay revolt underlines the fact that the question of whether or not to fight is not laid down in advance. Especially in a crisis, the question of political leadership becomes crucial. The union bureaucracies are very unlikely to provide it. Their social position, balancing between workers and bosses, leads them towards compromise and to hold back from confrontation. They can sometimes be pushed into struggle by pressure from below and by their own interests in maintaining some degree of workers' organisation. But even then they can never be relied on.

The bureaucratic strangling of the public sector pay revolt does not mean that pay will cease to be an issue. Everyone, including most union officials, parrots the line that inflation will soon be zero (or less). But in February 2009 the officially sanctioned rate of inflation was 3 percent, still steadily eroding the living standards of those millions who have received "rises" of 2 or 2.5 percent. And the real rate of inflation was far higher, with food prices still up by 10 percent or more and energy prices by 40 to 50 percent. At least some workers in some sectors will fight over pay, and that will be an especially important sign that workers will not pay for the crisis. But undeniably the union leaders (aided and abetted by the rest of the left apart from the Socialist Workers Party) did close off this phase of the public sector pay battle.

Rank and file organisation

The recent rise in struggle has given a lift to the organisation of the rank and file. But because they have been quite limited and short lived, the strikes have not produced a lasting rank and file movement. For example, the strikes

---

26: "NUT Scraps Call For Strikes Over Pay", *Times Educational Supplement*, 7 November 2008, www.tes.co.uk/article.aspx?storycode=6004737

in local government over pensions (2006) and pay (2002 and 2008) were big and important struggles. But they were only one or two-day actions, and therefore when the bureaucracy moved to choke off these strikes there was protest and outrage, but not a sufficiently strong movement to reverse the decision or carry on the battle without the bureaucracy's support.

The beginnings of rank and file strength are clearer in smaller struggles. An instructive example is on the London buses. There has been a gradual rise in militancy and organisation, starting in 2006 with strikes by 2,500 Metroline drivers, the first major bus strikes in the capital for seven years. The expansion of bus services and the consequent shortage of drivers helped make workers aware of their power. As *Socialist Worker* reported:

> There was an impressive level of involvement by rank and file bus drivers in the strikes. As well as workplace meetings, some union reps organised meetings open to members from across the garages. At these meetings drivers organised their action and discussed problems that they were facing. This gave drivers a chance to raise arguments they were dealing with—such as how to respond to management's claims that the strikes would lose the company bus routes. It also allowed drivers to discuss how to support weaker areas. This meant that the second day of strike action was stronger than the first... "The strikes raised people's confidence," said one driver. "They brought together people who have worked on the buses for years and a layer of newer recruits, including many migrant workers".[27]

The main union involved, Unite, felt under pressure from a new generation of reps who were more attuned to the mood of the workforce. And union officials were also anxious about signs of a drift in some garages towards the RMT union, which was offering to organise a fightback. The new layer of reps and activists launched *Busworker*, a rank and file paper, and several thousand copies of each issue were distributed. But then one company, Metrobus, got a legal ruling that a strike ballot was invalid and its drivers did not join a one-day strike with 5,000 other bus workers in October 2008. Emboldened by this success, all the companies applied for legal injunctions to halt a further cross-London strike.

Until then the bureaucracy and rank and file had worked quite easily together, differing only over the speed of getting a cross-London strike. Suddenly the bureaucrats' fear of the anti-union laws and the determination

---

27: "Bus Drivers' Strikes Shake Bosses", *Socialist Worker*, 16 December 2006, www.socialistworker.co.uk/art.php?id=10353

not to risk the union's funds proved disastrous. There was talk of reballoting across the capital once "all the legal issues had been tied up". But if such a state of affairs were ever possible it never seemed to arrive. Bus workers kept rejecting pay offers, and at one company, Sovereign, the rank and file was strong enough to get a strike called. But as the months dragged on it became clear that there was never going to be a renewed cross-London pay fight for 2008-9 and nearly all bus workers settled for increases of between 4 and 4.5 percent—hardly a defeat, but well short of the hopes of the summer of 2008.

Activists will have to work hard to stop the bitterness turning into apathy or disengagement from the union, but a network of stewards and activists now exists and has the potential to draw in more workers. It is important to recognise that this has not been some spontaneous development but depended crucially on the initiative of socialists, with the Socialist Workers Party playing an important role in assisting the process. As struggle develops there will be many more such opportunities to strengthen rank and file organisation. There will also be opportunities to link together different groups of rank and file workers. Can the tube workers and the bus workers come together to discuss how to coordinate strikes and campaigns? Can the postal workers meet with civil service workers to discuss the fight against privatisation? During the public sector pay revolt workers from different unions began to come together for public meetings, rallies and demonstrations. But real change requires organised rank and file groups in unions to meet to plan consciously coordinated strategies.

In the 1960s stewards' organisation could be created in the important engineering and car industries through sectional disputes, which could win economic demands in a period of expanding capitalism. The model then spread to other industries and played a key role in driving the struggle forward when the bureaucracy wanted to retreat. We are not going to see the movement recreated through the methods of the past. Instead we need to develop the best of what exists and seek constantly to raise the level of struggle, politics and organisation.

It is important to recognise that neoliberalism can have unforeseen consequences. The attempts to localise bargaining in order to weaken and isolate workers can sometimes have the effect of reviving workplace networks. Let's look at three examples.

Further education colleges were effectively set up as competing businesses following an act in 1992 which set in train the process of "incorporation". They no longer had to implement agreements negotiated with the unions nationally over pay and conditions. So, for example, by the end of 2008 a third of all general further education colleges had still not implemented a pay deal from 2004, and the UCU union began strikes over the issue. Of course we should fight for the full implementation of such deals, and the return of national bargaining, but it is also true that the need for local strength has forced numbers of colleges to rely on their own structures and their own organisation. The result is that some colleges have much more powerful local structures than they would have had if everything could be "left to the officials".

A similar process has taken place in Glasgow's schools, where the introduction of school by school bargaining over key issues has led some schools' union groups to develop their own local muscle. In 2008 15 schools voted against changes in the structure of the school week which would have meant that teachers were forced to do more work. Some weaker school groups have suffered harshly from the break-up of negotiations, but others have gained from being forced to engage closely with their members and concentrate on winning over every person in their school.

The imposition of "single status" deals in local government, which has affected the pay and job descriptions of some 800,000 workers, has forced some union branches to organise more effectively. Although negotiated nationally, the deal has been implemented in many different ways locally, and union reps have been involved in highly complex and extended battles over who gains or loses, how much money comes from the government as opposed to the workforce, how much is taken from council reserves and so on. The need for local organisation has been greatly increased by the total failure of the unions to provide a national fight over the issue, with unions claiming that legal factors make it impossible to discuss the matter openly, let alone coordinate the fightback. And at one Unison conference it became impermissible to mention the words "equal pay"! This has weakened the overall resistance. But it has also seen big battles at councils such as Coventry, Falkirk, Stafford, Greenwich and Birmingham. Some of these have greatly developed sectional strength.

So it may be that in some areas sectional strength is growing because of the way capitalism is organised today. But a central method of building the rank and file is through political trade unionism.

Political trade unionism
Political trade unionism has four key elements:

(1) The recognition that virtually every dispute at present raises the issue of the Labour Party.
Labour is in government and is imposing the attacks on pay and pensions

and conditions. Labour went to war alongside George Bush in Iraq and Afghanistan. Labour refuses to repeal the anti-union laws and sides 'with employers in disputes. It is therefore not surprising that in almost all strikes the issue of hostility to giving money to Labour will emerge. Raising the issue of a political alternative to Labour is a crucial part of solidifying the politics of rank and file revolt. It is the necessary inoculation against the idea that we must not rock the boat because it weakens "our government".

(2) Many strikes raise inescapable political issues.

The most obvious examples were the strikes at construction sites in February 2009. They raised issues of genuine concern such as insecurity, job losses, the defence of national conditions against undercutting and the toxic system of subcontracting. But that was not the half of it. Strikers raised the slogan "British jobs for British workers" on virtually all the picket lines. This led to a major argument inside the working class about whether this was the right way to oppose the effects of the crisis. No lasting rise in the struggle can be achieved through such slogans—the politics of unity and solidarity are critical to any recovery of organisation.

The London Underground cleaners' strikes of 2008 were inseparable from the issue of immigration controls and migrant workers' rights. On one level the strikes were a simple issue of pay and rights. But this was a strike of mainly black, mainly migrant workers. And bosses responded with a fierce assault on the strike activists, examining their national insurance records and immigration histories in an effort to punish those who raised their heads. Several workers were deported and some strike leaders were sacked. The basic trade union role of defending the members had to include a much wider political vision.

(3) Politics is a major source of radicalisation and union-building.

Union strength grows not just by militant struggle but by taking up political issues. This is important in pulling activists together, especially during years of low class struggle, as was shown by the positive impact of the very large numbers of trade unionists involved in the anti-war protests. Being part of an anti-war movement or a demonstration over Third World debt does not automatically mean you will fight at work, but you are much less likely to heed calls to sacrifice your living standards "to keep Labour in office" if you think Blair and Brown are mass murderers in Iraq and Afghanistan.

An example of the right approach comes from further education lecturer Sean Vernell: "We not only successfully organised large turnouts on the anti-war demonstrations and walkouts but also organised events in the college.

What we have found is that rather than simply trying to organise meetings though the auspices of the union we have organised meetings/forums through the college's Enrichment Programme and also different departments."

The trade unionists who did a collection for Medical Aid for Palestinians during the Israeli attack on Gaza will be the ones best prepared to combat redundancies. The trade union branch which is affiliated to the Stop the War Coalition and Unite Against Fascism will most likely be the one that fights hard over victimisation and bullying. And this approach is not just something to occupy activists in slow times. It is making concrete Lenin's stress on the necessity for active socialist and working class support for political struggles: "Working class consciousness cannot be genuine polit-ical consciousness unless the workers are trained to respond to all cases of tyranny, oppression, violence and abuse, no matter what class is affected".[28]

(4) The politics and ideology of the work we do is important.
Trade unionists cannot be indifferent to the politics of the work they do. Organising around these issues is the crucial mediating link between agitating around questions such as pay and hours, and the overarching political questions such as war, racism and climate change. It is also a way to make unions more effective. One obvious sphere in which this is true is education. Narrow trade unionists who see their role as simply driving up pay and defending professional standards will be constantly outflanked by management and government who say that workers fighting over these questions don't care about the children. Teachers have to engage at every level of the educational debate, and be firmly on the side of the children against the truncated and limited education they receive. Initiatives such as the "Rethinking Education" conferences have given parents and educa-tors a chance to talk about campaigns against academies and trust schools as well as the issues of war, racism, community learning, testing and democ-racy in schools.

The same applies in Further and Higher Education which, according to one lecturer, have "for more than a decade been war zones" with staff supposed to perceive students as "customers" and courses "strictly subject to market criteria". Socialist teachers who argue that the principles of edu-cation must be defended "strike a chord with the bulk of lecturers", as has been shown with recent conferences held under the title "Education Is Not for Sale". In social work, conferences around the theme of "Social Work: A Profession Worth Fighting For?" have raised the issue of the content

---

28: Lenin, 1961, p423.

of the job as "New Labour's 'welfare reforms' have turned many areas of social work into a business" and "managing budgets and saving money have become more important than improving people's lives—what one writer describes as 'neoliberal social work'".[29]

Health workers also have a clear need to link their trade unionism to a defence of the NHS and demands for better treatment for all. One of the great strengths of the campaign to defend victimised activist Karen Reissmann was that it engaged with the issue of mental health provision. During the London bus strikes many of the best activists discussed the need for a publicly owned system of public transport—not just because it might deliver better workers' rights but because it would be more efficient for Londoners and reduce climate change.

There are many other examples, but the point is that trade unionists have to fight around pay and the content of their job, and the national and global political questions. Missing out any of these limits the fightback.

Four things to do now

(1) Agitate for resistance.
Socialists have to be organising and arguing for resistance against the effects of the crisis—particularly job losses, closures and unemployment. Without a revival in struggle the working class is going to be steam-rollered by the crisis. Making the struggle effective will require a consistent challenge to the union bureaucracies and their support for Labour. Socialists should be particularly aware of the possibilities created in areas of expansion even in a period of general recession. In the 1930s one such area, the car industry, was a centre of stormy struggles.

(2) Put socialist politics at the centre of a fightback.
Political trade unionism is not separate from the agitation for a fightback—it is integral to it. We cannot afford for the movement to be dragged behind toxic slogans such as "British jobs for British workers". And the question of the relationship of the workers' movement to Labour will become ever more pressing. We cannot allow the resistance to unemployment to be stilled by the union leaders' closeness to Brown. The issues of war, racism and climate change need to be addressed consistently. All of that will mean united front work with others, not a retreat into propaganda. But it is also true that a

29: "Conference Planned On Social Work: 'Ethical Career' Or Excuse For Social Control?", *Socialist Worker*, 3 March 2007, www.socialistworker.co.uk/art.php?id=10818

fight against recession and capitalist chaos will be massively strengthened by the growth of a revolutionary socialist organisation which can put forward an alternative worldview to the collapsing system we see around us.

(3) Build networks of political solidarity.

Confidence is a precious commodity, and one aspect of confidence is knowing that other people will support you in times of need. Socialists need to create and strengthen networks of political solidarity. If there is a fightback, some networks of support can be brought into existence virtually overnight but they will be far stronger if they are built in advance.

The tradition of doing collections for other groups of workers in dispute is much weaker than it was 20 years ago. We need to reinstate this with regular collections for disputes and for political campaigns. Many workplaces could host delegations of strikers, but this almost never happens in the union movement today. We need to repeat the excellent work done in this respect round the Karen Reissmann campaign. The networks created by such methods can be the embryo of rank and file movements in the future.

(4) Build a culture of "No"!

Under capitalism, especially at a time of crisis, managers are constantly looking for ways to ratchet up exploitation. One NHS code of conduct I saw last year demanded that hospital workers should not simply perform their jobs safely and efficiently but also "quickly". And such pressures do have an effect. Britain is the long-hours capital of Europe, with one in eight workers regularly doing more than 48 hours a week. Such hours are illegal in most of the EU but Labour has tenaciously defended the right of employers to be able to "offer" workers the chance to opt out of limits on hours—although two million of those who do more than 48 hours a week say they have never even been asked if they consent to it. Some 60 percent of union safety reps report that stress is a big issue for the members at their workplace.[30] Over five million people at work in Britain regularly do unpaid overtime, giving their employers £27 billion of free work every year.[31] One in three workers do not take their full holiday entitlement because they cannot face the backlog of work when they return or fear that they will be passed over for promotion or selected for the sack unless they show willing to "go the

---

30: "Stress, Overwork and Office Hazards Top Workers' Safety Concerns", TUC website, 24 October 2008, www.tuc.org.uk/h_and_s/tuc-15517-f0.cfm

31: "More Than Five Million People Are Working Unpaid Overtime In The UK", TUC website, 8 January 2009, www.tuc.org.uk/work_life/tuc-15798-f0.cfm

extra mile". A survey of women in their 30s showed, "About 85 percent of those polled said they 'frequently feel tired', and 59 percent of these 'feel tired all the time' ".[32] Finding ways to resist compulsion from management is one way of rebuilding workplace strength.

Conclusion

Far too many opportunities for a fightback have been missed during the New Labour years. And this has weakened the workers' movement. But at the same time the working class has had the infusion of strength from the anti-war and anti-capitalist movements. That means it will be a struggle to overcome the bureaucracies and get resistance, but there is also a good chance that if struggle does take place it will be politically powerful.

And when we speak of "workers fighting back" it does not mean that everyone has to realise the necessity for resistance all at the same time. The example of an occupation, especially if it wins, is far more potent than speeches and leaflets. The Republic Windows and Doors occupation in Chicago in the United States in December 2008 lasted only six days. But it won its demands and provides a example to encourage others. As I write, Waterford Glass in Ireland is occupied and has already inspired others to talk seriously of resistance. In an earlier period of crisis in Britain occupations at Upper Clyde Shipbuilders (1971), Fisher Bendix (1972) and Lee Jeans (1981) also rebuffed the notion that "nothing can be done" when redundancies are announced.

It may well be that the groups involved will be unexpected ones. Nobody would have put money on the match girls in 1888 (or the poorly organised and casualised dockers for that matter). Trotsky wrote in 1930:

> In discussing the radicalisation of the masses, it should never be forgotten that the proletariat achieves "unanimity" only in periods of revolutionary apex. In conditions of "everyday" life in capitalist society, the proletariat is far from homogeneous. Moreover, the heterogeneity of its layers manifests itself most precisely at the turning points in the road. The most exploited, the least skilled, or the most politically backward layers of the proletariat are frequently the first to enter the arena of struggle and, in the case of defeat, are often the first to leave it. It is exactly in the new period that the workers who did not suffer defeats in the preceding period are most likely to be attracted to the movement, if only because they have not yet taken part in the struggle.[33]

32: *Daily Mail*, 27 September 2007.
33: Trotsky, 1976, p32.

Today, when world capitalism is in deep general crisis, calls for militancy alone are not enough. As Tony Cliff wrote in 1979, "General social and political questions have to be faced. The battle of ideas becomes crucial. To build a bridge between industrial militancy, rank and file activity and socialism, we must relate the immediate struggles to the final struggle—the struggles inside capitalism to the struggle against capitalism".[34]

References

Bryson, Alex, and Rafael Gomez, 2003, "Why have Workers Stopped Joining Unions?", LSE, http://cep.lse.ac.uk/pubs/download/dp0589.pdf

Charlwood, Andy, and John Forth, 2008, "Workplace Employee Representation, 1980-2004", NIESR discussion paper, www.niesr.ac.uk/pdf/240708_152852.pdf

Cliff, Tony, 1979, "The Balance of Class Forces in Recent Years", *International Socialism* 6 (autumn 1979), www.marxists.org/archive/cliff/works/1979/xx/balance1.htm

Dix, Gill, John Forth and Keith Sisson, 2008, "Conflicts at Work: The Pattern of Disputes in Britain since 1980", NIESR discussion paper, www.niesr.ac.uk/pdf/240708_152632.pdf

Hallas, Duncan, 1977, "The CP, the SWP and the Rank and File Movement", *International Socialism*, 95, 1st series, February 1977, www.marxists.org/archive/hallas/works/1977/02/cp-swp-rfm.htm

Harman, Chris, 2008, "Snapshots of Union Strengths and Weaknesses", *International Socialism* 120 (autumn 2008), www.isj.org.uk/?id=483

Kimber, Charlie, 2002, "Pressure That Makes Union Leaders Buckle", *Socialist Worker*, 14 December 2002, www.socialistworker.co.uk/art.php?id=4207

Lenin, Vladimir, 1961 [1902], *What is To Be Done?*, in *Collected Works*, volume five (Moscow).

Trotsky, Leon, 1924, "Report on the World Economic Crisis and the New Tasks of the Communist International (part two)", in *The First Five Years of the Communist International*, www.marxists.org/archive/trotsky/1924/ffyci-1/ch19b.htm

Trotsky, Leon, 1976 [1930], "The Third Period of the Comintern's Errors", in *Writings of Leon Trotsky*, 1930 (Pathfinder).

WERS, 2004, *Workplace Employment Relations Survey 2004*, www.wers2004.info

Woodhouse, Michael, and Brian Pearce, 1975, *Essays on the History of Communism in Britain* (New Park).

34: Cliff, 1979. I am grateful to the many trade unionists who took the time to talk to me in the process of preparing this article. I am also aware that it is far from a wholly comprehensive treatment of all the issues and welcome further comment and debate on it.

1934: year of the fightback

John Newsinger

There was a great strike wave in the US in the aftermath of the First World War. It was beaten back with the decisive defeat of a rank and file driven campaign to organise the steel industry.[1] Brutal repression was compounded by, at best, only half-hearted support from the American Federation of Labour (AFL).

Once the unions had been contained the employers prepared for what has been described as "a war of extermination against organised labour".[2] An open shop drive was launched across the country to smash the unions once and for all. Taking advantage of the sharp recession of 1921-2, when US Gross National Product (GNP) fell by an astonishing 24 percent and unemployment shot up to five million (worse than in 1929-30), employers cleared out union members and destroyed union organisation. In 1920 union membership stood at 5,110,000; by 1923 it had fallen to 3,592,000. The defeat of the craft unions in the railroad shopmen's strike of 1922[3] convinced the AFL leadership that the only hope for the survival of the trade union movement was for them to throw themselves on the mercy of the employers,[4] to proclaim their conservatism, hail the virtues of

---

1:   For the 1919 steel strike see Brody, 1987. See also Foster, 1920.

2:   Soule, 1947, p200.

3:   For this strike see Davis, 1997.

4:   According to Melvyn Dubofsky, from 1922 until his death in 1924 the AFL president, Samuel Gompers, "acted the beggar, beseeching employers to give the unions a break... His successor as president, William Green, proved even less militant and more deferential to employers"—Dubofsky, 1994, p97.

the capitalist system, expel militants and "reds", and embrace class collaboration. Symbolising all this was the expulsion of the veteran militant and socialist William Dunne from the 1923 AFL convention for his membership of the Workers Party (the then incarnation of American communism). The vote to expel him was carried by 27,837 to 198.[5]

But class collaboration required a collaborator and the American employers were not interested. Union membership continued to fall in the 1920s. In 1920 16.7 percent of American workers had been union members; by 1929 the figure was only 9.3 percent—less than one in ten. The unions had retreated into their craft strongholds, although even these were shaken. In 1920 the Machinists (metalworking and engineering workers) had 282,000 members, but this had fallen to only 148,000 in 1922 in the face of the employers' offensive and was down to only 70,000 by 1929. And in the mass production industries trade unionism had been almost exterminated so that in 1929, in the car industry, the Carriage, Wagon and Automobile Workers Union had only 1,500 members out of a workforce of 450,000.[6]

Over four million workers had taken part in some 3,600 strikes in the United States in 1919. By 1929 the number of strikers had fallen to 289,000 and the number of strikes to 900. For many commentators, it seemed that the class war was over and that industrial peace and harmony were within reach.

Repression and secret police

The weakness of American unions was not due to any "exceptionalism" on the part of American workers, but rather the "exceptionalism" of the American capitalist class. "Unionisation rates did not differ substantially from those in Great Britain and Germany around 1900. The gap...widened between the early 1900s and the 1920s" because "American employers have opposed trade unions with a vehemence unequalled in other OECD nations".[7]

On 23 March 1928 Richard Mellon, the brother of the Secretary of

---

5:   Foner, 1991, p167. Dunne had been one of the leaders of the insurgent labour movement in Butte, Montana. After the kidnapping and murder of the Industrial Workers of the World organiser Frank Little in the city in 1917, an attempt was made to lift Dunne. "I had a .32 Colt in my coat pocket—with my hand on it—and I shot twice. Two of the men dropped and the third ran." The next day he searched the press for a report of the shootings but found instead "headlines announcing that W F Dunne had disappeared"—Howard, 1924, pp192-193. William Dunne was for most of the 1920s a close ally of James P Cannon in the Communist Party but he went on to become a hardline Stalinist. His younger brothers, Ray, Miles and Grant, were to follow Cannon out of the party and became stalwarts of the Trotskyist movement.

6:   Down from a membership of 40,000 in 1920. Peterson, 1987, pp113, 126.

7:   Robertson, 2000, p23.

the Treasury, appeared before a congressional committee in Washington. He was questioned by the United Mine Workers' attorney about his family's extensive Pittsburgh mining interests and was asked about the use of machine guns. When the attorney asked, "Would you approve of that?", he replied, "It is necessary. You could not do without them."

This was not the testimony of some renegade backwoods employer, but of one of the pillars of the American establishment, the brother of the man widely regarded as the architect of the 1920s boom, talking about the family business.[8] It testifies to a dimension of class conflict in the United States that is usually not given enough weight of class: repression was a vital factor in the defeat of the unions after the First World War and in the subsequent maintenance of the open shop.

Trade unions operated in conditions of "semi-outlawry".[9] The readiness of the courts to grant injunctions against the unions seriously curtailed the right to strike, on occasions removing it altogether. Instead of a strike involving a confrontation with an employer, who might well be armed to the teeth anyway, it often also involved a confrontation with the courts.[10] Unions were also hobbled by the legal recognition given to "yellow dog" contracts. (The name supposedly derives from an employer saying he would rather employ a yellow dog than a union man.) In 1917 the Supreme Court had upheld the legality of contracts whereby workers agreed not to join a union. For a union organiser to ask a worker who had signed such a contract to join a union was illegal.

Among the organisers imprisoned for contempt in the 1917 trial was Fannie Sellins, whose career provides a useful case study on the role of repression. Later, in 1919, she was shot down in cold blood by company guards while picketing the Allegheny Coal and Coke Company mine, western Pennsylvania. Her skull was crushed with a blow from a club while she lay dead or dying. A coroner's jury returned a verdict that her killing was "justifiable and in self-defence", and went on to condemn "anarchy and Bolshevism".[11]

Finally, trade unionists were the victims of a secret police regime. There were 230 private detective agencies engaged in spying on the unions, providing armed guards or strike-breakers, with an absolute minimum

---

8:   Cannadine, 2006, p361.
9:   The phrase is from Forbath, 1991, p98.
10:   Montgomery, 1980, p160.
11:   Accounts of Fannie Sellins's death differ over detail, something which reflects the determination of the authorities not to inquire too deeply. See however Cassedy, 1992, and Meyerhuber, 1986, pp42-59.

number of undercover agents at work in industry at some 40,000.[12] Such, labour spies were part of everyday experience for union militants and activists. Abraham Muste, when looking back over his own time as a militant trade unionist, remembered that he "soon learned that on any strike committee or union executive board there would be one or more labour spies". Indeed, when he was one of the leaders of the 1919 textile workers' strike in Lawrence, he was taken aside by one of the other strike leaders, John Mach, the man in charge of relief operations, who revealed that he was a private detective.[13] Another self-confessed spy was the president of the Philadelphia Central Labour Union, a key body in the struggles of the time, and yet another was the Machinists' own district organiser.[14]

The decision to fight for the union was a much bigger decision for American workers than for those in Britain, a decision that often required an uncommon degree of anger and resolve. Once that decision was made they fought all the harder. In the 1920s, however, with wages rising, most workers were not prepared to make that decision. Then in 1929 came the Great Crash and the start of the Great Depression.

The Great Depression

The Great Depression was a catastrophe. US GNP fell from $104.4 billion in 1929 to $94.4 billion in 1930, a less dramatic fall than in the depression of 1921-2, but on this occasion the collapse continued, reaching a low point of $72.7 billion early in 1933. For American workers the consequences were disastrous. The unemployment figures tell the story. They rose from 1,550,000 in 1929 to 12,830,000 in 1933.[15] The real figures were certainly higher than these "official" figures with Sidney Lens, for example, arguing that in 1933 unemployment "was probably 16 or 17 million, with just about the same number working part-time".[16] By 1931 employers began cutting wages across the board and by 1933 some 87 percent of firms "had lowered wage rates at least once, and some several times for an average reduction of 18 percent".[17]

The depression doomed the presidency of Herbert Hoover. His administration was swept away in the 1932 presidential election and the Democrat Franklin Roosevelt was elected by a popular landslide

12: Huberman, 1937, p6.
13: Muste, 1970, pp65, 66.
14: Brooks, 1978, pp51-52.
15: Chandler, 1970, p5; Watkins, 1999, p40.
16: Lens, 1949, p256.
17: Chandler, 1970, p34; Watkins, 1999, p44.

(Roosevelt received 22,821,857 votes to Hoover's 15,761,841). Roosevelt took office in March 1933.

While this is not the place to discuss the politics of Roosevelt's New Deal in any detail, some points are worth making. Roosevelt had fought the election on a programme that was in many respects to the right of Hoover. He condemned Hoover's "reckless and extravagant spending" and promised "to reduce the cost of the current federal government operations by 25 percent". He was, as his Secretary of Labour, Frances Perkins, observed, "no political or economic radical" and took "the status quo in the economic system for granted". As for his promised New Deal, in 1933 it "was not a plan with form and content. It was a happy phrase he had coined during the campaign, and its value was psychological. It made people feel better".[18]

Roosevelt had been a New York State senator before the First World War. He had shown no enthusiasm for reform except insofar as it advanced his career. Most telling was his response, or lack of it, to the 1911 Triangle factory fire that cost the lives of 146 workers, overwhelmingly young women. The fire raised a storm of protest but Roosevelt's "copious correspondence did not even mention the Triangle fire". At this time Roosevelt showed no sympathy for the labour movement, supporting judicial decisions that were intended to cripple the union, "taking for granted the use of force to suppress disturbances during strikes".[19] By the time he became president his attitude towards the working class had not markedly changed. He was, as David Kennedy observes, "a rather diffident champion of labour, and especially of organised labour unions...his fundamental attitude toward labour was somewhat patronising".[20] It was his commitment to save American capitalism that drove him forward and saw him adopt policies never even entertained in 1933. This was to involve concessions to the unions, concessions that Roosevelt had little sympathy for and that had to be extracted by rank and file revolt.

"A virtual uprising of workers for union membership"

In June 1933 Congress passed the National Industrial Recovery Act (NIRA), a cornerstone of the so-called "First New Deal". It provided state sponsorship for firms to form trade associations charged with the regulation of their particular industry, including common standards that

18: Martin, 1976, p259; Perkins, 1948, pp135, 256. The best account of Roosevelt as a politician is that offered by David Shannon who characterises him as "an extraordinarily gifted political broker... He did not design the New Deal; he 'brokered' it"—Shannon, 1979, p178.
19: Freidel, 1952, p121.
20: Kennedy, 1999, p297.

included pay, hours and conditions for the workforce. As one contemporary critic observed, the administration had adopted a corporatist strategy "to restore industrial stability by guaranteeing the status quo of worker and employer, one in possession of little, the other in possession of much".[21]

The NIRA included what Sidney Lens described as "a sop to the working class"—section 7(a).[22] This gave employees the right "to organise and bargain collectively through representatives of their own choosing".[23] While Roosevelt did not intend this to do any more than prop up the AFL, it had an electrifying effect on the working class.

Years of defeat and hardship boiled up in anger and rage. Even with between 12 and 17 million unemployed, the working class seized the opportunity to fight back. Roosevelt, or so it seemed, had guaranteed workers' right to join a union. Underpinning this explosion of militancy was the widespread belief in 1933 that the economic decline had actually bottomed out. Now was the time to fight. As the AFL reported, there was "a virtual uprising of workers for union membership". In factory after factory workers were holding mass meetings that then "sent word they wanted to be organised".[24] The open shop was under attack.

In July 1933 there were nearly 300 strikes and in August 400, as workers demanded the right to organise. By the end of 1933 there had been more strikes than in any year since 1921. This rank and file revolt met with fierce resistance from employers, while the government paid only lip service to the protection of workers' rights and the AFL leadership stood by helpless. Only the United Mine Workers and the handful of other industrial unions actually gave an official lead to the revolt. More typical was Teamsters president Daniel Tobin's dismissal of the men and women now signing up to join the unions as "rubbish".[25] According to the American Civil Liberties Union, the months from July until the end of 1933 saw "widespread violations of workers" rights by injunctions, troops, private police, deputy sheriffs, labour spies and vigilantes".[26]

21: Lundberg, 1938, pp459-460.
22: Lens, 1949, p272. One aspect of Section 7(a) that is often ignored is its impact on black workers. Attempts by black organisations to have anti-discrimination written into the codes, banning unions from barring black workers from membership, were shamefully opposed by the AFL and eventually dropped. See Wolters, 1969.
23: Bernstein, 1970, p34.
24: Watkins, 1999, p218.
25: Zieger, 1994, p42.
26: Preis, 1972, p17.

By the end of the year at least 15 workers had been "killed by police, company guards or vigilantes".[27]

General Hugh Johnson, the man Roosevelt put in charge of the National Recovery Administration (NRA), told delegates at the AFL convention in October 1933 that "unions were no longer needed and that strikes had become superfluous since the president had created new mediation machinery under the NRA". The unions should "be under government supervision" anyway.[28] Roosevelt himself warned the unions in October 1933 that "horses that kick over the traces will be have to put in the corral".[29]

Employers completely ignored the NRA codes with respect to pay, conditions and union recognition. Johnson stood by while there was the wholesale victimisation of union members and sanctioned the formation of company unions into which a million workers found themselves enrolled. Johnson even provoked his own NRA staff to strike when he sacked one of them for union activity!

The AFL opposed workers taking industrial action to protect themselves and instead insisted that they should place their faith in Roosevelt and the NRA, even though William Green, the AFL president, was informed as early as August 1933 that as far as the textile industry was concerned there was not a single mill in the South "living up to the code as signed by the president".[30] William Collins, the man sent by Green to organise Detroit, assured some of the most ruthless employers in the country that "I never voted for a strike in my life. I have always opposed them".[31] Under such inspired leadership the outcome was predictable. By the start of 1934 it appeared that the working class revolt had either been contained or was actually being beaten back.

The role of the left
Looking back at the period Sidney Lens, then a young Trotskyist, remembered how "a radical mood replaced...the despair of the very early 1930s". It was a time when "one leftist among a thousand workers was enough to give the group direction and stimulus". On one occasion:

27: Bellush, 1975, p56.
28: Ohl, 1985, p198; Bellush, 1975, p94.
29: Dubofsky, 1994, p118.
30: Bellush, 1975, pp55, 79-80.
31: Fine, 1963, p148.

We hired a hall that seated 30 people and gave out leaflets inviting workers of a certain shop to a meeting. Of the 275 employees more than 200 turned up; we had to adjourn to a nearby parking lot, where all the workers present signed application cards.

It was, he remembered:

An exhilarating time for young radicals. When I got on the bus, strangers were talking freely about how the union drives were going in their shops. I have never seen anything like it before or since. "This must be", I thought to myself, "how things are during a revolution".

There were hundreds of strikes, most of them spontaneous. The ferocity of the strike wave was demonstrated by "the figures on casualties. From August through October 1933 15 strikers were killed on the picket line and another 40 were slain in 1934." With the AFL leadership failing to give a lead, the American left, even though few in numbers, had a strategic role to play:

A group of workers enraged over wages or an unresolved grievance would be taken in hand by a leftist fellow worker who just knew what to do or, if not, where to get the best advice. The radicals brought to their task a number of a priori concepts, which were immensely helpful in organising the unorganised. They opposed in principle any collaboration with business. They considered the government an implacable enemy to be fought without restraint. And they were unequivocal about the "labour *fakirs*"—heads of the established unions—whom they thought of as the concubines of the employers and the state, to be opposed with equal vigor.

How did he explain the revolt? Workers he argued, "undergo a saturation process—they silently absorb one affront after another until the moment is finally reached when they are saturated with the abuses heaped upon them. That is what happened in the red decade".[32]

The largest organisation on the left was the Communist Party. During this time it was following the Comintern's Third Period line, having, as one historian has put it, "a final stab at insurrection".[33] The Third Period involved the belief that revolution was imminent. It committed the

---

32: Lens, 1974, pp286-287; Lens, 1980, pp56-57, 63-64.
33: The phrase is from Ryan, 2004.

party to "dual unionism", the establishment of revolutionary trade unions. And it involved the embrace of a crazed sectarianism that labelled the AFL as "fascist" and others on the left as "social fascists". The only redeeming feature of the politics of the Third Period was that it involved Communists in actively combating racism and fighting for black workers' rights in a way that had never been seen in the United States before.

At the start of 1930 the Communists had only 7,545 members, a figure that had risen to 19,000 by the start of 1934. Much of this recruitment came from the party's work among the unemployed. The party organised unemployed councils that fought for relief, resisted evictions and established gas and electricity squads to switch these utilities back on when the companies cut them off. It organised occupations of relief offices and protest marches that frequently involved violent clashes with the police. Party members often showed incredible courage in the face of police brutality. On 6 March 1930 the Communists organised nationwide protest marches against unemployment, part of an international protest, which they claimed mobilised over a million people in the United States. One historian argues that 500,000 is a much more realistic figure, but this is still a remarkable achievement.[34]

The achievement is all the more impressive when one considers the routine repression that Communists suffered. In Chicago the police raided one neighbourhood meeting in the run-up to 6 March and arrested 14 activists. They were handed over to the city's "Red Squad". Steve Nelson, one of those arrested, was strapped to a chair, worked over with a blackjack and then kicked unconscious. When he rejoined the others, "Harold Williams was stretched out, his torn pants revealing an enormous rupture, and B D Amos had his front teeth knocked out. Joe Dallet was bleeding from his mouth and had a gash on his cheek." Two of their number were untouched: "This, we figured, was done deliberately so as to throw suspicion on their integrity." The reason for detailing this episode is that there are beatings and there are beatings—and in the United States at this time a systematic working over by professionals was the norm. The so-called "third degree", to be blunt, the use of torture to extract information and confessions, was widespread and routine in many US police departments. This helps illustrate why Communists were often held in such high regard despite their sectarian politics. The party still managed to put out 200,000 leaflets and 50,000 stickers in Chicago. On 6 March 30,000 people, black and white, demonstrated in the city.[35]

34: Watkins, 1999, p119.
35: Folsom, 1994, pp246-257. For the Third Degree see Leo, 2008.

On 31 August 1931, once again in Chicago, a large crowd of black workers, led by the Communists, assembled to protest against evictions. In a scuffle with the police two protesters were shot dead and later that day the body of another who had been "taken for a ride" by the police was found, having been tortured and shot in the head. The party organised a massive funeral for the three men with 60,000 people, including at least 20,000 white workers, following the coffins.[36] On 7 March 1932 the Communists led a "hunger march" to the Ford River Rouge plant in Dearborn, Detroit. In the clashes with police and company guards four of the protesters were shot dead. Another died of his wounds later. Once again party members displayed tremendous courage. One of the dreadful ironies of Soviet state capitalism is that while American Communists were being shot down outside the plant, there were Russian Communist officials inside, at that very moment, "receiving instructions in Ford methods of production. This was part of a highly lucrative contract Ford had signed with the Communist regime".[37]

Nevertheless, as Sidney Lens acknowledged, whatever one thought about their politics, individual Communist Party members "faced hardships, beatings and the threat of jail with great courage". The other side of this coin was the routine violent disruption of the meetings of others on the left. This climaxed on 16 February 1934 when the Socialist Party held a broadly based rally at Madison Square Garden to protest against the military assault launched against workers in Austria by the Dolfuss regime. The rally was broken up by hundreds of Communists "armed with the usual bats and brass knuckles" who succeeded in making "a shambles of the affair".[38]

A strike at the open shop Hormel packinghouse in Austin, Minnesota, in November 1933 demonstrates quite marvellously the coming together of working class unrest and strategically placed revolutionaries. One of the company foreman was Frank Ellis, an Industrial Workers of the World[39] veteran, who "had been thrown into almost every jail from Texas to Minnesota". As foremen he had employed every good union man he could find. The consequence was that when the workers' discontent reached "saturation" point (over deductions for a compulsory insurance scheme), Ellis and his supporters held meetings and established an independent Wobbly-style union, the Independent Union of All Workers. Continual conflict with the company finally came to a head on 10 November with a strike vote. Pickets

---

36: Storch, 2007, pp100-102.
37: Widick, 1989, pp49-50.
38: Lens, 1980, pp24, 54.
39: The Industrial Workers of the World, known as the "Wobblies", was a large revolutionary syndicalist trade union organisation in the 1910s and 1920s.

were put on the gates, but on 11 November some 400 workers stormed the plant and cleared out management, company guards and any scabs they found. One foreman made his escape by rowboat across the Red Cedar River accompanied by loud cheering when the boat sank halfway. When the sheriff arrived at the plant the strikers bodily picked up his car with him in it, turned it round and sent him away. The workers had effectively occupied the plant.

With the threat of the National Guard being sent in, the workers agreed to mediation on the assurance of the governor, Floyd Olson, that their interests would be looked after. Olson was the leader of the Minnesota Farmer-Labour Party, a reformist politician, whose electoral base included the labour movement.[40] Although he often boasted of his radicalism, he told the strikers that they were putting him "on the spot because if I have to choose between my proper duty and my sympathy, I will be obliged to choose duty"—the excuse of the reformist politician throughout the ages. The strikers returned to work with only a partial victory, but the open shop had been busted. The union was entrenched in the plant and went from strength to strength.[41]

The tide turns

"Strikes continued to be broken, pickets continued to be imprisoned or slain, and the dreams and aspirations of union members continued to be shattered" despite the NRA, concludes Bernard Bellush. At best, "the door to labour's rights was slightly opened".[42] It was to be rank and file action that kicked down the door. In 1934 over 1.5 million workers were to take part in nearly 2,000 strikes.

Three strikes in particular—the Auto-Lite strike in Toledo, the Teamsters' strike in Minneapolis and the longshoremen's strike in San Francisco—were to completely change the strategic context for the American working class. All three were led by radicals or revolutionaries. All three defied the AFL leadership, confronted the state and were fought with fierce determination. They served notice on the Roosevelt administration that the working class could not be ignored.

Toledo

The AFL had paid some lip service to organising workers in the mass production industries, recruiting them into Federal Labour Unions (FLUs). By and large, they were short-lived, deprived of help and assistance, regarded

---

40: For the Farmer-Labour Party, see Valelly, 1989.
41: Engelmann, 1974.
42: Bellush, 1975, p178.

with suspicion and certainly never a central concern of the AFL leadership. This situation became critical as hundreds of thousands of workers demanded unionisation. By mid-1934 there were 350,000 workers in 1,700 FLUs. The only advice the AFL gave them for confronting the most anti-union employers was to trust the government.

FLU Local 18384 in Toledo, near Detroit, had organised throughout the city, recruiting members in all the car component firms. The employer the local had to organise to survive was Auto-Lite. On 23 February 1934 the local called a strike there, demanding a pay rise and union recognition. Only a minority of the workforce walked out, but enough to cause the company problems. After five days it conceded a 5 percent pay rise and promised negotiations on recognition. In reality Auto-Lite prepared for another strike, taking on extra workers, trying to undermine the union by intimidation and then reneging on the promised negotiations. On 12 April union members walked out again. With most workers crossing the picket line, the strike looked like ending in a crushing defeat, one of many such setbacks at the time. On this occasion, however, the strikers turned to the American Workers Party (AWP) for help.

The AWP, almost completely forgotten today, was largely the brainchild of one of the most remarkable men in the history of American radicalism, Abraham Muste.[43] He was a Protestant clergyman, radicalised by his opposition to the First World War, who threw himself into the post-war workers' struggles. He was one of the leaders of the 1919 textile workers' strike in Lawrence and emerged from that conflict as the general secretary of the radical United Textile Workers. After the union was driven out of existence by the employers' open shop offensive he became dean of Brookwood Labour College, making it a centre of radical opposition to the AFL leadership and training union organisers to build industrial unions committed to socialist politics. Muste's radicalism led to determined efforts by the AFL president, William Green, to close the college down. In 1929 Muste and his supporters established the Conference for Progressive Labour Action (CPLA) to campaign for "progressive" trade unionism and to actively support workers in struggle. Its organisers in North Carolina were supporting striking mill workers when police in the town of Marion opened fire on pickets on 2 October 1929, shooting 36 men and women, most of them in the back as they ran for their lives. Six of the pickets were killed. One of them, 65 year old George Jonas, was shot dead when he was already under arrest and in handcuffs. When the workers came to bury their

---

43: For Muste see in particular Robinson, 1988.

dead, none of the local preachers was prepared to defy the mill owners and officiate, so Muste "stepped forward".[44]

The Depression transformed Muste from a radical into a revolutionary and a Marxist. In 1932 the CPLA began setting up Unemployed Leagues to fight for relief, to resist evictions *and* to support workers on strike. By the end of 1933 the Leagues had successfully established themselves in Ohio (100,000 members) and Pennsylvania (40,000 members).[45] Encouraged by this, Muste and his supporters established the American Workers Party in December 1933. It proclaimed itself a revolutionary socialist party. It was anti-Stalinist in politics, but part of that stance involved a rejection of Bolshevism. It was one of a number of such organisations internationally trying to find a middle way between reformism and Stalinism in the 1930s. It attracted a number of Marxist intellectuals, such as Sidney Hook[46] and James Burnham, but its orientation was very much on mass struggle.

In Toledo two of its members, Sam Pollock and Theodore Selander of the Lucas County Unemployed League, offered to reinforce the picket line with unemployed volunteers. The offer was accepted and the party secretary, Louis Budenz, quickly became a key adviser to the strike committee, the strategist directing the conflict.

The decisive moment came when the company secured a court injunction restricting picketing. Urged on by the American Workers Party, the strikers decided to defy the injunction. The police began making arrests, but this only led to the picket numbers growing as the strike came to be seen as a battle affecting the whole of the Toledo labour movement. Workers from other factories joined the strikers and the unemployed on the picket line and by the morning of 23 May there were 6,000, swelling to 10,000 as the day went on. That afternoon the police once again began making arrests and their brutality provoked resistance:

> The fighting went on from mid-afternoon until midnight. In effect the great crowd outside imprisoned 1,500 strike breakers inside the factory. Auto-Lite barricaded its doors and turned off the lights. From the roof and upper-story windows deputies rained tear gas bombs on the people in the streets below… The crowd replied with a seven-hour barrage of stones and bricks…heaved through the factory windows. Fires broke out in the shipping room and the

---

44: Salmond, 2004, pp7-8, 22-23, 63-64.
45: Rosenzweig, 1975.
46: For a very interesting discussion of Sidney Hook's involvement with the AWP see Phelps, 1997, pp109-123.

parking lot…cars were overturned, saturated with gasoline and set on fire. During the evening strikers broke into the factory at three points and there was hand to hand fighting before they were driven out. The area for blocks around was blanketed with tear gas.[47]

The strikers improvised catapults out of inner tubes and bombarded the factory through the night, breaking every window.[48] The National Guard arrived the following day to rescue the besieged scabs. The workers were in no mood to submit and the fighting continued, driving the guardsmen back to the factory gates with a hail of bricks. They responded with bayonet charges and when this failed they opened fire, shooting two pickets dead, both unemployed. Still the fighting continued. At last, on 31 May with the Toledo Central Labour Union threatening a general strike, the company agreed to shut the plant. The troops were withdrawn and negotiations got under way. On 2 June Local 18384 won recognition. The strikers did not win all their demands but they had inflicted an unambiguous defeat on Auto-Lite.

The strike was, as Muste put it, "an expression of the pent-up suffering of many years".[49] How did William Green of the AFL respond to it? He wrote to the Toledo Central Labour Union condemning the strike as a mistake and making it clear that there should be no thought of a general strike. With the fighting raging in the streets, he wrote to one of his organisers that "I hardly know what to do in this situation at the present moment".[50] All that can be said in his favour is that his desertion to the other side was no great loss. Instead the strike was won by working class militancy given direction by revolutionary socialists.

Minneapolis

Local 574 of the Teamsters union in Minneapolis had 75 members at the end of 1933. It had relied for its survival on sweetheart agreements with a handful of coal yards, but in November 1933 it was taken over by a remarkable group of militants. Carl Skogland, Ray Dunne and his brothers, Miles and Grant, and Farrell Dobbs were all members of the Trotskyist Communist League. Inspired by the success of the Hormel strike in nearby Austin (Skogland had actually assisted in the strike), they developed a strategy for organising the trucking industry in the city. They recruited not

---

47: Bernstein, 1970, pp222-223.
48: Fine, 1963, p279.
49: Muste, 1970, p157.
50: Phelan, 1989, pp86-87.

just the drivers but the indoor warehouse workers as well, transforming the Teamsters from a craft into an industrial union.

This was accomplished in defiance of the Citizen's Alliance, one of the most powerful and ruthless open shop organisations in the United States, which ran a network of informers and spies, operated blacklists and broke strikes, boasting that "the open shop is more firmly established in private industry than any time in the history of the city".[51] In 1920 there had been 27,000 union members in Minneapolis; by 1928 the number had been driven down to 14,000, and under the impact of the Depression, fell to 7,000 in 1934.[52] The Teamsters had not won a strike in the city since they had been crushed in the great strike of 1916.

The first step in building the union required a victory to show that the employers could actually be beaten. To this end Skogland set about organising the coal yards, recruiting enough drivers to be able to call a strike on 7 February 1934. Some 700 drivers struck across 67 yards. As Charles Walker admiringly observed:

> Preparation had been surprisingly detailed and painstaking. A map of the coal yards of Minneapolis was prepared, and mimeographed instructions were issued to each picket captain before the strike. Within three hours 65 coal yards out of 67 were closed as tight as a bull's eye in fly time.

The tactic that decided the strike was the brainchild of a "rank and file coal heaver": "the militant use of cruising picket squads".[53] Instead of trying to maintain stationary pickets at 67 yards, the union put its men in cars and trucks and they patrolled the streets looking for scab trucks. They knew the routes, intercepted and stopped scab trucks, dumping their loads into the road. Sub-zero temperatures aided the strikes and, after three days, the employers surrendered. In the aftermath of the success thousands of drivers joined the union.

The next step was to organise the trucking industry across the city. This required closing the market district and the union prepared with military precision. Farrell Dobbs wrote in his Trotskyist classic, *Teamster Rebellion,* "Seldom anywhere…has there been such a well-prepared strike". With the aid of advisers from the Cooks and Waiters Union volunteers were ready to serve food to 4,000 to 5,000 people daily. The union established its

51: Millikan, 2000, p219.
52: Faue, 1991, p56.
53: Walker, 2005, p90.

own medical centre to treat those injured in the struggle so they could not be arrested at the hospital. It was manned by sympathetic doctors, nurses and volunteers. As for the picketing:

> We had a special staff at our disposal to handle the telephones and operate a shortwave radio used to monitor police calls. Teenage volunteers with motorcycles were organised into an efficient courier service… They served as the eyes and ears of the picket dispatchers and as a swift means of contact with picket captains.[54]

Once again they relied on "cruising picket squads", operating their own repair shop to keep dozens of cars and trucks on the road. The union headquarters itself was guarded by men "equipped with tommy guns" to deter vigilante attacks.[55] The pickets were unarmed and included members of the Women's Auxiliary. Brutal beatings by police and deputised volunteers left many seriously injured on 19 May, including "20 blood covered women…several with broken legs or unconscious".[56] After this women were withdrawn from picket duty and pickets were armed with clubs. The union prepared for confrontation and hid 600 men in the AFL hall, unnoticed by the police. When fighting broke out between pickets and police on 21 May, instead of the pickets receiving a beating, 600 men armed with clubs marched to their assistance, taking the police completely by surprise. When the police brought in reinforcements the union motored in its reserve of 900 men from union headquarters and broke the police lines by the simple device of driving a truck through them. Over 30 police and deputies were hospitalised in hand to hand fighting.

The following day another battle took place for control of the market district. The police were reinforced by large numbers of deputies provided by the Citizens Alliance, the teamsters by hundreds of striking building workers. In the ensuing "Battle of Deputies Run" two deputies were killed, one of them a leading member of the Citizens Alliance. The forces of law and order were driven from the market district and the pickets were left in control, "directing the traffic".[57]

The employers now agreed to negotiations under the auspices of the Farmer-Labour Party. Governor Floyd Olson, known to be a bitter enemy,

---

54: Dobbs, 1972, p103.
55: Walker, 2005, p272.
56: Millikan, 2000, p272.
57: Dobbs, 1972, p94.

of the Citizens Alliance, had donated $500 to the strike fund. But he had no wish to strengthen the position of the Trotskyists in the Minneapolis labour movement and his concern was to end the strike as soon as possible, before it could become an electoral liability, rather than to ensure victory on the union's terms. He led the union to believe that the employers had accepted their terms and it recommended acceptance on 25 May.

Local 574 had won a stunning victory over a feared opponent but quickly discovered the May agreement was only a truce. Both sides prepared for another confrontation. The second Teamsters' strike began on 17 July. The union had immeasurably strengthened its organisation, recruiting more members and establishing an unemployed auxiliary with 5,000 members. It had started a weekly newspaper, *The Organiser*, edited by Max Shachtman. During the strike it became a daily. This was to prove absolutely vital in order to counter the "red scare" that the Citizens Association ran in the press, aided and abetted by Teamsters president Daniel Tobin.

Once the strike began, the union's picketing operation swung into action. To begin with pickets were once again unarmed. This time, however, the police had orders not to allow a rerun of the May strike and staged an ambush on 20 July, opening fire with shotguns on a truckload of pickets as they tried to stop a scab truck. When other pickets on foot went to the rescue, they too were shot down. By the time the shooting stopped 69 pickets and bystanders had been shot, two pickets killed and many more seriously wounded.[58]

This deliberate, calculated attack was intended to put an end to picketing, break the strike and smash the union. The union took steps to prevent its members picketing with guns. Dobbs describes taking firearms off the pickets "as the hardest thing I ever did in my life".[59] A shoot-out with the police would give the authorities just the excuse they needed to destroy the union by open repression. But they continued picketing with "cars and trucks trailing scab vehicles, forcing the police to provide large

---

58: In his biography of Floyd Olson, George Mayer writes of this incident that the Local 574 leadership "played an equally reprehensible role as the police". He claims that "the strike leaders sought the shedding of blood to reinforce working class solidarity" and that they deliberately sent pickets into an ambush where they knew men would be killed—Mayer, 1987, pp209-210. Bernstein agrees, writing that Dunne and Dobbs deliberately sent "unsuspecting pickets into the rain of police gunfire". He puts this down to the "Marxist doctrine of class warfare, with its inversion of ordinary ends and means"—Bernstein, 1970, p243. The problem with this is that the only evidence for it is the authors' distaste for Trotskyism. The slander seems to have originated with people on Olson's staff, who had their own reformist political agenda.
59: Dobbs, 1972, p156.

escorts, up to 20 police cars for one scab truck, and therefore severely limited the number of scab trucks they could run".[60]

Governor Olson sent 4,000 National Guardsmen into the city and declared martial law on 26 July, claiming this was necessary to prevent any further loss of life. But while he claimed he was being even-handed, in practice the troops set about breaking the strike and the employers had thousands of scab trucks running within days. The Local 574 leadership had to convince its membership to confront Olson, who was trusted as a man who was on the side of the workers and had opposed the Citizens Association in the past. Ray Dunne insisted to the strikers, "Submit to the governor and the strike is lost." As Charles Walker points out, he did not use Marxist theory to explain the role of reformism; he simply pointed "to the 6,000 trucks moving in Minneapolis".[61]

The union took the crucial decision to defy the martial law regime and reinstate the cruising picket squads as a guerrilla-style operation. Dobbs describes how it worked:

> A series of control points was set up around the town, mainly in friendly filling stations, which cruising squads could enter and leave without attracting attention. Pay phones in the stations and couriers scouting the neighbourhood were used to report scab trucks to picket dispatchers. Cruising squads were then sent to the reported locations to do the necessary and get away in a hurry. Trucks operating with military permits were soon being put out of commission throughout the city... Troops in squad cars responded to the calls usually to find scabs who had been worked over, but no pickets.[62]

Olson responded with a raid on the union headquarters and the arrest of the union leadership, but then found the only way he could get the picketing called off was to release the people he had just arrested and force the Citizens Association to come to terms with them. Olson was, as the Trotskyist leader, James P Cannon pointed out, trapped in contradiction. He was "on the one hand supposedly a representative of the workers; on the other hand, he was the governor of a bourgeois state".[63] He had taken action to break the strike but there was a limit to how far he could go without losing the support of the working class on whom his electoral

---

60: Dobbs, 1972, p157.
61: Walker, 2005, p198.
62: Dobbs, 1972, pp170-171.
63: Cannon, 1944, p161.

survival depended. Having failed to break the union he turned his attention to the Citizens Association. In a gesture of even-handedness he ordered their headquarters raided by troops. More to the point, on 8 August he met with Roosevelt, who agreed to put pressure on the banks that were financing the employers. The federal government's Reconstruction Finance Corporation threatened to withdraw its loans which were saving the banks from bankruptcy and the employers' resistance collapsed.[64]

Against all the odds Local 574 had won a decisive victory in one of the best conducted strikes in the history of the American working class.[65]

San Francisco

San Francisco had been one of the best organised cities in the US. This changed after the First World War when the open shop drive, spearheaded by the Industrial Association, broke union power. On the docks the longshoremen (dockers) were defeated in 1919, with the employers establishing a company union, known as the Blue Union. Conditions on the docks inevitably worsened with the onset of the Depression. There were big wage cuts and speed-ups which produced a growing toll of accidents.

A group of left militants—mostly syndicalists (many of them former Wobblies) but open to Communist Party influence—had started a rank and file paper, the monthly *Waterfront Worker*, in December 1932. As one of its founders, Mitch Slobodek, put it, "There was an undercurrent of restlessness on the waterfront when we started putting out the paper but no direction. The paper gave one".[66] It urged its readers to form "small undercover groups of those whom we know on each dock"[67] as a covert network of militants, the nucleus of a union, ready to come out in the open when the time was right. Later on in the year the International Longshoremen's Association (ILA) appointed an organiser in San Francisco, Lee Holman, who began signing up members.

The Communist Party were committed to the formation of

64: Mayer, 1987, p221.
65: The May and July strikes provoked the publication of a minor Stalinist classic: *Permanent Counter-Revolution: The Role of the Trotskyites in the Minneapolis Strikes* by William Dunne and Morris Childs. They condemn the Trotskyists' "defeatist strategy and tactics", accuse them of "strike-breaking", of writing "another miserable page in the history of class collaboration", of being "spineless and unprincipled leaders", and of following "a counter-revolutionary and, therefore, anti working class policy"—Dunne and Childs, 1934, pp3, 21, 22, 23, 47.
66: Larrowe, 1977, p13.
67: Selvin, 1996, p57. The best account of the strike along the whole Pacific coast is Markholt, 1988.

revolutionary trade unions in opposition to the supposedly "fascist" AFL. The failure of this policy was not brought home because the AFL unions were not growing either. But in 1933, with the rush of workers into the AFL, many Communist Party members began ignoring the party's policy. This was the case in San Francisco where the rank and file group that had developed around the *Waterfront Worker*, with Communist support, resolved to take over the ILA, democratise it and turn it into a militant fighting organisation.[68] In Seattle and Portland, Communist Party branches stuck to the party line, condemning the ILA as "social fascist", and consequently they had no influence on events whatsoever.

As more and more dockers joined the ILA they increasingly came into conflict with the Blue Union and the employers. The official ILA position, argued by Holman, was that they should place their trust in the NRA and at all costs avoid trouble. But the militants around the *Waterfront Worker*, led by Harry Bridges, decided to act. In September 1933 on the Matson dock men refused to show their Blue Union cards and four of them were suspended for wearing ILA buttons. Holman refused to support them but the militants led a walkout that threatened to spread throughout the port and the employer backed down. The Blue Union was finished. As Bridges put it, that "was the end of the fear and intimidation".[69] A small tactical victory had been carefully calculated so as to have a decisive strategic result.

Rank and file dockers the length of the Pacific coast were taking control of their union. They endorsed a policy based on union controlled hiring halls that would effectively establish the closed shop and give the union control of the docks—voting at the end of March by 6,616 to 699 for strike action if their demands were not met. ILA president Joseph Ryan, the worst type of AFL bureaucrat, stepped in to suspend the strike when Roosevelt promised mediation. The employers refused to give any ground, and were preparing to break the threatened strike and smash the union. The militants succeeded in having Holman, by now completely discredited by his opposition to strike action, suspended from office, and elected a strike committee. Mass meetings across the Pacific coast voted on 8 May for immediate strike action. On 9 May 12,000 dockers stopped work.

The walkout was quickly joined by the seamen, coming out both in solidarity and to win their own demands. Crucial, however, was the

---

68: The party organiser in California, Sam Darcy, had little time for "dual unionism". On one occasion, when he was being berated by an emissary from party general secretary Earl Browder for rightist deviations, he threw the man out of the window. See Kimeldorf, 1992, p8.
69: Larrowe, 1977, p21.

decision by the San Francisco teamsters, defying their full-time officials, to boycott the docks. Even when the employers got scabs to load and unload ships they could not move goods off the docks because of the teamsters' decision to respect picket lines. Every day there were clashes between pickets and police. The first fatalities occurred at San Pedro on 14 May when police and company guards shot two pickets dead during an attempt to storm a scab compound. The strike remained solid.

ILA president Joseph Ryan (on occasions he claimed the union initials stood for "I Love America") intervened to try to bring the strike to an end. His support in the union rested on the New York docks, where the union worked in close collaboration with the employers and organised crime, and he was not accustomed to the idea of actually having to put agreements to the membership . He negotiated a deal over the heads of the west coast strikers, only to have it repudiated at mass meetings.[70]

When union leaders failed to deliver a sell-out the employers determined to open the San Francisco docks by force. The Industrial Association set up a trucking firm with scab drivers who would cross picket lines and carried goods off the docks with a massive police presence. There was fierce fighting between pickets and police on 3 July, with the police making free use of clubs and tear gas. On 5 July some 20,000 pickets (dockers, seamen, unemployed, teamsters and others) assembled to stop the trucks. Bridges and his picket captains marshalled their forces to fight a regular battle. By the end of the day two pickets had been shot dead and dozens more were seriously injured.[71] The state governor, Roger Lapham, seized on the shootings as an excuse to send in the National Guard, although, just as in Minneapolis, the union disarmed pickets who turned up for duty with firearms.

It was by now clear to more and more workers that what was at stake was not just the longshoremen's cause but the fate of the San Francisco labour movement. On 12 July the teamsters voted, once again in defiance of their officials, for an indefinite all-out strike. Workers across the city were walking out in sympathy in growing numbers in what one historian has

---

70: Ryan was a friend to employers, gangsters and politicians, including Roosevelt when he was Governor of New York State. Incredibly, his political friends made him head of the New York State Parole Board, which was very useful to his gangster friends. Many of the ILA's New York officials were gang members, most notably the head of the union in Brooklyn, Albert Anastasia, whose brother, Tony, ran Murder Incorporated for the New York mob. In the aftermath of the Pacific strike, a rank and file opposition developed in New York, led by Peter Panto. He built up widespread support but then suddenly disappeared in 1939. His body was eventually found in a secret mob cemetery in 1947; he had been strangled. See Kimeldorf, 1992, p124.
71: For a graphic account see Bernstein, 1970, pp272-279.

described as "a creeping general strike".[72] The AFL officials on the Central Labour Union reluctantly bowed to the inevitable and called a general strike on 14 July, beating off attempts to establish a rank and file controlled strike committee. One official admitted that it "was an avalanche. I saw it coming so I ran ahead before it crushed me".[73] It was the only way they could keep the strike firmly under official control.

There was serious discussion at government level about whether or not to send in federal troops, with Governor Lapham arguing, "We can cure this thing best by bloodshed".[74] Roosevelt was on holiday, and both acting President Cordell Hull, the Secretary of State and Attorney General Cummings were in favour of the use of force. Secretary of Labour Perkins was strongly opposed, arguing it would mean "regular shooting and a lot of people will drop in the streets". Bloodletting would cause "frightful resentment" and would do serious damage "politically and morally and for the basic labour-industry and labour-government relationship".[75] Roosevelt backed her judgement, a decision that, in effect, determined the direction of the New Deal. If the administration had sent in the troops, it would have alienated working class support. Instead the decision was made to rely on the union leaders to police their members, keeping them aboard as allies, even if it meant making concessions that Roosevelt had little sympathy with.

This did not preclude action against the left. On 17 July there was a well organised wave of vigilante attacks across California. With the police conveniently absent, gangs of armed vigilantes wrecked offices and meeting halls, and administered beatings, with the Communist Party the favourite target. Once the vigilantes had done their work the police arrived to arrest the victims. By the end of the day over 450 people had been arrested and charged with vagrancy, with bail set at $1,000 instead of the normal $10. This carefully organised assault was celebrated in the press as a popular uprising against the "reds". Earlier a group of businessmen had got together to discuss having Bridges killed (he had already turned down a $50,000 bribe) but one of their number warned he would go public if they did.[76]

On 20 July the Central Labour Union called off the general strike on the grounds that acceptable mediation was now on offer. This effectively outmanoeuvred the longshoremen. The Teamsters voted to end their boycott of the docks and the now isolated dockers voted for mediation. Bridges was

---

72: Crook, 1960, p123.
73: Nelson, 1990, p149.
74: Selvin, 1996, p178.
75: Martin, 1976, p320.
76: Larrowe, 1977, pp99-100.

criticised by some on the left for this, but in retrospect it seems he accurately judged the balance of forces. On strike the balance of forces was against them; back at work it was in their favour. The final settlement gave the dockers a coast-wide contract with a six-hour day, time and a half for overtime and a union appointed dispatcher in joint union–employer hiring halls. On the job action soon cleared any scabs off the docks, ended the speed-ups and established the closed shop.[77] It was a historic victory.

Defeat

The victories in Toledo, Minneapolis and San Francisco changed the strategic picture as far as the class struggle was concerned. Whereas the Roosevelt administration had once felt that it could ignore the working class, it had now been forcibly brought home that this was no longer the case. And as far as the working class itself was concerned, it had been demonstrated that militant action, amounting on occasions to virtual insurrection, could triumph. Even in conditions of mass unemployment militancy and solidarity could defeat the most ruthless employers. In all three strikes the formula for victory was rank and file militancy and radical or revolutionary socialist leadership confronting employers, the union leadership and the state. The year 1934 was to see another great strike that proved the importance of this formula in a negative sense.

On 1 September 1934 the United Textile Workers called a national strike, the largest stoppage in US history up to that point. Between 350,000 and 400,000 workers walked out. Three weeks later, on 21 September, it was called off by the leadership on the basis of "assurances" given by the president personally. The result was a crushing defeat.

Textile workers were among the hardest hit by the Depression, with wages driven down and work relentlessly intensified by the "stretch out". The union had virtually collapsed with only 15,000 members in February 1933. Section 7(a) revolutionised the situation and union membership had increased to 40,000 by September that year and to 340,000 by August 1934. This explosion in membership was driven by rage, but the rage was regarded as a dangerous embarrassment by a union leadership looking to Roosevelt and the NRA for justice. It was only under intense rank and file pressure that the union leadership finally called a strike.

While the mills in New England and Maine were shut down, the region where the strike would be decided was acknowledged to be in the South, in the Carolina Piedmont. Here the workers formed "flying

---

77: Nelson, 1990, pp156-162.

squadrons", car and truck convoys of pickets that motored from mill to mill, closing them down. The tactic met with great success and the authorities responded by mobilising the National Guard. In Georgia governor George Talmadge, "a friend of the workers", declared martial law and ordered the internment of strikers. There were violent clashes. On 6 September company guards opened fire on a group of about 70 strikers picketing the Chiquola mill in Honea Park and killed seven. Secretary of Labour Perkins described this as "an unfortunate situation".[78] Altogether 15 strikers were killed in the three weeks of the dispute. The union retreated in the face of this repression, suspending the flying squadrons and effectively abandoning any serious attempt to spread the strike. Having given up any attempt to win, they threw themselves on the tender mercies of the Roosevelt administration.

After the strike was called off on the basis of Roosevelt's assurances one union leader, Francis Gorman, proclaimed it "one of the most amazing victories ever recorded in the annals of the AF of L".[79] In fact the union had surrendered. Roosevelt's assurances were worthless and thousands of workers found themselves sacked, evicted from company housing and denied relief by agencies run by men appointed by the "millocracy". The employers' intention was to strike a blow that would deter attempts at unionisation for a generation. Union membership collapsed from 340,000 in August 1934 to only 79,000 in the summer of 1935. The importance of this defeat for the American labour movement was that it left the South an open shop stronghold.

Was defeat inevitable? Certainly the textile workers confronted ruthless employers, armed to the teeth and with the full support of the police and the National Guard. The union had few financial resources and it received no help from the AFL. Nevertheless, when the strike was called off, union members were still fighting and still believed they could win. Between the end of the strike and the end of July 1935 there were 94 textile strikes across the South as the workers tried to protect themselves with or without the union.[80] Instead of even a fighting retreat the union leadership chose surrender and proclaimed the disaster a historic victory. The union leader who made this proclamation, Francis Gorman, belatedly recognised, two years after the strike, "Many of us did not understand fully the role of government in a struggle between labour and industry... Government protects the strong, not the weak, and...yields to that group which is strong enough to assert itself over the other".[81]

78: Irons, 2000, pp148-150. For a nationwide account of the strike see Salmond, 2002.
79: Hodges, 1986, p117.
80: Hodges, 1986, p146.
81: Irons, 2000, p163.

References

Bellush, Bernard, 1975, *The Failure of the NRA* (W W Norton).

Bernstein, Irving, 1970, *Turbulent Years 1933-1941* (Houghton Mifflin).

Brody, David, 1987, *Labor in Crisis: The Steel Strike of 1919* (University of Illinois).

Brooks, Thomas, 1978, *Clint: A Biography of a Labor Intellectual* (Athenium).

Cannadine, David, 2006, *Mellon* (Alfred Knopf).

Cannon, James P, 1944, *The History of American Trotskyism* (Pioneer).

Cassedy, James, 1992, "A Bond of Sympathy: The Life and Tragic Death of Fannie Sellins", *Labor's Heritage*, volume 4, number 4.

Chandler, Lester, 1970, *America's Greatest Depression* (Harper and Row).

Crook, Wilfred, 1960, *Communism and the General Strike* (Shoestring Press).

Davis, Colin, 1997, *Power At Odds: The 1922 National Railroad Shopmen's Strke* (University of Illinois).

Dobbs, Farrell, 1972, *Teamster Rebellion* (Monad).

Dubofsky, Melvyn, 1994, *The State and Labor in Modern America* (University of North Carolina).

Dunne, William, and Morris Childs, 1934, *Permanent Counter-Revolution: The Role of the Trotzkyites in the Minneapolis Strikes* (Workers Library), www.marxists.org/archive/dunne/1934/10/

Engelmann, Larry, 1974, "'We Were The Poor People'—The Hormel strike of 1933", *Labor History*, volume 15, number 4.

Faue, Elizabeth, 1991, *Community of Suffering and Struggle: Women, Men and the Labor Movement in Minneapolis 1915-1945* (University of North Carolina).

Fine, Sidney, 1963, *The Automobile Under the Blue Eagle* (University of Michigan).

Folsom, Franklin, 1994, *Impatient Armies of the Poor* (University of Colorado).

Foner, Philip S, 1991, *The TUEL to the End of the Gompers Era* (International Publishers).

Forbath, William, 1991, *Law and the Shaping of the American Labor Movement* (Harvard University).

Foster, William Z. 1920, *The Great Steel Strike and its Lessons* (B W Huebsch), www.archive.org/details/greatsteelstrike00fostuoft

Freidel, Frank, 1952, *Franklin D Roosevelt: The Apprenticeship* (Little, Brown).

Hodges, James, 1986, *New Deal Labor Policy and the Southern Cotton Textile Industry 1933-1941* (University of Tennessee).

Howard, Sidney, 1924, *The Labor Spy* (Republic Publishing).

Huberman, Leo, 1937, *The Labor Spy Racket* (Modern Age Books), www.archive.org/details/laborspyracket00huberich

Irons, Janet, 2000, *Testing The New Deal: The General Textile Strike of 1934 in the American South* (University of Illinois).

Kennedy, David, 1999, *The Oxford History of the United States* (Oxford University).

Kimeldorf, Howard, 1992, *Reds or Rackets: The Making of Radical and Conservative Unions on the Waterfront* (University of California).

Larrowe, Charles, 1977, *Harry Bridges: The Rise and Fall of Radical Labor in the US* (Lawrence Hill).

Lens, Sidney, 1949, *Left, Right and Center* (Henry Regenery).

Lens, Sidney, 1974, *The Labor Wars* (Anchor Books).

Lens, Sidney, 1980, *Unrepentent Radical* (Beacon Press).

Leo, Richard, 2008, *Police Interrogation and American Justice* (Harvard University).

Lundberg, Ferdinand, 1938, *America's 60 Families* (Vanguard Press), www.archive.org/details/americas60famili035216mbp

Markholt, Ottilie, 1988, *Maritime Solidarity: Pacific Coast Unionism 1929-1938* (Pacific Coast Maritime History Committee).

Martin, George, 1976, *Madame Secretary: Frances Perkins* (Houghton Mifflin).

Mayer, George, 1987, *The Political Career of Floyd B Olson* (Minnesota Historical Society).

Meyerhuber, Carl, 1986, *Less Than Forever: The Rise and Decline of Union Solidarity in Western Pennsylvania* (Susquehanna University).

Millikan, William, 2000, *A Union Against Unions* (Minnesota Historical Society).

Montgomery, David, 1980, *Workers' Control in America* (Cambridge University).

Muste, Abraham Johannes, 1970, "Sketches for an Autobiography", in Nat Hentoff, *The Essays of A J Muste* (Simon and Schuster).

Nelson, Bruce, 1990, *Workers On The Waterfront* (University of Illinois).

Ohl, John Kennedy, 1985, *Hugh Johnson and the New Deal* (Northern Illinois University).

Perkins, Frances, 1948, *The Roosevelt I Knew* (Hammond).

Peterson, Joyce Shaw, 1987, *American Automobile Workers 1900-1933* (State University of New York).

Phelan, Craig, 1989, *William Green* (State University of New York).

Phelps, Christopher, 1997, *Young Sidney Hook* (Cornell University).

Preis, Art, 1972, *Labor's Giant Step* (Pathfinder).

Robertson, David Brian, 2000, *Capital, Labor and State* (Rowman and Littlefield).

Robinson, Jo Ann Ooiman, 1988, *Abraham Went Out: A Biography of A J Muste* (Temple University).

Rosenzweig, Roy, 1975, "Radicals and the Jobless: The Musteites and the Unemployed Leagues 1932-1936", *Labor History*, volume 16, number 1.

Ryan, James, 2004, "A Final Stab at Insurrection: the American Communist Party 1928-1934", in Matthew Worley, *In Search of Revolution: International Communist Parties in the Third Period* (IB Tauris).

Salmond, John, 2002, *The General Textile Strike of 1934: From Maine to Alabama* (University of Missouri).

Salmond, John, 2004, *Southern Struggles* (University Press of Florida).

Selvin, David, 1996, *The Terrible Anger: The 1934 Waterfront and General Strikes in San Francisco* (Wayne State University).

Soule, George, 1947, *Prosperity Decade: From War to Depression 1917-1922* (Rinehart).

Storch, Randi, 2007, *Red Chicago: American Communism at its Grassroots 1928-1935* (University of Illinois).

Valelly, Richard, 1989, *Radicalism in the States: The Minnesota Farmer-Labor Party and the American Political Economy* (University of Chicago).

Walker, Charles Rumsford, 2005, *American City: A Rank and File History of Minneapolis* (University of Minnesota).

Watkins, T H, 1999, *The Hungry Years* (Henry Holt).

Widick, B J, 1989, *Detroit: City of Race and Class Violence* (Wayne State University).

Wolters, Raymond, 1969, "Section 7a and the Black Worker", *Labor History*, volume 10, number 3.

Zieger, Robert, 1994, *American Workers, American Unions* (John Hopkins University).

Culture and socialism

Terry Eagleton

All human beings are prematurely born, helpless and dependent, unable to look after themselves. This applies not just to Oxbridge dons but to the whole of the human species. Later on, if all goes well, we will achieve a degree of autonomy—but only on the basis of a continuing dependency, this time on culture rather than nature. Only through the form of dependence on others we call culture can we come to be self-sufficient, which is no doubt one reason why the word "monster" in classical antiquity meant among other things one who sees himself as self-dependent and to that extent is in conflict with his or her creaturely nature. Sophocles's Oedipus is a case in point—that canny entrepreneur of himself whose suppressed parentage will return to destroy him. We all like to fantasise that we have a posher pedigree than we actually do or (even more deludedly) that we have no pedigree at all—that we sprang from our own heads or loins. Since that which was never born can never die, this yields us the comforting illusion of immortality.

This is certainly the case with what we might call bourgeois man, or Faustian Man, whose desire is infinite and whose will is unconfined. He must therefore secretly regard himself as wholly immaterial, since materiality is a constraint. This is a creature who recognises no end, origin, ground or goal but himself. When his phallic tower is demolished by terrorist aircraft he instantly resolves to build an even bigger one in its place. A case of slow learning if ever there was one...

Since we are all born prematurely, with a donnish inability to cope, we will all die very quickly unless culture moves in on us right away. I don't mean by this that Stendhal or Shostakovich are essential for our survival. I mean culture in the sense of a system of nurture, "nurture" being a word which for Shakespeare mediates between nature and culture. The playwright Edward Bond speaks of the so-called "biological expectations" with which we are born—the expectation, he writes, that "the baby's unpreparedness will be cared for, that it will be given not only food but emotional reassurance, that its vulnerability will be shielded, that it will be born into a world wanting to receive it, and that knows how to receive it". Unless one of those faces around the cradle actually speaks to the infant it will never become a person at all. It will be human, of course, since this is a matter of the sort of body it has, but becoming a person is a project, not a given. Measuring contemporary capitalism by this single criterion, Bond refuses to grace it with the title of a culture.

Culture, one might note, is here a descriptive and a normative term at the same time. It describes in a neutral way what must actually happen for us to survive, but it also refers to a kind of loving and is thus a value term as well. Without some culture of caring geared up to greet us we simply won't flourish. In this sense, the word "culture" leaps the gap between fact and value—between what is the case and what is desirably the case. Far from just rising shakily on our paws and licking ourselves down, we are born with an enormous hole in our natures, which culture must instantly plug if we are not to die. It is natural to us to be lacking. And since our premature birth results in an unusually long period of dependency on those human beings immediately to hand it gives rise to an unusually intense intimacy with them. This in turn results in a particularly traumatic severance from them at a later point, which is what gives rise to that curious human invention known as psychoanalysis. Psychoanalysis is a science concerned among other things with how the *fact* of our interaction with other bodies breeds certain conditions relevant to *value*: fantasy, neurosis, psychosis, denying that the grey-haired old codger who arrives at the school gates is your father rather than grandfather, pretending he's just a wrinkled old family retainer and so on.

All of which is to say that culture is of our nature. A very different proposition, note, from the postmodern claim that culture *is* our nature. For the postmodern ideology we might dub culturalism, culture goes all the way down. It is, so to speak, wall to wall. You can't ask *what* is being culturally constructed, since the answer to that must also be a cultural construction. This fashionable brand of culturalism, one which is rife all the way from Al Qaida to the Institute of Contemporary Arts, is among other things a disavowal of our fragility and mortality. Al Qaida is culturalist because it believes that values, religious ones in particular, are what matters, more so than material matters. For both Al Qaida and the American Dream, materiality is constraining rather than enabling, which is no doubt one reason why both parties have a somewhat casual way with human flesh and blood. Neither the ICA nor the American Dream (I haven't consulted Al Qaida on this point) would agree that, whatever else we may be, we are in the first place natural material objects. Anything more glamorous, sexy and fascinating we can get up to has to be got up to on this basis. For the anti-culturalist view I'm proposing here culture is required by our peculiar kind of creatureliness, by the sort of species-being we share, by the kind of material bodies we have.

Only a linguistic animal—that is to say, one which moves within a world of meaning—can be said to have a culture. To live in a world of meaning is to share a sensory world with others of one's kind in a way that transcends mere bodily contact. It isn't just to add something extra to a sensory world but to transform it at a stroke. It is to extend the body outwards into a complex set of networks and institutions, and this in turn extends the body inwards, lending it its spiritual depth and interiority. The whole of civilisation is an extension of our bodies. Technology is a kind of prosthesis. And this is made possible by the kind of labouring, linguistic, conceptual, self-transformative, self-transcending bodies we have (or are). (Whether we "have" bodies or "are" bodies is a fascinating issue we must leave aside here.) As Ludwig Wittgenstein remarks, if you want an image of the soul, look at the human body.

Now this is both our delight and our disaster. The linguistic, culture building creature has the edge over its fellow animals in all sorts of ways. Indeed, it is hard to suppress a shudder of humanistic contempt when one thinks about all that we can do and they can't. We can stockpile nuclear weapons, torture Muslims and blow the heads off small children, for example, none of which are within the capacity of moles or badgers (unless they're being remarkably furtive about it). Language or conceptual thought allows us to sit loose to our own bodies, as well as to the bodies of others, unhinging us to some extent from our constraining sensuous responses. It is hard to strangle someone with your bare hands since the intra-specific inhibitions on killing a member of one's own species would kick in and succeed in making us sick. And though it is unpleasant to have someone throw up over you, it is a great deal more agreeable than being strangled.

We can, however, override these sensuous inhibitions by killing each other at long range, an ingenious strategy which squirrels and earthworms have so far disastrously failed to come up with. (Why? Because a non-linguistic being can't invent a rifle.) Language, and the cultural or conceptual world of which it is the medium, is the catastrophic triumph we have over our fellow animals. If this dangerously two-edged sword permits us to torture, it also allows us to perform major surgery without just throwing up over the patient's body all the time. It does this because it helps to objectify the world, set it over against us, which is a source of alienation *and* achievement. Unlike aardvarks and alligators, we can be ironic and play the trombone, write *Little Dorrit* and care for the sick. Linguistic culture also means that we can enter into relations with others more intimate and intense than just bodily interaction, which is what we mean by spirit, soul or consciousness.

Consciousness is more something between us than within us, more like dancing than a rumble of the gut. Because of this unique form of communication, we can dissolve the walls of our bodies and get closer to each other than touching. Sexual relationships, for example, are mostly a matter of talking (or am I missing out on something?). For sign-making animals like ourselves, physical action isn't a way of getting closer to each other than words. In fact, actions like hugs or handshakes only make sense within a world of meaning. Sharing signs isn't a substitute for sharing things; it is a way of sharing them more deeply.

Entering into language was certainly a fall. But like all the best falls it was one up and not down. It was a fall up from sheer innocent animality into the guilt laden domain of culture and history. It was, as the theologians say, *felix culpa*—a fortunate fall. To live in a world of meaning is both our glory and our terror. Language, or conceptuality, sets us free from the dull constraints of a biological routine into that form of collective self-determination we known as history. I don't want to be odiously patronising here: I'm sure moles and badgers are splendid little chaps in their own way, and no doubt slugs and tapeworms make marvellous companions once you get to know them. It is just that their existence looks from the outside just a trifle boring, which is the last thing one can say of the flamboyant career of a species apparently set on destroying itself.

Because we live culturally and historically, our existence is at once enthralling and spectacularly precarious, whereas the lives of our fellow creatures are for the most part tedious but secure. Or rather they are insecure only because *we* are around. Being eaten by a tiger is not in the least tedious for us, but it is routine for the tiger. Having history means that we are never able to be fully identical with ourselves. Like language itself we are constitutively unfinished—and this means that death is always arbitrary and gratuitous even when we see it coming. As Lady Macbeth recognises but her husband does not, it belongs to our natures to transgress our natures. Living in a world of meaning also allows us to reflect on the grounds and validity of our meanings—in other words to do theory—which is another way in which we are not self-identical. In reflecting on ourselves, we divide ourselves into two, becoming both subject and object of our thought.

A creature doomed to meaning is one constantly at risk. It would seem, for example, to have no solid ground to its existence, since there is always more meaning where that came from, and meaning is in any case inherently unstable. There can be no such thing as a final interpretation, in the sense of an interpretation which does not itself need to be interpreted. There could be no final word because a word only has meaning in terms of other words. We are able to live historically because the kind of bodies we have are self-transcending, which is to say that they allow us within certain limits to determine the way in which we are determined. We are determined in such a way as to be able to make something creative and unpredictable of what makes us. Language offers a model of this, because it is a regular, fairly predictable system of conventions but one which all the time allows us to generate strikingly original speech acts which no one has ever heard before. A poem is the best example of such utterances.

Language allows us to make present what is absent. It punches a hole in the indicative mood and ushers in the subjunctive—the sphere of imagination and possibility. With language both futurity and negation are born. A dog may be vaguely expecting its master to return, but it can't be expecting him to return at precisely 3.57pm next Tuesday. As for negation, it is language which allows us to do this as there is no negativity in reality. Speech introduces nothingness into the world.

The problem with this constant negating and transcending of the present (which is what we mean by history) is that linguistic creatures can develop too fast. Evolution, by contrast, is mind-blowingly slow and boring but safe.

Linguistic animals are perpetually in danger of overreaching themselves and bringing themselves to nothing. Their chronic condition is what the ancient Greeks knew as hubris or which modernity knows as the myth of Faust. We are always likely to be undone by our desire. In fact there is something perversely self-doing about it: a self-delighting, self-squandering, demonic recklessness which Freud called the death drive. When it comes to taking a gratuitous delight or obscene pleasure in the destruction of others simply for the hell of it, this recklessness is traditionally known as evil.

So what has all this got to do with Gordon Brown? Let me try to sidle my way from culture to politics by way of *King Lear*. Shakespeare, in

Lear but also elsewhere, sees culture as a kind of surplus or excess, a super-fluity over and above strict necessity. But he also sees that this superfluity is necessary to us as well. Superfluity belongs to our natures. Culture is a sup-plement—but it is one which is built into our being. Shakespeare sees that to overflow the measure, as he writes in *Antony and Cleopatra*, is somehow part of our measure, that transgressing the norm belongs to what we are. This is why Lear cries, "O reason not the need!" when he is asked by his brutally utilitarian daughters why he needs even one knight in his retinue.

At one point in the play Shakespeare seems to be arguing his way from the idea of surplus and the senses to the idea of socialism. Struck by the unfamiliar sight of the naked, defenceless poor, Lear exclaims, "O, I have ta'en Too little care of this! Take physic, pomp; Expose thyself to feel what wretches feel, That thou mayst shake the superflux to them, And show the heavens more just." What Lear means is that power is without a body. Power is fleshless. If only it had a body, if it had senses, it would feel the misery it inflicts, and thus might stop doing so. What blunts the senses of power is a surplus of material property, which provides it with a kind of surrogate body, a fat-like swaddling of material possessions. And this is what insulates it against compassion. So the point is for power to shuck off its surplus fat to the poor ("shake the superflux to them"), which will then both improve the conditions of naked wretches and allow power itself (Lear himself) to *feel,* to re-appropriate its body, to be rehumanised. (The nearest thing to the play on this score, incidentally, is Marx's *Economic and Philosophical Manuscripts* of 1844, a document which similarly seeks to argue its way up from the material body to communism, from the somatic to the socialistic. Marx, too, sees that socialism is essential if we are going to start feeling our bodies again.)

As Lear goes on: "Let the superfluous and lust-dieted man That slaves your ordinance, that does not see Because he does not feel, feel your power quickly, So distribution should undo excess, And each man have enough." If the senses of the rich and powerful weren't so swaddled and pampered, the rich might be moved by the deprivations of the poor to share with them the very goods which currently prevent them from feeling their misery. The rich are quarantined from compassion by an excess of property, whereas the poor are impoverished by too little of it. The renewal of the body and a radical redistribution of wealth are closely allied. Communism and corpore-ality, here as elsewhere in Shakespeare, are closely related ideas.

"O reason not the need!" Gift, gratuity, lavishness, non-necessity, superabundance: these things are constitutive of what we are, or rather, of what we could become in politically transformed conditions. This, surely, is one reason why artistic culture is so vital all the way from the romantics to Oscar Wilde. It represents a form of production which is radically for its own sake, done just for the hell of it. As such, it is an implicit critique of utility simply by the miracles of its existence, a living rebuke to the Benthamites and avatars of exchange-value.

Art becomes that mysterious thing which, like the God from which it tries to take over, is its own ground, end and origin, which keeps conjuring itself spontaneously up from its own unfathomable depths for the sheer delight of it, which stoops to no external law and refuses to be judged by any grim faced tribunal of history, *Geist*, production, benevolence or utility, but which lives only by the law of its own autonomous being (auto-nomus)—and which in doing so resembles nothing quite so much as us, as men and women, or at least what men and women might be in a society in which we, too, would be treated as ends in ourselves, in which human existence might no longer be bent to the imperatives of a bloodlessly instrumental reason but could become, as Marx puts it in the *Grundrisse,* a matter of "the absolute working out of creative potentialities...with the development of all human powers as such as an end in itself", which is to say, in his idiom, the realm of freedom rather than the domain of necessity.

Astonishingly, then, from romanticism and aestheticism to modernism, art is most profoundly political when it's *least* functional. It is most politically engaged and instructive when it broods over the miracle of its own being in a civilisation where, strictly speaking, it ought to be well-nigh impossible. Ours is a culture where the commodity, whose reason for being lies entirely outside its sensuous being, is the norm for what defines an object and where the work of art thereby becomes the very opposite of the commodity, even if it is now in fact for the first time part of general commodity production.

In the battle between nature and culture, nature always finally has the upper hand. It's known as death. In the shorter term, however, the aim of socialism is for culture and self-delight to be where labour and necessity once were. There's an important conflict within the socialist tradition over how this is to be best accomplished: do you try to make work creative in the manner of a William Morris, so that artistic culture becomes a paradigm of non-alienated labour, or do you try to abolish work altogether, in the style of Marx and Wilde? Is the best possible reason for being a socialist the fact that you object to having to work? For Wilde this is certainly the case. In his view, once the realm of necessity has been automated, we will simply lie around the place all day in loose crimson garments in various interesting postures of *jouissance*, reciting Homer, sipping absinthe and being our own communist society. Indolence is a sign of the coming socialist kingdom.

It's absolutely nothing to feel guilty about. The aristocrat is the forerunner of the communist, rather as the landowner has a sneaking affection for the poacher as opposed to the petty bourgeois gamekeeper. The culture which is at present the preserve of the privileged few is also a utopian image of a future beyond the commodity, on the other side of iron necessity.

This, however, involves a shift in the very meaning of culture, from the more restricted sense of the term, roughly, art, to the broader sense of a whole way of life. Art defines certain qualities of living which it's the task of a radical politics to generalise to social existence as a whole: this, I take it, is a key insight of Raymond Williams, who died twenty years ago last year. Let me put these points in rather baldly propositional form:

(1) Culture in the broad sense—culture as language, symbol, kinship, community, tradition, roots, identity and so on—can be summarily defined as that which men and women are prepared to kill for, or die for. This isn't true, as you may have noticed, of culture in the sense of Stendhal and Shostakovich, except perhaps for a few seriously weird types hiding out in caves somewhere too shamefaced to come out and confront the rest of us. As capitalist civilisation develops, this *gemeinschaftlich* idea of culture grows more and not less powerful, as an abstract globalism breeds a myopic particularism.

(2) This means that culture has on the whole ceased to be part of the solution, as it was in the heyday of liberal capitalism, and has instead in advanced capitalism become part of the problem. The generous, utterly well-meaning, hopelessly idealist view that culture could provide the common or universal ground on which we could all ultimately meet, regardless of our social, sexual, ethnic and other differences, and could thus offer a much needed form of spiritual cohesion in a fragmentary society, has ceased to be viable even for most liberal bourgeois critics.

At the same time, however, culture as a radical utopian image of the kind I've discussed has ceased to be current too. Instead culture speaks the language of conflict and antagonism rather than consensus and universality. The three movements which have dominated the political agenda from the mid-20th century onwards—revolutionary nationalism, feminism and ethnic struggles—all see culture as the very idiom in which their demands are articulated, in a way that was not so true of the traditional industrial struggle.

(3) Finally, we are shifting from an opposition between civilisation and barbarism to one between civilisation and culture. The political left has always insisted that civilisation and barbarism are synchronous, not sequential—not just that civilisation was dredged laboriously from barbarism but that the two

are secretly sides of the same coin. No cathedral without a pit of bones; no high culture without wretchedness and exploitation. Nowadays, however, civilisation means individuality, universality, autonomy, irony, reflection, modernity and prosperity, whereas culture signifies spontaneity, conviction, collectivity, specificity, tradition and (generally speaking) impoverishment.

It isn't hard to map this opposition on a geographical axis. Whereas there used to be parts of the globe which were civilised and others which were barbaric, there are now bits which have civilisation and other bits which have culture. Who said there was no progress in our thinking? The only problem for the left, before it rushes to dismantle this flagrantly ideological contrast, is that there are, of course, aspects of so-called civilisation which are precious and progressive, and aspects of so-called culture which are bigoted and benighted. And on that I impeccably even-handed note, I leave the question as one for you to ponder...

An apologist with insights

Alex Callinicos

A review of Martin Wolf, **Fixing Global Finance: How to Curb Financial Crises in the 21st Century** *(Yale University, 2009), £18.99*

The great global economic crisis has put many institutions brutally to the test and destroyed them. One of these that has yet to come under sufficient scrutiny is mainstream economics. When the queen visited the London School of Economics in December 2008 she did ask, "Why did no one see it coming?". Alas, none of the culprits were hauled off to the Tower.[1] But plotting the course of a crisis that has undergone such dramatic twists and turns is a hazardous business even for those not intellectually imprisoned in the theoretical assumptions of neoclassical economics. For example, Leo Panitch and Martijn Konings, introducing a valuable collection of essays written from a broadly Marxist perspective about finance and American imperialism and published last autumn, rather unwisely expressed "some scepticism" about "strong claims concerning the disastrous outcome of the current liquidity crunch for the global system of finance and America's position in it".[2] They add, "The main upshot of the current situation is that the American state finds itself with a peculiar and unanticipated problem of imperial management".[3] I think it's fair to say the problem lies a bit deeper than one of "imperial management".

1:   For this anecdote, and the general embarrassment of mainstream economics, see Chris Giles, "The Economic Forecasters' Failing Vision", *Financial Times*, 16 December 2008.
2:   Panitch and Konings, 2008, p10.
3:   Panitch and Konings, 2008, p238.

A charitable response might stress that any reading of the situation written before the collapse of Lehman Brothers on 15 September 2008— described by George Soros as "a game-changing event with catastrophic consequences"—would be liable to be similarly embarrassed.[4] There is some truth in this: financial markets function chaotically, in the scientific sense. In other words, it's helpful in studying them to draw on the understanding of complex systems developed by chaos theory: according to this, a quite small change in the initial conditions governing a system can unleash a qualitative transformation of that system.[5]

Moreover, the sheer complexity of the capitalist economic system (of which, of course, financial markets are a subsystem) and the interaction of different tendencies that drive it reinforce this propensity for sudden flips in the overall state of the system, particularly at a time of acute crisis. Consider, for example, the dramatic shift from the preoccupation of policy makers and economic actors with accelerating inflation as late as the summer of 2008 to, by the autumn, increasing fears that the powerful recessionary forces that became evident after the financial crash precipitated by the Lehman collapse would generate a deflationary spiral—a flip reflected in the remarkable fall of the oil price by over $100 a barrel in the space of a few months.[6]

But simply to appeal to complexity would be a cop-out. A crisis on the present scale is a major test of different theoretical perspectives on contemporary capitalism. So Panitch and Konings haven't simply been caught out by events. They were misled by an analysis of imperialism that overstates both the global power of American capitalism and its success in overcoming the economic crises of the 1970s and early 1980s.[7] What about more mainstream approaches? Martin Wolf's new book, *Fixing Global Finance*, is a case in point. Wolf is one of the intellectual swells of neoliberalism. Chief economic commentator of the *Financial Times*, he went into the lists a few years ago to produce a wide-ranging defence of neoliberal globalisation.[8]

But, although Wolf is undoubtedly one of what Karl Marx called

---

4:   George Soros, "The Game Changer", *Financial Times*, 28 January 2009.
5:   On chaos theory, see especially Prigogine and Stengers, 1984.
6:   Indeed, so volatile is the state of capitalist animal spirits that, at the time of writing, bond markets seem to be switching again to reflecting expectations of increased inflation rather than of a deflationary spiral. See Krishna Guha, "Market Fears Of Deflation Abate", *Financial Times*, 15 February 2009.
7:   See Callinicos, 2005; Panitch and Gindin, 2006; Callinicos, 2006. In a recent interview Panitch, while now acknowledging the scale of the crisis, simply reaffirms this analysis—see Panitch, 2009.
8:   Wolf, 2004.

"the hired prize-fighters" of international capitalism,[9] he is very far from being a fool. He has consistently been highly critical of the euphoria surrounding the successive bubbles blown up by the financial markets in the past couple of decades. On the eve of the present crisis Wolf acknowledged that financial deregulation could lead to disaster.[10] And he was relatively quick to recognise the potential scale of the crisis once it hit. Thus he warned in February 2008 that the American economy was facing "the mother of all meltdowns": "The connection between the bursting of the housing bubble and the fragility of the financial system has created huge dangers, for the US and the rest of the world".[11]

So what Wolf has to say repays attention. Moreover, *Fixing Global Finance* isn't a polemical intervention like his previous book, but a more reflective work, developed from various academic lectures and seeking to address what he regards as tensions in the system that he so strongly defends. It seems to have been finished in the summer of 2007, on the eve of the present crisis, and has not been significantly updated, though there are passing references to what is (rather inadequately) described as "the subprime crisis". Given its vulnerability to the hazards of publishing schedules in volatile times, how well does Wolf's book stand up to the test of events?

The answer is mixed. Wolf's starting point was potentially valuable, in that he acknowledged that "the age of financial liberalisation was…an age of crises". He cited a study that estimates there were 139 financial crises between 1973 and 1997, twice the level of the era before 1914 that is often described as that of the "first globalisation", of a liberal world economy in which, under British hegemony, money flowed freely across national borders. There were, moreover, a mere 38 financial crises between 1945 and 1971, a period when capitalism was more nationally regulated.[12]

The problem is that Wolf went on to develop an analysis of the dynamics of financial crisis that presented it as largely something that afflicts so-called "emerging market economies"—that is economies in the Global South and in the former Soviet bloc that have over the past few decades been seeking integration into the world market by adopting (often partially and selectively) the distinctive institutions and practices of liberal capitalism. Hence the typical financial crisis is, according to a study by Frederic

---

9: Marx, 1976, p97.

10: Martin Wolf, "Risks and Rewards of Today's Unshackled Global Finance", *Financial Times*, 26 June 2007.

11: Martin Wolf, "America's Economy Faces Mother Of All Meltdowns", *Financial Times*, 19 February 2008.

12: Wolf, 2009, p31.

Mishkin that Wolf cited approvingly, "the product of at least one and often two errors: mismanaged liberalisation...and fiscal indiscipline".[13] The normal course of such a crisis involved increasing pressure on the currency of the state concerned until panic set in and capital fled the country, generating a deep recession.

This diagnosis is the intellectual equivalent of the generals who are always fighting the last war. It is a framework that was developed on the basis of the study of the financial crises of the 1980s and 1990s, which mainly affected Latin America, East Asia and Russia. In other words, financial crises happen somewhere else, outside the core of the system. It is true that Wolf occasionally mentioned cases that occurred closer to home, for example, the Savings and Loan crisis in the United States at the end of the 1980s. But his focus was on the "emerging markets". One might say in his defence that this was a reasonable inductive generalisation from the evidence to hand but this simply shows the inadequacy of induction as a way of providing theories with empirical support. The best theories are those that allow us, at least in broad terms, to anticipate future developments; this is the rational kernel of Karl Popper's philosophy of science.

The net effect is that Wolf provided an explanatory framework that is little use in understanding a financial crisis that started at the very core of the system, in the US itself, the state whose rulers have offered their own institutions and practices as the paradigm of neoliberalism that others should copy—a crisis, moreover, in which currency movements have been the symptoms of the larger forces at work rather than the precipitants of crisis. Nor will it do to say in Wolf's defence that he was overtaken by events. He had extraordinarily little to say about the collapse of Japan's bubble economy at the beginning of the 1990s and the resulting deflation and paralysis of the banking system. This was the most serious financial crisis to afflict an advanced capitalist state since the Great Depression (until, of course, the present one).[14]

Moreover, there has been widespread debate—provoked by, for example, semi-popular works such as Robert Shiller's *Irrational Exuberance*— for at least a decade over whether the US was heading towards a major speculative bust. Wolf's focus on "emerging market economies" whose crises can be put down to their failure to confirm to neoliberal norms (in the way that the East Asian crisis of 1997-8 was blamed on local "crony capi-

---

13:   Wolf, 2009, p34.

14:   Wolf has, however, now woken up to the possibility that the US may be experiencing a version of the same kind of crisis. See, for example, Martin Wolf, "Japanese Lessons For A World Of Balance-Sheet Deflation", *Financial Times*, 18 February 2009.

talism") allowed him to evade the really tough theoretical questions. Is it true, as neoclassical orthodoxy claims, that financial markets, when operating properly (ie without excessive state interference), are self-equilibriating, as is affirmed by the efficient market hypothesis, stated by George Gibson in 1883: "When shares become publicly known on an open market, the value which they acquire may be regarded as the judgement of the best intelligence regarding them"?[15] Or are financial markets inherently unstable, and hence liable to speculative cycles of euphoria and panic, as, for example, the "post-Keynesian" economist Hyman Minsky argued?[16] I leave out of the discussion Marxist analyses of money and finance, since Marx seems to figure in Wolf's vocabulary only as a swear-word.

So Wolf isn't much use in helping us to understand the general dynamics of financial markets under capitalism, even as the problem is posed within the framework of bourgeois economics. Where his book is valuable is in identifying one of the main dimensions of the present crisis. He pointed to the "puzzle" that, at the height of the mid-2000s boom, real interest rates were very low, despite the fact that the United States was running a huge balance of payments deficit, which should, in the normal course of things, have pushed global interest rates up because of the American need to borrow abroad. What made this state of affairs possible, Wolf argued, was that a global "savings glut" had developed. More precisely, several key regions—China and the rest of "developing Asia", Japan, the oil exporting countries, and the Euro-zone— had been running a surplus of savings over investments. In the US the reverse was true, reflecting growing government borrowing and a very low level of saving by households. As a result, "the United States has been absorbing about 70 percent of the surplus savings of the rest of the world".[17]

Wolf argued that the key element in this story was provided by the East Asian economies—Japan, South Korea, Taiwan and, above all, China. The lesson these countries' rulers drew from the crisis of the late 1990s was that they must never again allow themselves to run up big balance of payments deficits and thereby to become vulnerable to the kind of rapid inflows and outflows of foreign capital that proved so destructive then. So they pursued managed exchange rate policies whose aim was to prevent their currencies from rising too far against the US dollar and hence to keep their exports relatively cheap. One consequence of this policy was that the East Asian states had to buy foreign currencies (above all the dollar)

15: Quoted in Shiller, 2001, p172.
16: Minsky, 2008.
17: Wolf, 2009, p76.

to prevent their own from rising. So they accumulated, from the millennium onwards, vast foreign exchange reserves: "By March 2007 the total global stock of foreign-currency reserves had reached $5.3 trillion. China alone had $1.2 trillion and Japan had another $890 billion. Both Taiwan and South Korea held more reserves than the entire Eurozone. Asia held $3.3 trillion in all—just over three fifths of the global total".[18]

Much of this money was then lent back to the US, allowing it to finance its balance of payment deficit. The dollar makes up about two thirds of foreign exchange reserves, though Wolf suggested, "It would not be surprising if the proportion of Chinese reserves held in dollars was not substantially higher, given that the reserve accumulations are the by-product of an exchange rate target against the US currency".[19] Some economists have called this setup Bretton Woods Mark II, after the system of currencies fixed against the dollar that was established under the Bretton Woods Agreement of 1944 which collapsed in the early 1970s. They see it as a relatively benign and stable arrangement, in which developing economies are able to grow fast by fixing their exchange rates against the currency of the biggest developed economy, and then lend back to the US the dollars they earn in the process, allowing it to continue buying their exports.[20]

Wolf's position is more nuanced. In his book he was admirably brisk with various practitioners of voodoo economics who have tried to explain away the American deficit. (My favourites among these are two Harvard academics who claim that the official payments figures fail to take into account financial "dark matter": once this is added in, they claim, the US turns out to be a net creditor.) He also pointed out that, at the end of 2006, "almost two thirds of the foreign holdings of US assets (other than financial derivatives) took the form of debt". But the real return on American private and public debt held by foreigners was, over the period 1973 and 2004, a mere 0.32 percent.[21]

"Thus", Wolf observed, "the signal—and for the United States, very favourable—characteristic of foreign ownership is that a high proportion of foreign capital is invested in assets with low returns, denominated—even better for the United States—in depreciated dollars".[22] Indeed, he calculated that America's net financial liabilities—what it owes to foreigners minus its assets abroad (the foreign investments of US firms and citizens)—has risen

---

18: Wolf, 2009, p87.
19: Wolf, 2009, p95.
20: For example, Dooley, Folkerts-Landau and Garber, 2004.
21: Wolf, 2009, p124.
22: Wolf, 2009, p124.

much more slowly than the influx of capital required to finance the deficit. Simply on the basis of the cumulative current account deficits, "the US should have had net liabilities equal to 44 percent of GDP [gross domestic product] at the end of 2006. As it was, according to the Bureau of Economic Analysis, the net liability position was only 16 percent of GDP, down from 23 percent at the end of 2002".[23] This is partly because of the fall of the dollar against other major currencies (in the 1970s, the late 1980s and early 1990s, and 2002-8), but mainly because the prices of US-held assets abroad have risen relative to those of the assets held by foreigners in the US.

Wolf concluded that "the best argument for the view that high current account deficits are indefinitely sustainable is that Americans are 'savvy investors', fleecing the naive".[24] Indeed, quoting the former French president Valéry Giscard d'Estaing, who described "the ability of the United States to borrow cheaply and apparently without limit in its own currency as an 'exorbitant privilege'", he went on to write, "The United States (as is true also of the United Kingdom) has been a vast and hitherto very profitable hedge fund".[25] This is an interesting analysis because it seems to dovetail with the argument of various Marxist and radical scholars that the US derives massive advantages from its dominance of the financial system (though they often stress the strength of the dollar, whereas, according to Wolf, it has been the successive episodes of dollar devaluation that have been a key mechanism in boosting the relative price of US foreign assets).[26]

This state of affairs allows the US to play what critics of American imperialism would call a hegemonic role:

> The United States accommodates and offsets whatever the rest of the world throws at it because, as issuer of the world's key currency, it suffers from no external constraint: it has been able, at least up to now, to borrow as much as it wishes in its own currency, at modest interest rates... The result is that the Federal Reserve [the US central bank] is free to pursue policies that balance the US economy and, in doing so, also balance the world's, by absorbing the excess savings and so the surplus of goods and services, at given real exchange rates, of the rest of the world.[27]

23: Wolf, 2009, p126.
24: Wolf, 2009, p137.
25: Wolf, 2009, p112.
26: Two of the best examples of this kind of analysis are Wade, 2003, and Gowan, 2009.
27: Wolf, 2009, p100. Herman Schwartz argues the position of a hegemonic state is underpinned economically by it acting as the main market for other participants in the world economy—Schwartz, 2000, chapter 3.

This analysis of the financial imbalances particularly between the US and East Asia is important for two reasons. First, it highlights a crucial presupposition of the credit boom of the mid-2000s: it was the flood of lending from East Asia that made it so cheap to borrow and blow up the speculative bubble that developed in the American housing market and sucked in (via a cobweb of financial derivatives) much of the global banking system. Second, Wolf believed the US's role as "borrower and spender of last resort" was a positive one: "the US current account deficit is protecting the world from recession".[28] But he was ambivalent. On the one hand, this situation "is far better than the repeated financial crises that preceded it".[29] On the other hand, he was queasy about "a more liberal global financial system" that "generates a huge surge of capital that flows 'uphill'—not from the world's most advanced economy, as happened in the 19th century under British hegemony, but toward it".[30]

Wolf accordingly favoured a cautious and phased process of adjustment, in which the US would gradually save more and consume less, and China save less and consume more. In its final chapters the book descended into not very interesting Davos boilerplate about the reform of the International Monetary Fund and the like. Here it has most visibly been overtaken by events. Far from representing a break from "repeated financial crises", the pattern Wolf analysed has led to the biggest crash since 1929. Not that the global imbalances directly caused the present financial crisis, but that, in making possible "an apparently ongoing free banquet" for American capitalism,[31] they facilitated the credit boom whose collapse in 2007 has now paralysed the international banking system.

The resulting crisis has also underlined the pivotal role of the US in sustaining global demand. The American recession that started in early 2008 has now sent the great manufacturing and trading economies of the world—Germany, Japan and China—into a tailspin as their main export market has dried up. The fantasy that Asia could somehow "decouple" from the US and keep the world economy growing despite the financial crisis, a view still influential in the markets in the winter of 2007-8, has been demolished.[32] As Wolf has recently emphasised, "the US, it is clear,

---

28: Wolf, 2009, p110.
29: Wolf, 2009, p150.
30: Wolf, 2009, p113.
31: Wolf, 2009, p112.
32: These illusions are recorded in Sundeep Tucker, Joe Leahy and Geoff Dyer, "Asia's Continued Rise Spurs 'Decoupling' Debate", *Financial Times*, 1 November 2007.

remains the core of the world economy".[33]

In the face of this spectacular reversal, Wolf has moved to the left somewhat. He now declares that "Keynes offers us the best way to think about the financial crisis", and praises Minsky for his critique of the efficient market hypothesis. Consistent with the stress on the necessity of massive state intervention to prop up the banking system that has been one of the main themes of his *Financial Times* column since the onset of the crisis, he calls for measures, in the short term, "to sustain aggregate demand, as Keynes would have recommended", and, in the longer term, "to force a rebalancing of global demand".[34] This second theme is more or less a cliche of contemporary policy discussion. "There is no longer any choice for Asia," pontificates Clyde Prestowitz of the Economic Strategy Institute. "Asia has to start consuming more... The export-led model has outlived its usefulness".[35]

The trouble with such pronouncements is that they ignore the concrete interests that sustain different economic models. Worse still, they ignore class. Concepts such as savings and investment that Wolf uses in his analysis of global imbalances refer to macroeconomic aggregates, the analysis of which Keynes helped to pioneer. Despite their undoubted usefulness, these concepts grasp the behaviour of capitalist economies at a relatively superficial level. To go deeper we need the Marxist concept of capitalist relations of production and the understanding of antagonistic class relationships that this allows. Thus it isn't "Asia" that will decide to consume more or less. Patterns of consumption reflect deeply entrenched class relations. At one point Wolf acknowledged these realities:

> Chinese households save enormously. But the core of the Chinese savings story over the past five or six years has been the rise in corporate savings... The Chinese government told state enterprises to become profitable, and they have done what they were told. The corporate sector has become profitable by disposing of surplus workers, yet the government has not taken some of the increased profits as dividends on the assets it owns, even to finance a safety net for displaced workers. Remarkably (and shockingly), the government has left the money with enterprise insiders. But the government

33: Martin Wolf, "Japanese Lessons For A World of Balance-Sheet Deflation", *Financial Times*, 18 February 2009.
34: Martin Wolf, "Keynes Offers Us The Best Way To Think About The Crisis", *Financial Times*, 24 December 2008. Compare his much more even-handed response to the death of Milton Friedman, the founder of monetarism: "Keynes v Friedman: Both Can Claim Victory", *Financial Times*, 21 November 2006.
35: David Pilling, "Unlucky Numbers", *Financial Times*, 13 February 2009.

itself is also a large saver. China has about 800 million poor people, yet the country now consumes less than half of GDP and exports capital to the rest of the world. This is highly peculiar. It is also why the country has such a huge current account surplus.[36]

So what is generally presented as "China" not consuming "enough" is really intensified exploitation via the extraction of relative surplus-value—fewer workers are producing a growing output. Low consumption by Chinese workers is matched by high profits for Chinese capital. But the same realities govern the other end of the circuit that has sustained the world economy, namely the US. Analysing the American balance of payments deficit, Wolf points to:

A startling contrast between business and the household sector... The business sector moved into a large deficit during the investment boom triggered by the bubble economy of the late 1990s and 2000. It then cut back sharply on investment and, after a short period of squeeze, built up profits again. More important, it also avoided any repeat of the investment surge of the 1990s. As a result, the business sector ran a financial surplus from the fourth quarter of 2001 to the first quarter of 2007.[37]

So the gap between savings and investment is to be found in the US business sector. I will return to this shortly. Let us first note that, as Wolf observed, "the household sector is quite a different story. It has been running historically unprecedented financial deficits, consistently spending more than its income on consumption and residential investment".[38] The obvious way of interpreting this is that ordinary Americans have been engaged in a high-consumption splurge. Such a view informs all the chatter about the crisis being "our" fault because we've been so busy borrowing and spending.

The trouble is that this doesn't fit with another important piece of the economic puzzle. As Edward Luce puts it:

Between 2000 and 2006, the US economy expanded by 18 percent, whereas real income for the median working household dropped by 1.1 percent in real terms, or about $2,000... Meanwhile, the top tenth saw an improvement

36: Wolf, 2009, p69.
37: Wolf, 2009, p104.
38: Wolf, 2009, p104.

of 32 percent in their incomes, the top 1 percent a rise of 203 percent and the top 0.1 percent a gain of 425 percent. Part of this was because the latest period of economic growth failed to create jobs at nearly the same rate as in previous business cycles and even led to a decline in the number of hours worked for most employees. Unusually for a time of expansion, the number of participants in the labour force also fell. But mostly it was because the fruits of economic growth and soaring productivity rates went to the highest income earners.[39]

One does not have to look much further than these figures to understand the deep anger in American society that has been directed against the Wall Street bankers. But, from a scientific point of view, it represents, once again, a higher rate of exploitation thanks to an increase in relative surplus-value.[40] Workers at both ends of the circuit have been squeezed. The difference is that Chinese workers, at a much lower standard of living than their counterparts in the US, are pressured to save in order to provide the security against illness, unemployment and old age that the Chinese state no longer offers them. American workers, by contrast, have been encouraged to borrow in order to sustain their basic consumption at a time when their real wages have actually fallen. This both helped to maintain effective demand and thereby to keep the American and world economies growing after the collapse of the dotcom boom in 2000 and to provide profits for the banks that lent them the money. It is the bursting of the resulting bubble that precipitated the present crisis.[41]

But there is one final piece to the puzzle. As we have seen, Wolf argued that American firms were hanging onto their profits rather than investing them. But he also noted that this is a general phenomenon in the

---

39: Edward Luce, "Stuck In The Middle", *Financial Times*, 28 October 2008.

40: One note of caution about simply extrapolating, as I do in the text, from national-income statistics: naturally the concepts used in these statistics do not correspond to those of Marxist value theory, with potentially misleading consequences. For example, part of what is classified as labour income—the earnings of senior corporate executives—should probably be understood as a portion of surplus-value, which is redistributed to this layer of employees in order to ensure their loyalty and efficiency. Doing so wouldn't contradict the point made in the text, since it would mean that the rise in the rate of exploitation (profits relative to wages) is even higher than the official statistics indicate because the mass of surplus-value would then comprise these "earnings" in addition to profits, interests, and rent, but the rate of profit (profits relative to investment) would then also turn out to be higher. I owe this point to Gérard Duménil.

41: Costas Lapavitsas has rightly highlighted the significance of the increasing extension of the credit system to lending to workers, but his suggestion that this has led to the "direct exploitation" of workers by the banks doesn't seem particularly helpful—Lapavitsas, 2008.

"aftermath of what we may now confidently call the global stock market bubble of 1999-2000":

> In most economically significant countries, corporations are very profitable but cautious about investing... The shift on income from labour to capital is an important phenomenon across high-income economies. Interestingly and significantly, the biggest shift from labour income has not been in the United States and other Anglo-Saxon countries, but in Japan and the Eurozone.[42]

So one key dimension of the "savings glut" is that capitalists in the advanced economies during the 2000s increased their profits through wage repression but then not invested these profits in expanded production. There are various ways of explaining this phenomenon. The one I prefer is that, on the evidence available, capitalists may have succeeded in increasing the rate of surplus-value, the mass of profits relative to wages, but they have failed to push up the rate of profit, the mass of profits relative to total investment (in means of production as well as in labour-power), to a level where they feel confident enough to invest on a large scale. If this explanation is correct, then it puts the credit bubble in another perspective, where we can see it as an effort (engineered especially by the Federal Reserve while Alan Greenspan was its chairman) to allow the US economy (and hence, thanks to its central role in maintaining global demand, the world) to continue to grow, despite its failure to overcome a chronic crisis of profitability that dates ultimately back to the 1960s.[43]

Where does this leave Wolf's book? It contains, as the foregoing analysis indicates, important elements for an explanation of the present crisis. But these are present in a fragmentary way. This is partly a consequence of the—to be frank—apologetic framework in which Wolf approaches the specific issue of financial crisis, but more fundamentally because of his reliance on the concepts of neoclassical orthodoxy, which are completely incapable of identifying the real mechanisms governing capitalist economic relations. Therefore, for all the intelligence of the author and the value of the material that he provides, I couldn't recommend *Fixing Global Finance* as a way into the present crisis. From this point of view, it is inferior to

---

42: Wolf, 2009, p64.

43: The question of whether the rate of profit has been falling is a matter of great controversy even among Marxist economists. For recent analysis and discussion, see Brenner, 2006, Harman, 2007, and the discussion inspired by the latter article—Kincaid, 2008, Harman, 2008, and Moseley, 2008. Brenner traces the relationship between low profitability and successive bubbles in Brenner, 2002, and Brenner, 2004.

Graham Turner's *The Credit Crunch*,[44] which, though written from a theoretical perspective closer to Irving Fisher's theory of debt deflation than to Marxist political economy, has a much better sense of the dynamics of the crisis, particularly through the relationship that Turner posits between wage repression and financial speculation. At a time such as the present, those who remain within the boundaries of mainstream thinking are lost.

44: Turner, 2008.

References

Brenner, Robert, 2002, *The Boom and the Bubble* (Verso).

Brenner, Robert, 2004, "New Boom or New Bubble?", *New Left Review* 25 (January-February 2004), www.newleftreview.org/A2490

Brenner, Robert, 2006, *The Economics of Global Turbulence* (Verso).

Callinicos, Alex, 2005, "Imperialism and Global Political Economy", *International Socialism* 108 (autumn 2005), www.isj.org.uk/?id=140

Callinicos, Alex, 2006, "Making Sense of Imperialism: A Reply to Leo Panitch and Sam Gindin", *International Socialism* 110 (spring 2006), www.isj.org.uk/?id=196

Dooley, Michael P, David Folkerts-Landau and Peter Garber, 2004, "The Revived Bretton Woods System", *International Journal of Finance and Economics*, volume 9.

Gowan, Peter, 2009, "Crisis in the Heartland", *New Left Review* 55 (January-February 2009), www.newleftreview.org/A2759

Harman, Chris, 2007, "The rate of profit and the world today", *International Socialism* 115 (summer 2007), www.isj.org.uk/?id=340

Harman, Chris, 2008, "Misreading and misconceptions", *International Socialism* 119 (summer 2008), www.isj.org.uk/?id=462

Kincaid, Jim, 2008, "The world economy—a critical comment", *International Socialism* 119 (summer 2008), www.isj.org.uk/?id=461

Lapavitsas, Costas, 2008, "Financialised Capitalism: Direct Exploitation and Periodic Bubbles", May 2008, www.soas.ac.uk/economics/events/crisis/43939.pdf.

Marx, Karl, 1976 [1867], *Capital*, volume one (Penguin); an alternative translation is available from www.marxists.org/archive/marx/works/1867-c1/

Minsky, Hyman, 2008 [1986], *Stabilizing an Unstable Economy* (McGraw-Hill).

Moseley, Fred, 2008, "Some Notes on the Crunch and the Crisis", *International Socialism* 119 (summer 2008), www.isj.org.uk/?id=463

Panitch, Leo, 2009, "The Financial Crisis and American Power", *The Bullet* 186, 16 February 2009, www.socialistproject.ca/bullet/bullet186.html

Panitch, Leo, and Sam Gindin, 2006, "'Imperialism and Global Political Economy'—A Reply to Alex Callinicos", *International Socialism* 109 (winter 2006), www.isj.org.uk/?id=175

Panitch, Leo, and Martijn Konings, 2008, "Demystifying Imperial Finance", in *American Empire and the Political Economy of Global Finance* (Palgrave Macmillan).

Prigogine, Ilya, and Isabelle Stengers, 1984, *Order out of Chaos* (Bantam).

Schwartz, Herman, 2000, *States versus Markets* (Palgrave Macmillan).

Shiller, Robert, 2001, *Irrational Exuberance* (Princeton University).

Turner, Graham, 2008, *The Credit Crunch* (Pluto).

Wade, Robert, 2003, "The Invisible Hand of the American Empire", *Ethics and International Affairs*, volume 17, number 2, www.columbia.edu/itc/sipa/U6800/readings-sm/Wade_Invisible_Hand.pdf

Wolf, Martin, 2004, *Why Globalization Works* (Yale University).

Wolf, Martin, 2009, *Fixing Global Finance: How to Curb Financial Crises in the 21st Century* (Yale University).

Social work after "Baby P"

Iain Ferguson and Michael Lavalette

In August 2007 the UK media reported the tragic death of a 17 month old boy (who became known as "Baby P"). In November 2008 two people were convicted of causing or allowing the death. The court was told that Baby P had been used as a "punch bag" and that his mother had "manipulated and lied to social workers and health visitors", even smearing him with chocolate to cover his bruises. The baby was eventually found dead in his blood-splattered cot just 48 hours after a doctor had failed to notice that he had a broken spine.

This happened in the London borough of Haringey, where seven years earlier the death of eight year old Victoria Climbié at the hands of a great-aunt and her boyfriend had led to a national outcry, followed by an investigation into social work practice (both in Haringey and nationally) by Lord Laming, and increased regulation and inspection of social work in Britain. This new death led to a similar outcry.

The *Sun* newspaper ran a petition calling for the sacking of the social workers involved in the case—and over 850,000 people signed.[1] The government announced a new national child protection review, again headed by Lord Laming, which would look at current practice in implementing safeguarding procedures, inter-agency work, effective public accountability and "developing and deploying workforce capacity". The children's secretary,

---

1: "Baby P Petition Reaches 850,000", the *Sun*, 24 November 2008.

Ed Balls, announced a review of serious cases and of Local Safeguarding Children Boards. He also brought in a temporary head of children's services from Hampshire, and suspended and then sacked Haringey's children's director, Sharon Shoesmith, as well as a number of frontline staff.

Initially the events were framed in a familiar guise: that "politically correct" social workers were a "soft touch" for manipulative parents; that social workers and their way of working were, at best, problematic, at worst completely failing; that there was a need for more regulation and controls over what social workers do; that the solution was more managerialism and marketisation of social care services.

Yet quite quickly other arguments began to develop. In the face of the suggestion that social workers were "failing" in their work, Polly Toynbee argued in the *Guardian* that "the number of children killed has fallen steadily—down 50 percent in England and Wales since the 1970s... Britain was fourth worst among Western nations in the 1970s. Now it is among the best: only four countries have fewer child murders per million. Compare America, where child murders have risen by 17 percent since the 1970s".[2]

And gradually evidence started to emerge of an under-resourced childcare system where budgetary constraints and market methods of care delivery had made child protection, and social work generally, more difficult. Childcare social workers in Haringey were still working with caseloads similar to those prior to the inquiry into the death of Victoria Climbié. A survey by the Unison union for the new Laming inquiry suggests that average caseloads for social workers working with children and families have increased since 2003.[3] It quotes one social worker: "I have 30 cases—all of which are child protection. I have been working in social work for 22 years, but it has never been as bad as it has in the last year".[4]

In Haringey there were large numbers of agency staff working in the borough, filling gaps where people had left or were on long-term sick leave. The survey suggests this is far from unusual. Six out of ten respondents claimed that there were more than 20 percent of posts vacant in their area, and a fifth claimed over 30 percent.[5] People without a social work qualification or newly qualified staff without experience, Unison suggests, are filling the gap of undertaking difficult child protection work.

2:   Polly Toynbee, "This Frenzy Of Hatred Is A Disaster For Children At Risk", the *Guardian*, 18 November 2008, www.guardian.co.uk/commentisfree/2008/nov/18/comment-social-services-child-protection
3:   Unison, 2009, p4.
4:   Unison, 2009, p4.
5:   Unison, 2009, p3.

The computerised Integrated Children's System being rolled out across the country is unfit for purpose and takes social workers away from face to face work with clients. "Social workers report spending between 60 percent and 80 percent of their time at the computer screen," according to Sue White, who has just conducted research into the impact of the new system.[6]

The Baby P case has thrown up a range of issues about the nature and scale of child abuse, the extent and impact of poverty on children's lives, the role of social work in the modern welfare state and to what extent there is space for an alternative, more engaged social work practice.

The abuse of children in Britain today

"Childhood" is not a natural stage of human growth common to all societies, despite commonsense assertions to the contrary, nor is it a life stage that we all experience in the same way. It has been shaped by the development of modern capitalism. And this did not bring a new "enlightened approach" to children and childhood, as much academic writing holds.[7] For working class children capitalism brought increased exploitation and oppression. They were forced to work in cottage industries, mines and factories, and they found themselves facing a brutal state determined to control their activities through the "justice" and penal systems. For children in bourgeois families, by contrast, there was education by governesses and teachers in public schools and "training" for a future life of privilege and authority. The vast differences and inequalities in the lives led by children of the different classes remain at the start of the 21st century.

Society has never been wealthier—and this means that there is the potential to deal with the vast range of problems that children face. Yet children in Britain continue to face all manner of societal abuse. The evidence shows that Britain, in comparison to other economically advanced countries, is failing its children. It also shows that the lives of poor and working class children are worse, more restrictive and more dangerous than their middle class peers on every front.

The most comprehensive recent survey of children's lives was produced by Unicef in 2007.[8] The UK ranked bottom of 21 industrialised countries in its child "well-being assessment", based on 40 separate

---

6:   White, 2008.
7:   For the debates around these issues, see, for example, Goldson, Lavalette and MacKechnie, 2002.
8:   Unicef, 2007.

indicators—including relative poverty, child safety, educational achievement and drug abuse. Britain has a higher number of children in poverty, defined as living below 60 percent of the typical income, despite 11 years of New Labour government and its much trumpeted target of eradicating child poverty by 2020. In Britain 22 percent of children are poor, compared to 8 percent in Sweden and 10 percent in Denmark. Thirty years ago the British figure was only 13 percent.[9] One in ten five to 16 year olds now have clinically significant mental health difficulties, but only a quarter of children who are seriously troubled or disturbed by mental health difficulties are getting any kind of specialist help.

The impact of poverty starts before birth. Children born to poor mothers are more likely to be born underweight and are ten times more likely to suffer from sudden death syndrome. They are also more vulnerable to a range of chronic illnesses, including cerebral palsy and various mental disorders. As they age they are 50 times more likely to suffer type two diabetes and 25 percent more likely to suffer chronic heart disease.[10] Toddlers from disadvantaged families experience slower rates of social and educational development so that, by the time they turn six, previously less able children from wealthier backgrounds will be ahead of them.[11] Children from poor households are more likely to leave school at 16 with fewer educational qualifications—only 28 percent of children in the most deprived quarter of schools gained five or more GCSE passes at A to C, compared to 67 percent of children in the least deprived quarter of schools.[12] A boy brought up in Calton, in the East End of Glasgow, can expect to live 28 years less than one brought up in Lenzie, a few miles away; one born in Hampstead, London, will live around 11 years longer than a boy from St Pancras, five stops away on London Underground's Northern Line.[13]

Finally, there is significant data to show that accidents, injuries and deaths of children are all profoundly influenced by class and poverty. Every year over a million children in the UK under the age of 15 are involved in accidents in the home for which they require hospital treatment. Accidents are the commonest cause of death in children over one year old and every

9: "The Good Childhood Inquiry", report summary, The Children's Society, http://tinyurl.com/tgcirs

10: "Study Links Child Poverty To Ill Health And Sudden Death Syndrome", Warwick University, http://www2.warwick.ac.uk/newsandevents/news/study_links_child/

11: "Charities Demand Action Over Child Inequality", the *Guardian*, 11 June 2007.

12: "The Good Childhood Inquiry", report summary, The Children's Society, http://tinyurl.com/tgcirs

13: "UK Trailing On Ill-health And Life Expectancy, UN Says", the *Guardian*, 29 August 2008.

year thousands suffer permanent disability or disfigurement. The age group most at risk from a home accident are the nought to four years.[14] Traffic accidents are the biggest killer of children and young people, causing 169 deaths of under 15 year olds in 2006 and seriously injuring 3,125.[15] Again children from poor areas are more likely to be the victims. Overcrowding in the home pushes them onto busy streets to play, so children from deprived areas are four times more likely to be seriously injured than pedestrians and three times more likely than cyclists.[16]

So the evidence shows that there continues to be a high level of societal abuse directed against the poorest and most vulnerable, but what about violence and abuse of individual children in the home?

Child abuse and the family

The family is a deeply contradictory institution. On the one hand, it seems to offer a haven, a place away from the pressures, inequalities and alienation of modern life, providing common support against the outside world; a place where people (usually women) care for children, partners and older relatives. Yet, on the other hand, it is also a deeply oppressive institution—at the heart of women's oppression and restrictive to so many people's lives.

The evidence shows it can be a very violent institution. One incident of domestic violence is reported to the police every minute, and on average two women a week are killed by a current or former male partner.[17] Yet the common sense is that children are in danger of violent abuse, sexual abuse and murder not from a family member, but from a stranger (so-called "stranger danger"). The figures tell a different story. The NSPCC data shows that while "child homicides"[18] are rare, the most likely culprits are family members. Every ten days in England and Wales one child is killed at the hands of a parent. This compares with an annual average of 11 children a year who are killed by strangers.[19] Infants aged under one are most at risk of being killed, and almost two thirds of children

14: "Child Safety...A Very Comprehensive, Useful Action List for Parents and Carers", Home Security Action, www.home-security-action.co.uk/child-safety.html

15: "Child Fact Sheet—Child Casualties in Road Accidents Great Britain: 2006", Department for Transport, http://tinyurl.com/cciragb

16: "Children In Poor Areas 'More At Risk Of Traffic Accidents'", *Families First for Health*, Great Ormond Street Hospital, www.childrenfirst.nhs.uk/families/news/2008/april3.html

17: "Domestic Violence Statistics", Women's Aid, http://tinyurl.com/wastat

18: That is, murder, manslaughter and infanticide.

19: "What you Need to Know about Child Abuse", NSPCC, www.nspcc.org.uk/whatwedo/aboutthenspcc/keyfactsandfigures/keyfacts_wda33645.html killed are aged under five. The younger the child, the more likely it is that the perpetrator is a parent.[20]

The figures for sexual abuse suggest that 16 percent of children under the age of 16 experience some form of sexual abuse: 11 percent of this is "contact abuse" and the rest is non-contact. The vast majority of "contact abuse" will involve more than one single event and is likely to be carried out by family members, relatives and family friends. The most common perpetrator is likely to be a brother or stepbrother. The most common site for abuse is the family home, or other known home. In 5 percent of cases the perpetrators are adult strangers or someone the child has just met; these are much more likely to be single event "non-contact" forms of abuse (eg flashing).[21] There is a similar pattern for physical abuse: 21 percent of children experience some degree of physical abuse at the hands of their parents or carers.[22]

What is the relationship between child abuse and poverty? Of course, the majority of poor parents do not abuse their children, but the few studies there are of the relationship between class and child abuse suggest a clear link between poverty and maltreatment. Some 60 percent of children on the child protection register for the Strathclyde region in Scotland in the 1990s lived in Glasgow, which has the highest concentration of poverty but only 27 percent of the population. The three poorest areas of Glasgow accounted for four times as many registered children as the city's other areas.[23] Some 25 percent of the children on the protection register in Coventry lived in just one electoral ward (the poorest in the city), although it only held 12 percent of the city's children.[24] More recently John Devaney has suggested that there is a significant "positive relationship" between a range of indicators of deprivation (unemployment and dependence on state benefits, overcrowding, living in social housing, non-car ownership) and children on the protection register.[25]

Two additional factors are important to take note of: parental age and parental history. There are a disproportionate number of parents on child protection registers who were under the age of 20 at the time of the child's birth.[26] And important research suggests that a parent's own

---

20: NSPCC, 2007a.
21: NSPCC, 2007b.
22: NSPCC, 2007c.
23: Baldwin and Spencer, 1993.
24: Baldwin and Carruthers, 1998.
25: Devaney, 2009.
26: Bunting and McAuley, 2004.

experience of child abuse will lead a significant proportion to encounter a range of problems associated with drug and alcohol abuse, depression, low self-esteem and poor physical health, with a minority then mistreating their own children.[27]

When money is tight, housing poor, living conditions overcrowded, life becomes stressful and the family home becomes a pressure cooker where parents can explode into rage at their children. That anger and frustration is more likely to be focused on the family's children if the parents are also younger and have a history of being abused themselves. The consequences are tragic, but it is the social conditions created by poverty and inequality which provide the context for the eruption of violence. It is also here, alongside the very poorest and most marginalised in society, that social workers spend most of their working lives.

"Care and control"—welfare under capitalism

Social work, sometimes described as the "fifth social service", after health, housing, education and social security, has always differed from these other arms of the post-war welfare state in being a residual, as opposed to a universal, service. Its primary concern, in other words, has traditionally been with the welfare only of those who belong to the very poorest sections of the working class, including those for whom age, or physical or mental disability creates problems for themselves or others. In Strathclyde in the 1990s, for example, nine out of ten social work clients were in receipt of state benefits.[28]

The statutory remit of social workers requires them to manage the perceived problem behaviour of poor parents, including, on occasion, taking their children into care. This has two consequences. They are often regarded with suspicion and hostility within working class communities— to a greater extent than, say, health visitors, who have no such statutory powers. And their association with stigmatised groups, such as abusing parents, young offenders, asylum seekers and people with severe mental health problems, makes them an easy target for right wing politicians and tabloids, who can portray social workers as being "soft" and "naive"— particularly since professional social work ideology emphasises the importance of being "non-judgemental", in the sense of seeking to understand the reasons for clients' behaviour.

Professional social work brings out particularly sharply the

27: Anda, Brown, Felitti, Bremner, Dube and Giles, 2006.
28: Becker, 1997.

contradiction between the "care" and "control" aspects of welfare provision under capitalism, which are present in all areas of welfare as the product of a mixture of complex and competing factors.[29]

First, welfare reforms are sometimes the direct outcome of working class struggle.[30] In France, for example, the social welfare settlement of the 1930s was strongly shaped by the wave of working class struggles that led to the election of a Popular Front government in 1936 against the background of a million on strike in Paris and mass factory occupations.[31] Again in France, in 1995-6 it was the threat of cuts to the social welfare budget (the so-called "Juppé plan") that brought two million people onto the streets, defeated the cuts and ignited an atmosphere of class conflict that still continues.[32]

More generally, the fear of working class revolt destabilising the existing order can be a major, if indirect, factor in producing reforms from above. Examples might include Bismarck's social legislation in 19th century Germany (which went hand in hand with the repression of the emerging socialist political parties) or the cross-party consensus on the need for change in Britain at the end of the Second World War, reflected in the statement of the Tory MP Quentin Hogg (later Lord Hailsham) in 1943, "If you do not give the people social reform, they are going to give you social revolution".[33] In that sense, the creation of a "welfare state" in Britain by the 1945-51 Labour government, with a National Health Service at its heart, mirrored the balance of class forces at the beginning of the post-war period.

It would, however, be inaccurate and misleading to portray welfare provision under capitalism as always being the product of struggle from below. Welfare also plays an important role for the ruling class as a form of social control, both political and ideological. Since its origins in the Poor Law of the 1830s it has been important in ensuring that those who are capable of selling their labour power are forced to do so. Provision for the rest has been made as unpleasant and stigmatising as possible, restricted to very limited categories of people (the old, the severely disabled and so on). This meant that, for much of the 19th century, the dreaded workhouse was the only alternative to destitution for many. The first social work organisation in Britain, the Charity Organisation Society created in 1869, was rightly described by Clement Attlee as "essentially designed for the defence

---

29: Ferguson, Lavalette and Mooney, 2002, chapter 2.
30: Lavalette and Mooney, 2000.
31: Danos and Gibelin, 1986.
32: Wolfreys, 1999.
33: *Hansard*, 17 February 1943.

of the propertied classes".[34] The dominant ideology within the organisation was a pathologising one, which blamed clients for their alleged character failings rather than locating misery within wider socio-economic structures. For its journal, the *Charity Organisation Review*, "the poverty of the working classes of England" was due "not to their circumstances" but "to their improvident habits and thriftlessness".[35]

The social control function of welfare is no less important today. This is shown by New Labour's attempt to force thousands of lone parents into the workplace and to reduce the number of disabled people claiming incapacity benefit by one million by new work tests—all justified by spurious claims that "work is the route out of poverty". More generally, welfare policy is crucial in shaping and reinforcing dominant ideologies about family and nation. Much welfare policy is based on familial assumptions,[36] assuming, for instance, that most women will raise children and provide domestic labour. It also reflects judgements about who should qualify for welfare benefits or services, invariably including a notion of "British citizenship" that questions the legitimacy of claims for benefits from "outsiders" such as asylum seekers.[37]

Finally, welfare provision matters to capitalism for another important reason. No individual capitalist nation can hope to compete successfully with its rivals without a healthy, well educated workforce. Thus ensuring at least a very basic level of health and education is in the interests of the capitalist class as a whole. Marx noted this in his discussion of the 19th century Factory Acts, which placed some limits on the hours worked by women and children in particular. "Factory legislation...is... just as much the necessary product of large-scale industry as cotton yarn, self-actors and the electric telegraph".[38] Most of the key welfare reforms of the past 100 years have been driven by recognition of the need for a skilled, healthy workforce, capable of contributing not only to the nation's economic success but also (as the negative experience of the Boer War showed) to its military success.[39] Nor, as Chris Harman notes, is this simply a question of physical well-being: "It is also a question of morale. The capitalist wants contented workers to exploit in the same way that a farmer wants contented cows. Workers cannot be expected to labour

34: Cited in Lewis, 1995, p86.
35: Cited in Jones, 1983, p76.
36: Merrick, 1996.
37: Mynott, 2000.
38: Marx, 1976, p610.
39: On this see Thane, 1982.

with any commitment to their work if they expect to starve to death once they reach retirement age".[40]

Yet Marx also noted that "capital never becomes reconciled to such changes".[41] In almost every case such reforms had to be forced through parliament in the teeth of fierce opposition from capitalists, who bitterly resented being forced to give up part of their profits in the form of taxes to fund welfare provisions for workers, even if their class as a whole benefited. Ruling classes were reluctantly prepared to concede a higher level of welfare spending so long as the economy was growing during the "long boom" between the late 1940s and the early 1970s. However, when global economic crisis returned in the mid-1970s, cutting such expenditure became a central political priority for both Labour and Conservative governments.

Neoliberalism, welfare and managerialism

The main concern of Margaret Thatcher and her ministers during her first two periods of Conservative government in the UK (1979-87) was with crushing working class organisation, both through direct attacks on specific trade unions and also through allowing unemployment to rise to around three million. It was not until her third term, from 1987 onwards, that the Conservatives turned their attention to the restructuring of welfare. The key turning point was the passing of the National Health Service and Community Care Act 1990, based on a report by Sainsbury's managing director, Sir Roy Griffiths. It sought to introduce market principles into health and social care, by changing the role of local authorities from providers of services to purchasers of services, based on competitive tendering by private and voluntary sector organisations:

> The implementation of the NHS and Community Care Act (1990) changed fundamentally the operation of social service departments and the practice of social work. It spearheaded the establishment of the social work business through two inter-related developments: marketisation and managerialism.[42]

Managerialism[43] is primarily concerned with bringing the values and practices of private sector management (in reality a wholly idealised and inaccurate version of these practices) into the public sector in general, and

---

40: Harman, 2008, p115.
41: Marx, 1976.
42: Harris, 2003, p43.
43: For a discussion of the marketisation of social work and social care, see Harris, 2003, and Ferguson, 2008.

social work and social care in particular. Managers, operating within the parameters of "economy, efficiency and effectiveness", were depicted by the Audit Commission as the "Bolsheviks" of the managerial revolution,[44] which would revitalise what was seen as a "failing profession". They would do this by: putting in place a strategic vision (usually in the form of a mission statement); introducing common values, which in practice means identification with the organisation, rather than with core social work values; refashioning clients as "customers" and emphasising "customer care", in reality complaints procedures; an emphasis on "performance review", through inspectorates such as Ofsted; much tighter budgetary procedures, based on the view that efficient management, not increased resources, is the key to quality services; and "clear leadership", or in other words, stronger managerial structures.[45]

The widespread introduction of computerised technologies has underpinned all of these processes and has been a crucial factor in the commodification of social work skills and processes. It has been a means both of rationing services and of standardising the social work task. Such technologies now dominate the working lives of most social workers (and are, of course, the basis of the social care call centres which are springing up in different parts of the UK[46]).

The Unison study quoted earlier provides some evidence of the impact of the managerialism on the working practices and morale of front-line social work staff.[47] It highlighted a continuing lack of resources across social work, with only 9 percent of respondents saying that things had improved since the publication of the first Laming Report in 2003. While 43 percent of respondents agreed that the systems and procedures for safeguarding children had improved since 2003, a further 26 percent felt that the effect of changes to these systems and procedures based on Laming's recommendations had been "neutral" and a third felt that there had been no improvement at all. Some felt that the procedural changes that had been put in place had actually made things worse. One worker commented:

It is ironic that the Laming enquiry set up procedures to protect children but in some respects these procedures are now harming children because the increased admin and paperwork have let crucial events slip by unnoticed

44: Audit Commission, 1992.
45: Harris, 2003, pp47-48.
46: Coleman and Harris, 2008; see also Garrett, 2008.
47: Unison, 2009.

or not acted upon due to lack of time with the families and children we are trying to protect. Less office-based work would mean that we can bring the "social" back into social work.[48]

Respondents were particularly critical of the computerised Integrated Children's System (ICS). The Unison report called for a complete overhaul of the system, with one respondent commenting, "ICS is a hindrance to our work. It should be scrapped and replaced with a more child and family focused way of working".[49] Such criticisms are supported by a recent independent academic study of children's social work:

> ICS's onerous workflows and forms compound difficulties in meeting government imposed timescales and targets. Social workers are acutely concerned with performance targets, such as moving the cases flashing in red on their screens into the next phase of the workflow within the timescale. Switching off the flashing red light bears no relationship to protecting a child. That is something of which social workers and managers are acutely aware, but slippages carry sanctions.[50]

While the ICS records for Baby P may well have been complete and up to date, the time required to complete such records is likely to have reduced the time available to carry out direct work with the family and reflect on the very complex issues involved in such cases.

New Labour's managerialism has relied on inspection agencies, such as Ofsted, to guarantee quality, rather than the professionalism and commitment of staff. Yet preparation for such visits consumes a huge amount of staff time, which could be spent in direct work with children and families, and the reports can offer a false sense of security since they rely solely on written reports and records rather than on direct contact with front-line workers or service users. This was shown by the "good" rating received by Haringey three months after Baby P's death.

Workers surveyed by the Unison report, like those in earlier research by Chris Jones,[51] called for an end to the "cult of bureaucracy" ensconced by the managerial reforms of the past two decades. As one worker put it:

48: Unison, 2009, p2.
49: Unison, 2009, p9.
50: White, 2008.
51: Jones, 2001.

The focus of social work has become entirely procedural and the meaning of the work has been lost. The needs of children have become secondary to the needs of agencies responsible for protecting them. The contents of assessments appear insignificant as agencies are far more concerned about whether they are completed on time.[52]

Is Britain a broken society?

Conservative prime minister John Major sought 15 years ago to exploit the tragic killing of toddler James Bulger to shift politics to the right through a debate around law and order.[53] In similar fashion, current Tory leader David Cameron has tried to bolster his thesis that Britain has become a "broken society" by linking the death of Baby P with a recent wave of gun crimes and other cases of child abuse, like the widely publicised faked "disappearance" of a child, Shannon Matthews. Writing in the *Daily Mail* in December 2008, Cameron argued:

How can Gordon Brown argue that people who talk about a broken society are wrong? These children suffered at the very sharpest end of our broken society but all over the country are other young victims, too. Children whose toys are dad's discarded drink bottles; whose role models are criminals, liars and layabouts; whose innocence is lost before their first milk tooth. What chance for these children? Raised without manners, morals or a decent education, they're caught up in the same destructive chain as their parents. It's a chain that links unemployment, family breakdown, debt, drugs and crime.[54]

It is a familiar right wing diatribe, reminiscent of much "underclass theory" of the 1970s and 1980s. However, the broken society thesis requires some examination since "decline of community" was also identified as a key "social evil" by 2007 Joseph Rowntree Foundation survey of 3,500 people.[55] First, the overall child homicide rate in England and Wales appears to have remained broadly similar, or even declined, since the 1970s at around 67 a year.[56] Second, as the NSPCC points out:

52: Unison, 2009, p9.
53: Ferguson, 1994.
54: David Cameron, "There Are 5 Million People On Benefits In Britain. How Do We Stop Them Turning Into Karen Matthews?", *Daily Mail*, 8 December 2008.
55: Joseph Rowntree Foundation, 2008.
56: NSPCC, 2007a.

While [Home Office] classifications tell us how a child was killed, they can only hint at the events leading up to the death and its possible prevention. Cases where the child/ren are killed by monoxide poisoning in a car on a custody visit by a "loving" father who then commits suicide are very different from those where a child dies from multiple injuries, following a long period of ill treatment. There are also the cases where a lone mother, who had cared very well for her child in the past, starts showing increasing signs of mental disturbance and finally kills the child dramatically, in a psychotic outburst.[57]

The sheer diversity of these situations means that to attempt to draw from them generalised conclusions about wider societal trends, along the lines of Britain being a "broken society", is both misleading and irresponsible. The reality of life on estates like that where Shannon Matthews lived is very different to the portrayal of them by Cameron and the right wing press, for whom the inhabitants are stereotypically underclass, lazy, feckless and immoral. Male unemployment on the estate where Matthews lived was less than 10 percent. As Lynsey Hanley, author of a study of council housing,[58] pointed out, "It was a shock to the media that Shannon's step-father worked. In fact, most people on these estates work; it's just that they are very badly paid".[59] Local people were quick to respond to middle class attacks on their lives and relationships. As one woman told a *Telegraph* reporter:

> Look, I've got three kids from two different fathers. Aren't some middle class women the same? When they do it they are "having a second family". That's okay for them but not for us. People here talk to each other, help one another. Do they do that in middle class areas? Half the time they never know the name of the person they're living next to.[60]

The evidence of community was evident both in the large numbers who joined in the search for Shannon (and rejoiced when she was found) and in the collective anger then felt towards Shannon's mother both for her treatment of her daughter and for letting down their community. Nor does the estate conform to images of a racist "white working class". Several reports noted increasing numbers of Asian families moving into the area in

---

57: NSPCC, 2007a.
58: Hanley, 2007.
59: Quoted in Tweedie, 2008.
60: Quoted in Tweedie, 2008.

recent years—and feeling safe living there—while the area is represented by two Asian Labour councillors.

It is true that many working class communities have become more fragmented in recent years. However, Cameron, like Tony Blair before him, is pointing to the wrong decade by blaming the "permissiveness" of the 1960s. As Lynsey Hanley notes, "The real problem is segregation—the farming out of the poorest families to estates on the outskirts of towns, often badly served by transport and shops. The 'right to buy' scheme of the 1980s removed many of the more affluent families in council areas as they sold up and moved on".[61]

Any discussion of the "decline of community" in Britain has to start from the profound damage, both material and spiritual, wreaked on working class communities by Cameron's predecessors, in the 1980s in particular. As Nick Davies concluded in his powerful study of poverty in Britain:

> Labour thinking seems to take no account of the damage which has been inflicted on the poor in the past 20 years. It assumes that even though these communities have been riddled with drugs and drink and depression and stress; that even though tens of thousands of young people have abandoned their schools without any thought for the future; even though hundreds of thousands are now unskilled and alienated while millions have been drained of hope and motivation; that nevertheless by flicking the switches of the benefits machine, these people can be manipulated into families or into work or out of crime as though they were carefully calculating their self-interest, as though their lives and sometimes their personalities had not been scrambled by the experience of the last 20 years.[62]

Conclusion

Even before the economic crisis hit, it was clear that Labour was going to miss its goal of halving the number of children living in poverty. The crisis will mean more people are made unemployed, more families will become dependent on benefits, and more families will lose their homes and be forced into poverty. As all the evidence shows, this will mean more children living in misery, having restricted life chances, being more vulnerable to all manifestations of harm—and for some, it will mean greater exposure to violence and abuse.

61: Quoted in Tweedie, 2008.
62: Davies, 1998, p303.

The End Child Poverty Campaign suggested that an immediate £3 billion was needed to meet the 2010 target. As they noted in their pre-budget press statement:

> Families are struggling to pay their heating bills or afford a decent meal, and they can't imagine how they could pay for a new winter coat. Help for these children should not be too much to ask when banks funded by the taxpayer are giving away billions in bonuses. It is simply not credible to say that the money doesn't exist.[63]

Managerialism and marketisation of social care simply do not work. The attempt to run social services on business models has proved to be a disaster for both workers and service users. Social workers have less time to spend with service users, less time to consider and understand the problems that service users face and less resources to deal with the problems people have.

And this leads to a final point. Most social workers don't enter the job because they want to control people's behaviour or manage "care packages"; most become social workers because (in however unspecified a way) they believe that they can help make a difference to vulnerable people's lives. The impact of "neoliberal" social work has been so broad and so detrimental to their ability to do so that it has created a space within which it is possible to engage with people over the nature of social work and the goals and priorities of Labour and Tory governments over the past 20 years. This time, when social workers came under attack, both they and service users spoke out about what was happening on the front line.

Along with Chris Jones and Laura Penketh, we wrote an on-line "manifesto" for a new engaged social work four years ago.[64] We were unsure what impact it would have but were pleasantly surprised when over 1,000 people added their names to it. We were then involved in setting up the Social Work Action Network (SWAN), a loose network of front-line social workers, trade unionists, academics, service users and social work students. It has now held three highly successful annual conferences and two special one-day events about the implications of the Baby P events for social work. And it was SWAN that took up the cudgels and launched its

---

63: "Go On, Mr Darling, Show A Little Love To 3.9 Million UK Children Living In Poverty, Says The Campaign To End Child Poverty This Valentine's Day", End Child Poverty, 13 February 2009.
64: Available from www.socialworkfuture.org

own petition against the witch-hunt of social workers by the *Sun*. Feedback from social workers and students indicates the SWAN initiative has been discussed in classrooms and workplaces across the country.

But it wasn't just SWAN. As we have noted, Unison undertook their own research to find out what was happening on the social work front line and their significant report forms the basis of Unison's submission to the Laming Inquiry. The British Association of Social Workers and *Community Care* (both traditionally associated with an orientation on the "professional values" of social work) have launched their own petitions and made clear their opposition to the costs of "neoliberal social work" to both workers and service users.

In the aftermath of the tragic death of Baby P it is now possible to argue that "another social work is possible" and that, if we want to avoid more poverty, inequality and harm to children, "another social work is necessary".

References

Anda, Robert, David Brown, Vincent Felitti, J Douglas Bremner, Shanta Dube and Wayne Giles, 2006, "Adverse Childhood Experiences and Prescribed Psychotropic Medications in Adults", *American Journal of Preventive Medicine*, volume 32, number 5.

Audit Commission, 1992, *The Community Revolution: The Personal Social Services and Community Care* (HMSO).

Baldwin, Norma, and Lyn Carruthers, 1998, *Developing Neighbourhood Support and Child Protection Strategies: The Henley Safe Children Project* (Ashgate).

Baldwin, Norma, and Nick Spencer, 1993, "Deprivation and Child Abuse: Implications for Strategic Planning in Children's Services", *Children & Society*, volume 7, number 4.

Becker, Saul, 1997, *Responding to Poverty* (Longman).

Bunting, Lisa, and Colette McAuley, 2004, "Teenage Pregnancy and Motherhood: The Contribution of Support", *Child and Family Social Work*, volume 9, number 2.

Coleman, Nigel, and John Harris, 2008, "Calling Social Work", *British Journal of Social Work*, volume 38, number 3.

Danos, Jacques, and Marcel Gibelin, 1986, *The Class Struggle and the Popular Front in France* (Bookmarks).

Davies, Nick, 1998, *Dark Heart: The Shocking Truth about Hidden Britain* (Vintage).

Devaney, John, 2009, "Chronic Child Abuse: The Characteristics and Careers of Children Caught in the Child Protection System", *British Journal of Social Work*, volume 39, number 1.

Ferguson, Iain, 1994, "Containing the Crisis: Crime and the Tories", *International Socialism 62*, http://pubs.socialistreviewindex.org.uk/isj62/ferguson.htm

Ferguson, Iain, 2008, *Reclaiming Social Work: Challenging Neoliberalism and Promoting Social Justice* (Sage).

Ferguson, Iain, Michael Lavalette and Gerry Mooney, 2002, *Rethinking Welfare: A Critical Perspective* (Sage).

Garrett, Paul Michael, 2008, "How to be Modern: New Labour's Neoliberal Modernity and the Change for Children programme", *British Journal of Social Work*, volume 38, number 2.

Goldson, Barry, Michael Lavalette and Jim MacKechnie (eds), 2002, *Children, Welfare and the State* (Sage).

Hanley, Lynsey, 2007, *Estates: An Intimate History* (Granta).

Harman, Chris, 2008, "Theorising Neoliberalism", *International Socialism* 117 (winter 2008), www.isj.org.uk/?id=399

Harris, John, 2003, *The Social Work Business* (Routledge).

Jones, Chris, 1983, *State Social Work and the Working Class* (Palgrave Macmillan).

Jones, Chirs, 2001, "Voices from the Frontline: State Social Workers and New Labour", *British Journal of Social Work*, volume 31, number 4.

Joseph Rowntree Foundation, 2008, "What are Today's Social Evils?", www.socialevils.org.uk

Lavalette, Michael, and Gerry Mooney (eds), 2000, *Class Struggle and Social Welfare* (Routledge).

Lewis, Jane, 1995, *The Voluntary Sector, the State and Social Work in Britain* (Edward Elgar).

Marx, Karl, 1976 [1867], *Capital*, volume one (Penguin).

Merrick, Dave, 1996, *Social Work and Child Abuse* (Routledge).

Mynott, Ed, 2000, "Analysing the Creation of Apartheid for Asylum Seekers in the UK", *Community, Work and Family*, volume 3, number 3.

NSPCC, 2007a, "Child Homicides", key child protection statistics, December 2007, www.nspcc.org.uk/Inform/resourcesforprofessionals/Statistics/KeyCPStats/4_wda48747.html

NSPCC, 2007b, "Sexual Abuse", key child protection statistics, December 2007, www.nspcc.org.uk/Inform/resourcesforprofessionals/Statistics/KeyCPStats/6_wda48742.html

NSPCC, 2007c, "Physical Abuse", key child protection statistics, December 2007, www.nspcc.org.uk/Inform/resourcesforprofessionals/Statistics/KeyCPStats/5_wda48743.html

Thane, Pat, 1982, *The Foundations of the Welfare State* (Longman).

Tweedie, Neil, 2008, "Another Side Of Shannon Matthews' Moorside", *Telegraph*, 28 March 2008, www.telegraph.co.uk/news/features/3636060/Another-side-to-Shannon-Matthewss-Moorside.html

Unicef, 2007, "Child Poverty in Perspective: An Overview of Child Well-being in Rich Countries", Innocenti Research Centre, report card 7, www.unicef-irc.org//presscentre/presskit/reportcard7/rc7_eng.pdf

Unison, 2009, "Still Slipping Through the Net? Front-line Staff Assess Children's Safeguarding Progress", www.unison.org.uk/acrobat/B4416.pdf

White, Sue, 2008, "Getting IT Wrong? Despatches from the Front-line of Children's Social Care", *Social Work Action Network*, www.socialworkfuture.org/?p=83

Wolfreys, Jim, 1999, "Class Struggles in France", *International Socialism* 84 (autumn 1999), http://pubs.socialistreviewindex.org.uk/isj84/wolfreys.htm

Migration, migrant workers and capitalism

Jane Hardy

Consider these two scenarios. The first is in Ireland in December 2005 when 100,000 Irish, Polish, Lithuanian and Latvian workers demonstrated together against attempts by bosses to recruit migrant workers on worse pay and conditions than Irish workers. The second is in the UK in January 2009 with hundreds of workers taking industrial action under the slogan of "British jobs for British workers". The former reflects the possibility of solidarity and a rejection of "divide and rule". The latter is an alarming situation in which fearful workers turn on "foreigners" as the UK economy haemorrhages jobs and plunges into a deepening crisis.

Migration has always been high on the agenda of the ruling classes, particularly in the core capitalist economies, as they have sought to balance the need for migrant workers to fuel expansionary periods of capitalism against picking up the bill for reproducing and maintaining these workers. The large-scale movement of people has a long history.[1] The most important early migrations occurred in Asia, particularly China, the Middle East and Africa. From the late 16th century levels of migration in Europe grew as a result of the region's changing economic and military dynamics.[2] Political conflicts in eastern, southern and central Europe saw major displacements of ethnic groups across ever-changing boundaries, while mercantilist states

---

1: See Haywood, 2008; Emmer, 1993; Fagan, 1990.
2: Held, McGrew, Goldblatt, Perraton, 1999.

and empires drew on flows of skilled labour.[3] In the 17th and 18th centuries the European conquest and population of the Americas was intimately tied to the slave trade—the forcible and brutal movement of people, overwhelmingly from sub-Saharan Africa, across the Atlantic.

The expansion of capitalism often relied on naked violence. The forced subjugation and movement of people, and the use of indentured labour established coffee and tea plantations in Ceylon (now Sri Lanka), sugar plantations in the Caribbean, and mines and plantations in Brazil.[4] With the abolition of the slave trade in 1838 the mass migration of Asian labourers, known as the "coolie" system, allowed colonial economies to replace slave labour. Coolie labour was generally based on short-term contracts bound by penal sanctions, linked to debts incurred in transit and invariably to barbaric working conditions and levels of pay.[5] One of the largest migrations of the 19th century was that of Indian workers, both indentured labourers and administrative workers, to far-flung parts of the British Empire. One estimate is that between 1834 and 1937 30 million people left India (24 million returned).[6] Comparable to this were the waves of Chinese migration, temporary, seasonal and permanent, across South East Asia and the US, forming the backbone of a workforce that dug the earth in the gold rush and built the railroads.[7]

There were major transatlantic migrations from the mid-19th century to the beginning of the 20th century. The uneven development of capitalism produced large numbers of impoverished and displaced agrarian workers in Europe, who were needed to fuel the explosive growth of capitalism in North and South America. Between 1870 and 1914 50 million people left Europe. Two thirds went to the United States, the rest to Canada, Australia, New Zealand, South Africa, Argentina and Brazil.[8] This mass emigration amounted to one eighth of Europe's population in 1900—and between 20 and 30 percent of the population of countries such as Britain, Italy, Spain and Portugal.[9]

With the crisis and retrenchment of world capitalism after the First World War, these flows came to a halt as racism was used to tighten immigration laws to the US.

3: Held, McGrew, Goldblatt, Perraton, 1999.
4: Sassen, 1988.
5: See Kale, 1998; Northrup, 1995.
6: Nayyar, 2006, citing Tinker, 1974.
7: Nayyar, 2006, citing Lewis, 1977.
8: Nayyar, 2006, citing Lewis, 1977.
9: Stalker, 1994.

However, after the Second World War the advanced capitalist economies, particularly those in Europe, required immigration and they actively recruited labour. Britain, France and the Netherlands drew workers from their former colonies, while other countries recruited their labour force from the south east periphery of Europe, Turkey and North Africa. West Germany signed agreements with Italy (1955 and 1965), Greece and Spain (1964), Morocco (1963), Portugal and Turkey (1964), Tunisia (1965), Yugoslavia (1968) and even Korea (1962). By 1973 migrant workers in France and Germany made up about 10 percent of the labour force.[10]

The onset of recession in 1973 marked the end of open movements of labour. By the 1980s draconian immigration laws were in place across Europe. One feature of the post Second World War migration, particularly in the past three decades, has been the huge and forced displacement of people from developing countries through poverty, war and persecution.[11] The Iraq war, for example, has created a large number of refugees. The United Nations High Commission for Refugees reports that 4.2 million Iraqis have been forced out of their homes. About half have been displaced within Iraq and the rest have fled the country.

A reserve army of labour

Migrant workers play a distinct role in capitalism both as a "reserve army of labour" and as a means of raising the rate of exploitation. There is nothing new about the idea of a reserve army of labour. In 1845 Federick Engels wrote, "English manufacture must have, at all times save the brief periods of highest prosperity, an unemployed reserve army of labour, in order to produce the masses of goods required by the market in the liveliest months".[12]

Advanced capitalist economies regularly poach workers with particular skills, such as nurses, teachers and social workers, from developing countries. In the UK the supply of migrant workers from outside the European Union (EU) is turned on and off like a tap to provide flexible, seasonal, low cost labour. Employers use special schemes in agriculture and the so-called "hospitality" sector to import workers on a temporary basis.

After eight former Communist countries[13] joined the EU in 2004, bosses in existing EU states were able to cherry-pick workers from Central

---

10: Harris, 1995.
11: Marfleet, 1998; Marfleet, 2005.
12: Engels, 1962.
13: Latvia, Lithuania, Estonia, Hungary, Poland, Slovakia, Slovenia and the Czech Republic.

and Eastern Europe. One example that I came across involved a bus company from the Midlands hiring a hotel in Warsaw and putting leaflets around the city's bus depot. Large numbers of drivers who turned up to the meeting were promised what appeared to be good wages (in comparison with Poland at least), and the following week 20 drivers moved to the UK. The company paid the minimum wage but the contract said that there were no set hours and the drivers would have to work as needed. This meant that some weeks they did not make the salary they had been promised and other weeks they could be called up in the middle of the night and worked 60 hours. When they complained, an English test was sprung on them and three drivers were sacked.[14]

Migrant workers are especially useful as part of the reserve army of labour because they can quickly be expelled. The US, Belgium and France expelled foreign workers during the Great Depression of the 1930s. Nigeria expelled two million immigrant workers from other West African countries in the wake of the collapse of the oil market in the early 1980s.[15] After the 1997 economic crisis, which began in South East Asia, Japan, Hong Kong, Korea, Taiwan, Malaysia and Thailand stepped up border controls, enforcement and surveillance, and imposed fines for migration offences. South Korea, Thailand and Malaysia repatriated migrants, including those who were there legally.

The use of migrant workers also allows the receiver country to externalise the costs of renewing the labour force. The state uses migrant workers to fill gaps in the labour market but does not pay any of the costs of them or their families settling. For example, in the UK migrant workers from the new EU countries are denied benefits until they have worked there for 12 months. The new points system for immigrants (from outside to Europe) in the UK is a way of sifting workers who are highly skilled and ensuring that no one who arrives is going to be a "burden" on the state.

Migration to the richer countries has economic and social consequences for the poorer ones. In Moldova, for example, 26 percent of the population is employed outside of the country.[16] On a global scale the unevenness of capitalism can set in motion a whole chain of migration, with ever more degrading treatment the lower you are on the ladder. The gap left by welders who left the Gdansk shipyard in Poland was filled by

---

14: Some of the empirical material for this article was gathered as part of a project, "Cross Border Trade Union Collaboration and Polish Migrant Workers". This was funded by the Economic and Social Research Council between February 2007 and April 2008 with Ian Fitzgerald.

15: Strikwerda and Guerin-Gonzales, 1993.

16: *Migrant Remittances Newsletter*, http://migrantremittances.typepad.com/

workers from India and North Korea, working up to 16 hours a day under the control and surveillance of the North Korean Communist Party.[17]

Increasing the rate of exploitation

Employers do not simply want to obtain additional labour. They also want to get workers who can be used under specific conditions to raise the rate of exploitation. In general these conditions "embody a form of control over the workforce that presupposes the powerlessness of the workers".[18] In some cases bosses will try to employ migrant workers even when indigenous workers are available because they assume that migrants' status will make them easier to exploit.

Even when migrant workers are employed legally they face huge problems at work. The abuse of workers from Central and Eastern Europe legally in the UK over employment contracts and wages has been widely documented. Complaints include excessive working hours with inadequate breaks and no enhanced overtime. Recruitment and temporary labour agencies have been found to impose high charges for finding employment, lower payment than promised and the withholding of wages.[19] Tied accommodation, where bosses provide housing, has resurfaced and many complaints from migrants have focused on housing that is overpriced, overcrowded and shoddy.[20]

The vast majority of migrant workers have been used to fill the worst and most badly paid jobs. The Ken Loach film *It's a Free World* is a damning indictment of the exploitation of legal and illegal migrant workers in the UK. However, it focuses on "bad apple" employers on the fringes of the labour market, whereas in reality workers from Poland and other new EU members are central to British capitalism—and are indirectly or directly employed by some of the largest companies. Undoubtedly some employment agencies are run on a semi-criminal basis, but others are large transnational corporations themselves and could be regarded as traffickers with legal status.

The use of migrant workers is inextricably linked to the neoliberal agenda of increasing labour "flexibility" to ratchet up the rate of exploitation. This in turn is driven by increased competition between capitals. For instance, workers from the new EU countries are widely used in agriculture, food processing, distribution and supermarkets in East Anglia, and there is evidence of terrible working conditions and bullying, and of gangmasters

---

17: "Slaves From North Korea Work In Gdansk Shipyards", *Gazeta Wyborcza*, 24 March 2006.
18: Sassen, 1988, p39.
19: Fitzgerald, 2007; Hardy and Clark, 2007; Anderson, Ruhs, Rogaly and Spencer, 2006.
20: Jordan and Düvell, 2002.

running some small towns. However, it is not simply that bosses from this region are particularly nasty; rather they are locked into a highly competitive market. Supermarkets, which control the food chain in the UK (to a greater extent than other countries), continually force their suppliers to drive down prices. Lorry drivers from the new EU countries in supermarket distribution centres are often on zero hours contracts, and Polish workers I interviewed in a fruit-packing factory were continually told to work faster to meet the demands of supermarkets.

Migrant workers, wages and working conditions

What are the relationships between migrant workers and wider trends in wages and conditions? In the UK a plethora of bewildering econometric studies have reached contradictory conclusions and have been used to justify different positions within the ruling class.[21] One section of the ruling class does not benefit from migrant workers and therefore does not want to bear the costs, while another section has been keen to defend the benefits of immigration.

This split is evident in two reports by the UK government. The first, a Home Office report, citing the support of the Institute of Directors and British Chambers of Commerce, puts a strong case against linking immigration to depressed wages or increased unemployment.[22] Similarly, in a major speech on immigration in December 2007, home secretary Jacqui Smith spoke of the "purity of the macroeconomic case for migration". The then immigration minister Liam Byrne argued that "there are obviously enormous benefits of immigration... There is a big positive impact on the economy which is worth £6 billion".[23]

They have been keen to promote the views of economists who share this view such as David Blanchflower. In a speech to the Bank of England he concluded, "The empirical literature from around the world suggests little or no evidence that immigrants have had a major impact on native labour markets outcomes such as wages and unemployment. Recent work by a number of other authors for the UK is also consistent with this view".[24]

A second report, this time from the House of Lords, takes a more sceptical view, unconvinced that the economic impact of immigration justifies the additional costs.[25] Another study tells yet another story,

---

21: See Rowthorn, 2008, for a survey of the literature.
22: Home Office, 2007.
23: House of Lords, 2008, p22.
24: Blanchflower, Saleheen and Shadforth, 2007.
25: House of Lords, 2008.

concluding that immigration has a positive effect on the wages of higher paid workers but lowers the wages for those in lower paid jobs.[26]

While there is pressure on the wages of the worst paid workers, it is not the case that migrant workers are responsible for this. The drive for "flexibility" and lower wages goes back much further than the arrival of workers from Central and Eastern Europe in 2004. Privatisation, out-sourcing and subcontracting have intensified competition over the past two decades in industries such as cleaning and other badly paid service sector jobs as well as construction.

As Stobart points out, it is incorrect to talk about migration having a homogenous impact on wages and working conditions; rather the effects vary between and within sectors.[27] This will depend on the intensity of competition between capitals, the need for bosses to balance investing in skills against driving down wages and the ability of workers to resist across sectors and in individual workplaces.

Undoubtedly some employers in individual factories and workplaces have sought to employ migrant workers on poorer pay and conditions of service, in the Irish ferries dispute for example.[28] Forces are at work to try to drive down wages across Europe.[29] This was clearly illustrated by the disputes in construction in the UK in January 2009 when subcontractors brought in workers from Italy and Spain. The Posted Worker Directive, introduced in 1996, means that workers "posted" temporarily in another country by employers should get the guaranteed minimum provisions laid down by law or collective agreement in the host country. The reality is that bosses only need to pay the minimum, and even if they do not, migrant workers lack knowledge of their entitlements (particularly if they are housed on "floating accommodation"). It is unlikely that construction workers from another country, who may not speak English, are going to take their boss to a British industrial tribunal.

Under these conditions it is easy to see how employers could seek to employ workers on worse pay and conditions. But whether they succeed is a political question. It is worth recounting the landmark dispute in Sweden when Latvian workers were brought in to refurbish a school by the subcontractor of Alfa Laval on €9 an hour, rather than the nationally agreed €15 Euros.[30] The Swedish Byggnads union picketed the site and

---

26: Dustmann, Frattini and Preston, 2007.
27: Stobart, 2008.
28: "Irish Ferries Dispute Resolved After Bitter Stand-off", EIROnline, 21 December 2005.
29: Cremers, Dolvik and Bosch, 2007.
30: Woolfson and Sommers, 2006.

drew accusations of xenophobia from bosses and the Latvian government. The response of the Swedish union was not to demand "Swedish jobs for Swedish workers", but to place a full statement in the leading Latvian newspaper inviting workers coming to Sweden to join the trade union.[31] Therefore, although the existence of migrant workers offers the possibility of divide and rule, bosses have not always been successful in their unbridled exploitation of migrant workers.

The state and migration

Contrary to much rhetoric about globalisation, states have played a central and active role in managing outward and inward flows of labour across their boundaries. In the 19th century, for example, the active export of Europe's rural poor was facilitated by states that lifted restrictions on emigration, while state bodies, trade unions, philanthropic and colonisation societies made financial assistance available.[32]

The rise of the capitalist state saw the establishment of borders and categories of citizenship that demarcated immigrants as a separate group. Before the 19th century it was towns and guilds, not national governments, that determined whether "foreigners" could work.[33] Modern nationalism divided some groups and merged others. Saxons and Bavarians, who had migrated to France, the Netherlands and eastern Europe with their regional identities, suddenly became "Germans". National identity was often loosely defined because village, regional and religious identities could be stronger than national ones.[34] Immigrants to the United States before the First World War often defined themselves as Italian or Polish only once they were in the US. "International migration" in Africa now flows between areas that have long been connected by trade and cultural ties but have been divided by arbitrary boundaries imposed by European empires.[35]

By the First World War most modern states sought to control movements across their borders. Passports were the documentary expression of this and they were accompanied by a huge expansion of the immigration bureaucracy to police the system.[36] Although some kind of passport or travel document had been around for a long time, the modern passport was introduced in the UK and other European countries in 1914, for military reasons

---

31: Woolfson and Sommers, 2006.
32: Held, McGrew, Goldblatt, Perraton, 1999.
33: Strikwerda and Guerin-Gonzales, 1993.
34: Strikwerda and Guerin-Gonzales, 1993.
35: Strikwerda and Guerin-Gonzales, 1993.
36: Caplan and Torbey, 2001.

and in an effort to hold on to skilled workers.[37] By the 1920s most governments had taken steps to control the movement of people. Gubbay writes:

> Between them, the states…carve the populations of the world, each person in principle being the subject of a single state, possessing the privilege of citizenship and the right to freedom of movement within its territory, in particular in order to sell his or her labour power within the corresponding labour market… The legitimate function of citizenship, for which its possessor should feel gratitude and pride, depends in part upon the disprivileging of non-citizens and indeed the further buttress of finely graded rights conferred on non-citizens.[38]

Border enforcement is a mechanism facilitating the extraction of cheap labour by assigning criminal status to a segment of the working class—illegal immigrants. However, as Nick Clark points out, we have to take care not to see migrants in the way that bosses do, as simply units of production:

> It is [migrant workers'] humanity that causes authorities (and employers) problems. They don't only migrate to work. The categories—refugee, economic migrant, tourist, family member, business visitor, student—stubbornly merge one into another, and people impose their own wishes on the system. All of them, apart from the very rich, need some means of material support, but this is not necessarily the only reason why they move, or stay. When I asked a (small) sample of people who had settled, none of them planned to, but most of them did because they fell in love.[39]

Capitalist states must constantly intervene to recast the relationship between the state and labour in the interests of capital accumulation. War causes massive dislocations of people, but it is the combined and uneven nature of capitalism that produces a constant tendency towards labour mobility, with pull factors in expanding parts of the system and push factors where the landscape and workplaces of the system have been decimated. Capitalists need the constant movement of workers but also a degree of stability and embedded skills to compete with other capitalists. Governments have often been preoccupied with preventing emigration and the loss of skilled workers. David Harvey quotes Karl Marx's example of the cotton

---

37: Caplan and Torbey, 2001.
38: Gubbay, 1999, p44.
39: Correspondence with Nick Clark.

famine in Lancashire in 1860s when management acted secretly with the government to hinder emigration, "partly to retain in readiness the capital invested in the blood and flesh of the labourers".[40]

However, tensions between different capitalists, with different labour market needs, creates difficulties for states as they attempt to manage migration. This is well illustrated by the debates over Mexican migration to the US. As of July 2007 1,404 pieces of legislation related to immigration had been introduced by 50 states.[41] There were 170 pieces of legislation in 2007 alone, tightening up on illegal migrants enforced by 11,000 border guards with sophisticated surveillance equipment. But Mexican migrant workers are central to US capitalism. The number of migrant Mexican workers in the US has doubled since 1990—growing by 2.9 million. In 1990 migrant workers were concentrated in California and Texas, but by 2009 they were much more widely dispersed throughout the whole of the US.[42]

The American Health Care Association, the American Hotel and Motel Association, and the National Association of House Builders lobbied the Senate for a relaxation on migration. They represented the bosses of immobile sections of capitalist production such as restaurants, hotels, construction sites, hospitals and orchards, which depended on a constant supply of migrant workers. In June 2007 legislation introduced to relax migration with easier regularisation and more visas was defeated. However, the voting was not along Republican/Democrat lines but reflected the needs of different sectors of capital. Similarly in the UK the British Hospitality Association and National Farmers Union (an employers' association) have lobbied the government for access to more temporary foreign workers, with the effect that the government increased the quota by 5,000 in 2009.[43]

Organising migrant workers

In some accounts migrant workers are treated as passive victims of capital and/or as unorganisable because of the sectors they work in. However, migrant workers have often been at the forefront of strikes, union organisation and political activity, as Camille Guerin-Gonzalez and Carl Strikwerda document in their book *The Politics of Immigrant Workers*.[44] Many rank and file immigrant leaders brought with them a tradition of union activism or left wing political ties. There is no predisposition for some nationalities

40: See Marx, 1959, p89.
41: National Conference of State Legislatures, 2007.
42: American Immigration Law Foundation, 2002.
43: http://tinyurl.com/fruitjobs
44: Guerin-Gonzalez and Strikwerda, 1993.

to be more active in politics and unions than others. For example, while Italians were often seen as a conservative influence in the US, in Argentina and Brazil they supplied a disproportionate number of leaders of labour movements.[45] The high rate of union organisation among Turkish and Italian workers from the 1950s onwards in the former West Germany and their disorganisation in Switzerland was due to the relative strength of their unions, not entrenched national characteristics.

However, solidarity between workers is not automatic. In the Chicago meat packing yards, vividly portrayed by Upton Sinclair in his novel *The Jungle*,[46] the workforce comprised ethnically and racially diverse communities. Historian James Barrett found that "the existence of separate racial and ethnic continuities could lead to either unity or fragmentation, depending on the role played by important community leaders or institutions".[47]

The disputes in the UK construction industry and in oil refineries in January 2009, under the slogan of "British Jobs For British Workers", were a salutary lesson in the importance of uniting indigenous and migrant workers, and of the role of trade unions and socialists.

Some academics have talked about a segmented labour force in which migrant workers form a separate group, allowing them to be used to divide and rule. However, if we take the most recent wave of migrant workers from the new EU countries into the UK, it is not the case that they constitute a segmented and hermetically sealed part of the labour market. While it is true that some sectors are dominated by these migrant workers, for instance in agriculture and food processing, they are also employed alongside British workers as bus drivers, on building sites and in distribution centres.

Organising migrant workers in the US

The American working class has always consisted overwhelmingly of immigrants and their children. In her book *Organising Immigrants* Ruth Milkman looks at how migrant workers have been organised since their arrival in the United States in the 19th century.[48] Many craft unions of northern and western European origins were openly hostile to recent immigrants from southern and eastern Europe, who employers freely exploited as strikebreakers and who dominated the ranks of the unemployed. Although in the 1880s and 1890s the American Federation of Labour (AFL) made efforts to

---

45: Strikwerda and Guerin-Gonzalez, 1993.
46: Sinclair, 2006.
47: Barrett, 1987, cited by Strikwerda and Guerin-Gonzalez, 1993.
48: Milkman, 2000 and 2006.

incorporate these new immigrants, by the turn of the century most union leaders came to see them as unorganisable and supported restrictions on new immigration.[49] Racism, particularly apparent towards black and non-European workers such as those from China, pervaded even the most progressive unions.[50] New immigrants did organise themselves in some AFL affiliates, the most lasting results of which were in clothing and coal mining. Immigrant workers remained largely unorganised until the mass industrial union drive of the 1930s, which welcomed them into unions on a large scale, along with the African American working class. Historians documented the way immigrants were often more enthusiastic, easier to organise and quicker to sign up than indigenous workers:

> In the case of Slavic immigrants in meatpacking and steel and for the Jewish garment workers—as for English and German immigrants half a century earlier—receptivity to unionisation efforts was often linked to prior experiences with strikes and labour organisation in Europe.[51]

The 1965 amendments to the immigration laws set the stage for a massive influx of newcomers that would greatly enlarge the Latino community. Recruitment of migrant workers was central to rebuilding the labour movement and in the 1990s a series of dramatic successes demonstrated the potential for bringing foreign born workers into the unions. In 1995 a new progressive leadership won the contested elections of the AFL-CIO union federation, and some of its affiliates began pouring resources into organising on a scale not seen for decades. Immigrant workers were a crucial focus, especially in California.[52]

The Justice for Janitors campaign was a major success story of immigrant organisation. This was part of a top-down strategy to rebuild the Service Employees International Union (SEIU) but involved rank and file immigrant workers. It was defined by one of the SEIU organisers as "a war against the employers [the cleaning contractors] and the building owners, waged on all fronts without leaving any stone unturned".[53]

The militant demonstrations, violent response by the police and publicity stunts were vividly portrayed by Ken Loach in his film *Bread and Roses*. Immigrant workers were often willing to take risks in organising.

49: Milkman, 2000 and 2006.
50: Mink, 1986, cited by Milkman, 2000.
51: Barrett, 1987, cited by Milkman, 2000, p4.
52: Milkman, 2000 and 2006.
53: Milkman, 2000 and 2006.

One organiser, discussing the role of Salvadorians in the Justice for Janitors dispute, explained, "There, if you were in a union, they killed you...here you lose a job at $4.25 an hour".[54]

There were other major disputes organised by rank and file workers themselves. In 1990 there was a spontaneous strike at the American Racing Equipment Company by first generation Latino immigrants, who won higher wages, health insurance and union recognition.[55] In 1992, after months of preparation, thousands of Mexican immigrant construction workers achieved a stunning victory for higher pay after a five-month stoppage that shut down housing construction from North Angeles to the Mexican border.[56]

The lessons of these disputes were that immigrant workers could be recruited or take action themselves and win, even in the most difficult circumstances. The industries in which they organised had little or no union membership, or in the case of construction had faced a sustained attack by employers. The workers themselves, who often spoke little English, won in the face of intimidation, violence and the possibility of deportation.

In 2006 there were massive May Day demonstrations in every large city in the US (and many smaller ones) involving millions of migrant workers to protest against government legislation to tighten controls on immigration and criminalise undocumented workers, chanting slogans such as "*Queremos Justicia, Queremos Amnista*" ("We Want Justice And Amnesty").

Organising migrant workers in the UK

Post-war British capitalism was heavily dependent on migrant workers from the West Indies, India and Pakistan to provide labour for the worst paid jobs in the public sector and textile industry. In this journal Hassan Mahamdallie documented the way in which Asian migrant workers moved into confrontation with employers from the mid-1960s, often having to battle with racist union officials as well as bosses.[57] The strike by Asian workers at Imperial Typewriters in Leicester in 1974 became political when it moved from a dispute about wages to one over racism and democracy in the unions. The strikers fought against open and ugly racism on the part of both white union members and their leaders. The challenge to the trade unions of fighting for immigrant workers reached its height at Grunwick's two years later, in 1976, when mainly Asian women workers struck against appalling pay and

---

54: Waldinger and others, 1998, p117, cited by Milkman, 2000.
55: Zabin, 2000.
56: Milkman and Wong, 2000.
57: Mahamdallie, 2007.

conditions. There was a huge gap between the tepid support of the TUC and the massive support from rank and file trade unionists: "Grunwick's was the most important dispute in the history of the British labour movement concerning the ghost of black and brown workers not being prepared to join unions and under-cutting the wages of white workers".[58]

Twenty years later, in 2005, another group, mainly second generation British Asian women, struck against the union-busting Gate Gourmet at Heathrow Airport. While baggage handlers came out on unofficial strike in sympathy, as with disputes involving non-migrant workers, the union leadership were quick to stitch up a deal, rather than building on the solidarity that existed in the union movement.

The position of the Trades Union Congress (TUC) has not always been one of solidarity—even at a rhetorical level. In the 30 years following the Second World War the TUC and a number of affiliate unions were often openly hostile to immigrant and migrant workers and tried to exclude them from certain sectors. At workplace level there were very different responses ranging from refusing membership to black workers in some skilled unions to active recruitment drives with leaflets in a range of languages in other unions.[59]

From May 2004 workers from the new EU countries, two thirds of them Polish,[60] seeking work in the UK constituted its largest single in-migration.[61] This new wave of migrants was younger and more feminised than previous ones, with 82 percent aged between 18 and 34 and women comprising 43 percent.[62] The TUC and its affiliated unions responded positively, partly as a result of policies fought for by socialists in the movement, through the history of self-organisation of black workers, and partly as a result of a small section of the TUC having worked with Portuguese migrant workers. The response of the union bureaucracy was also driven by a recognition that between half a million and one million new workers were a fundamental change to the labour market—and not to organise these workers would weaken the movement as a whole.

The recruitment of Polish workers posed new challenges for unions. Large numbers were concentrated in the private sector and in agency employment where unions have less power and influence. Language barriers, a lack of bank accounts, aggressive and vicious employers, and stretched

---

58: Mahamdallie, 2007.
59: Castle and Kovack, 1973.
60: Border and Immigration Agency, 2007.
61: Salt and Millar, 2006.
62: Border and Immigration Agency, 2007.

union finances added to the problems. Nevertheless, British unions at a grass-roots level have showed themselves to be imaginative in deploying a new range of tactics. These included the secondment of a Solidarity union organiser from Poland to the north west TUC, using the Union Learning Fund[63] to recruit workplace representatives to provide English classes, and working with law centres, churches and community groups to organise "know your rights" events. In East Anglia the GMB union organised a fishing trip to build links between Polish and British workers. There had been antipathy to Polish workers who ate the fish they caught rather than throwing them back according to the apparent protocol of British fishing.[64]

Where Polish workers have been in organised workplaces they have been on strike alongside British workers. In December 2005 a strike took place at the Iceland distribution depot in Enfield, North London, over pay and management bullying. Some of the placards on the picket line read "*Strajk Oficjalny*" ("Official Strike"), reflecting the large number of Polish workers involved.[65] British and Polish TGWU[66] members were involved in a dispute over pay and pensions with First Bus in the Midlands.[67] Polish agency workers were bussed in to attempt to break a Post Office dispute over privatisation and pay in 2007. However, at Watford pickets climbed onto the bus, explained the dispute, and the Polish workers voted not to go into work.

A report by Bridget Anderson and others found that, despite claims by some that Polish migrant workers were suspicious of and hostile to unions, low membership did not represent antipathy to trade unions.[68] A clear majority were interested in joining and, according to the report, even on the most pessimistic assumptions, the interest in trade union membership was significantly greater than actual membership. Of the workers who were not interested in joining, half gave practical reasons such as cost, lack of information and brevity of stay. Less than 10 percent gave ideological arguments or bad experiences of unions as reasons for not joining. The reasons why workers were interested in joining a union were varied, and by no means all associated with individual protection, services or "insurance".

63: The Union Learning Fund was set up by the government in 1998 to promote activity by unions in support of the government's objective of creating a "learning society". The role of the Union Learning Representative is given recognised status similar to that of union health and safety representatives. See www.unionlearningfund.org.uk
64: Fitzgerald and Hardy, 2007.
65: "Chilling Anti-strike Tactics At Iceland", *Socialist Worker*, 16 December 2006.
66: Now part of the Unite union.
67: "Bus Drivers: 'Bosses Treat Us All The Same—Badly", *Socialist Worker*, 29 October 2005.
68: Anderson, Clark and Parutis, 2006.

The need for a "sword of justice" and a view of collectivism at work also motivated many. The four Polish union representatives I interviewed in one workplace all gave a desire to help others as a reason for being involved.

Debates over organising migrant workers

Organising migrant workers has provoked a number of debates for socialists, particularly around the questions of "community unionism" and separate organising. The idea of community unionism is most developed in the US, and often focused around worker centres.[69] These centres grew up because of the poor record of some sections of the union movement in organising migrant workers and addressing their problems at work, as well as wider concerns such as regularisation and housing. Worker centres combine servicing, legal help and organising, both for individuals and through collective campaigns. By May 2005 there were 137 worker centres in the US, 122 of them immigrant worker centres.[70] However, these centres have often relied on broad campaigns rather than putting workplace organisation at the centre of their politics. Fine comments, "Over the course of conducting the study, I was struck by how little workers' centres utilised the potential economic power of low wage immigrant workers themselves".[71]

Some worker centres have moved from union inspired radical pressure groups to operating as businesses—what is sometimes fashionably referred to as social entrepreneurship. The East Los Angeles Community Union, for example, was initiated by the United Auto Workers in the mid-1960s and campaigned successfully to get more public housing built. However, since then it has morphed into being a property developer and running for-profit businesses.[72]

There is no real equivalent of worker centres in the UK, although the "Campaign for a Living Wage" carries some of the same politics. The East London Community Organisation (Telco) managed to persuade some employers to pay the "living wage" of £7.20 (as opposed to the minimum wage). This was followed by a campaign by the TGWU union, which recruited about 1,500 cleaners and got agreements with leading contractors in Canary Wharf.[73] Winning improvements in the pay and working conditions of one of the most badly treated and poorly paid groups of workers was a significant achievement. Further, the campaign brought anti-racist ideas into

---

69: Fine, 2006.
70: Fine, 2006.
71: Fine, 2006, p257.
72: Pratt Center for Community Development, http://prattcenter.net/cdc-telcau.php
73: Wills, 2008.

the mainstream of the union movement. There are, however, some problems with the notion of community organising when it believes that a "wide diversity of actors with a multiplicity of interests" can operate in the place of workers' self-organisation.[74] The issue of class is sidelined as "workers' issues have been recast as community-wide concerns and class interests read through the lens of community, immigration, and race and religion".[75] Communities are very important in supporting strikes; they were key to the 1984-5 miners' strike. Often migrant workers have their own networks, communities and traditions. However, it is unity on the basis of class—bringing together men and women, migrant and indigenous workers—that has the power to win disputes in the workplace. Solidarity strikes from other workers at Heathrow and beyond are the sort of action that could have won the dispute for the Gate Gourmet workers in 2006, for example.

There is no single, principled position over community organising. After all in Argentina during the crisis of 2001 and in recent years in Venezuela it has been about occupying factories and taking over workplaces. It is a question of tactics. If community unionism means a broad alliance of classes that substitutes for the independent organisation of workers, or marginalises them, then it may be a problem. The real test is what happens when community unionising fails to win over or embarrass intransigent employers. In these circumstances the question must be one of focusing on groups of workers taking industrial action that can win.

The second debate focuses on the issue of separate branches for migrant workers, which some suggest is divisive. There is only one notable example in the UK—the GMB's Southampton Polish-speaking holding branch. The bottom line is that many Polish workers (and those from other new EU countries) do not speak English and have no access to language classes. The Southampton branch was set up in response to the demands of the Polish community, and the first meeting in August 2006 saw over 100 people crammed into a small pub room.[76] By 2008 it had grown from 50 to 500 members and produced a layer of Polish activists and full-time organisers.[77] This has acted as a catalyst for the recruitment and organising of other workplaces. In one case management at a workplace that employed a high number of workers from the new EU countries would not listen to grievances on health and safety, so 20 workers joined the union and 55

74: Wills, 2008, p306.
75: Wills, 2008, p309.
76: Fitzgerald and Hardy, 2007.
77: Fitzgerald and Hardy, 2007.

put their name to the grievances. When they tried to form a workplace union the management tried to set up a staff association, handed out leaflets as to why a union was not needed and suddenly produced the health and safety equipment that the workers had been asking for. According to the GMB organiser, "We went in [to the other factory] and recruited 40 people in one day—Latvians, Lithuanians, Russians as well as Poles. The key to recruiting these workers was a Latvian woman. Had she not been there we would not have been so successful".[78]

There are not many precedents for this, but it is worth noting that at the beginning of the 20th century the Socialist Party of America[79] created seven foreign language federations that successfully mobilised recent migrants. They were among the most radical sections of the party and were expelled with others in 1919 after the Russian Revolution for arguing that a revolution was possible in America. Separate trade union branches are not a long-term solution but may be a mechanism for organising workers and workplace activity as a step towards unity between British and Polish workers.

The crisis and migration

In the current crisis migrant workers are increasingly bearing the brunt of unemployment and facing deportation. The Czech government have given workers who have been laid off €500 and a ticket home. This is relatively altruistic in comparison with workers who have been summarily deported from countries such as Italy. Russia has ten million migrant workers, a disproportionate number of whom are facing increasing poverty and persecution, particularly as the construction industry goes into deep decline. One Moscow-based human rights group reported that in the past 12 months ten people had been killed in racist murders. There are other ramifications of the crisis for poorer and developing countries as remittances (the money sent home by migrant workers) have shown a sharp decline. These are often a significant part of the GDP of countries in South East Asia and a lifeline for individual families.[80]

In the UK, as the value of the pound fell spectacularly against other currencies (including the Polish zloty) from mid-2008, there were reports in the press of a mass exodus of Poles. With rising unemployment, and employment agency workers the first to be laid off, the UK looks less attractive for Polish

---

78: Interview with author.
79: The party was formed in 1901 and well entrenched in the labour movement.
80: "Countries Struggle With Rising Numbers Of Unemployed Migrant Workers", 10 February 2009. Available on www.findingdulcinea.com

workers. However, there are no figures for the impact on migration—only guesswork based on anecdotes. The current crisis is global and the only question is about the depth and precise form it will take in different economies. The Polish economy has been hailed as a great success story with high average rates of growth. Nevertheless in 2004 (on the eve of joining the EU) unemployment was 20 percent and by 2008 (after four years of outward migration) it was still nearly the highest in Europe. It is unlikely that the Polish labour market has much to offer young people. People trying to enter the UK from outside the EU will face the increasingly draconian implementation of the new points system, as these workers are now considered surplus to requirements.

Conclusion

Capitalism is a system based on divide and rule, and successive governments in Britain have played the race card or resorted to xenophobia to try to set workers against one another. The British and US economic bubbles have burst spectacularly, both economies are spiralling into crisis and jobs are haemorrhaging, with migrant workers bearing the brunt of unemployment. Workers are rightly fearful but the danger is that migrant workers will be used as scapegoats. It is crucial for socialists to argue in their workplaces and unions that blame does not lie with migrant workers. The imposition of neoliberal regulations across Europe has created cut-throat competition, which is compounded by a system with anarchy at its heart. History shows that migrant and indigenous workers can fight alongside each other for a better world and can win. We need to develop a socialist current among migrant workers just as we need to build an international perspective among British workers.

References

American Immigration Law Foundation, 2002, "Mexican Immigrant Workers and the US Economy: An Increasingly Vital Role", executive summary, Immigration Policy Focus, volume 1, issue 2, www.immigrationpolicy.org/?content=f200209

Anderson, Bridget, Nick Clark, and Violetta Parutis, 2007, "New EU Members? Migrant Workers' Challenges and Opportunities to UK Trade Unions: A Polish and Lithuanian Case Study", TUC, www.tuc.org.uk/extras/migrantchallenges.pdf

Barrett, James R, 1987, "Unity and Fragmentation: Class, Race and Ethnicity on Chicago's South Side", in Dirk Hoerder (ed), *Struggle a Hard Battle: Essays on Working Class Immigrants* (Northern Illinois University).

Blanchflower, David, Jumana Saleheen and Chris Shadforth, 2007, "The Impact of Recent Migration from Eastern Europe on the UK Economy", Bank of England, www.bankofengland.co.uk/publications/speeches/2007/speech297.pdf

Border and Immigration Agency, 2007, "Accession Monitoring Report A8 Countries, May 2004-June 2007", http://tinyurl.com/AMRA8C

Caplan, Jane, and John Torbey (eds), 2001, *Documenting Individual Identity* (Princeton).

Castle, Stephen, and Godula Kosack, 1973, *Immigrant Workers and Class Structure in Western Europe* (Oxford University).

Cremers, Jan, Jon Erik Dolvik and Gerhard Bosch, 2007, "Posting Workers in the Single Market: Attempts to Prevent Social Dumping and Regime Competition in the EU", *Industrial Relations Journal*, volume 38, number 6.

Dustmann, Christian, Tommaso Frattini and Ian Preston, 2007, "A Study of Migrant Workers and the National Minimum Wage and Enforcement Issues that Arise", Low Pay Commission, www.lowpay.gov.uk/lowpay/research/pdf/t0Z96GJX.pdf

Emmer, Pieter, 1993, "Intercontinental Migration as a Historical Process", *European Review*, volume I, number I.

Engels, Frederick, 1962 [1845], "The Condition of the Working Class in England", in Karl Marx and Frederick Engels, *On Britain* (Moscow).

Fagan, Brian, 1990, *The Journey From Eden: The Peopling of Our World* (Thames and Hudson).

Fitzgerald, Ian, 2007, "Working in the UK: Polish Migrant Worker Routes into Employment in the North East and North West Construction and Food Processing Sectors", TUC, http://tinyurl.com/WIUKPMW

Fitzgerald, Ian, and Jane Hardy, 2007, "Thinking Outside the Box: Trade Union Strategies and Polish Migrant Workers in the UK", paper given at the International Industrial Relations Association conference, University of Manchester, 3-7 September 2007.

Fine, Janice, 2006, *Worker Centers: Organizing Communities at the Edge of a Dream* (Cornell University).

Gubbay, Jon, 1999, "The European Union Role in the Formation, Legitimation and Implementation of Migration Policy", in Gareth Dale and Mike Cole (eds), *The European Union and Migrant Labour* (Berg).

Guerin-Gonzalez, Camille, and Carl Strikwerda, 1993, *The Politics of Immigrant Workers: Labor Activism and Migration in the World Economy since 1830* (Holmes and Meier).

Hardy, Jane, and Nick Clark, 2007, "EU Enlargement, Workers and Migration: Implications for Trade Unions in the UK", International Labour Organisation.

Harris, Nigel, 1995, *The New Untouchables: Immigration and the New World Order* (Penguin).

Haywood, John, 2008, *The Great Migrations: From the Earliest Humans to the Age of Globalisation* (Quercus).

Held, David, Anthony McGrew, David Goldblatt and Jonathon Perraton, 1999, "People on the Move", in *Global Transformations: Politics, Economics and Culture* (Polity).

Home Office, 2007, "Economic and Fiscal Impact of Immigration", cross-departmental submission to the House of Lords Select Committee on Economic Affairs, October 2007, www.official-documents.gov.uk/document/cm72/7237/7237.pdf

House of Lords, 2008, Select Committee on Economic Affairs, www.publications.parliament.uk/pa/ld200708/ldselect/ldeconaf/82/8202.htm

Jordan, Bill, and Franck Düvell, 2002, *Irregular Migration, the Dilemmas of Transnational Mobility* (Edward Elgar).

Kelly, John, 1998, *Rethinking Industrial Relations: Mobilisation, Collectivism and Long Waves* (Routledge).

Kale, Madhavi, 1998, *Fragments of Empire: Capital, Slavery and Indentured Labour* (University of Pennsylvania).

Lewis, William Arthur, 1977, *Growth and Fluctuations: 1870-1913* (Allen and Unwin).

Mahamdallie, Hassan, 2007, "Muslim Working Class Struggles", *International Socialism 113* (winter 2007), www.isj.org.uk/?id=288

Marfleet, Philip, 2005, *Refugees in a Global Era* (Palgrave Macmillan).

Marfleet, Philip, 1998, "Migration and Refugee Experience", in Philip Marfleet and Ray Kieley, *Globalisation and the Third World* (Routledge).

Marx, Karl, 1959 [1894], *Capital*, volume three (International), www.marxists.org/archive/marx/works/download/Marx_Capital_Vol_3.pdf

Milkman, Ruth (ed), 2000, *Organizing Immigrants: The Challenge for Unions in Contemporary California*, (Cornell University).

Milkman, Ruth, 2006, *LA Story: Immigrant Workers and the Future of the US Labor Movement* (Russell Sage Foundation).

Milkman, Ruth, and Kent Wong, 2000, "Organizing the Wicked City: The 1992 Southern Califronia Drywall Strike" in Ruth Milkman, 2000.

Mink, Gwendolyn, 1986, *Old Labor and New Immigrants in American Political Development: Union, Party and State, 1875-1920* (Cornell University).

National Conference of State Legislatures, 2007, "2007 Enacted State Legislation Related to Immigrants and Immigration", available from www.ncsl.org/programs/immig/2007Immigration831.htm

Nayyar, Deepak, 2006, "Globalisation, History and Development: A Tale of Two Centuries", *Cambridge Journal of Economics*, volume 30, number 1.

Northrup, David, 1995, *Indentured Labour in the Age of Imperialism* (Cambridge University).

Rowthorn, Robert, 2008, "The Fiscal Impact of Immigration on Advanced Economies", *Oxford Review of Economic Policy*, volume 24, number 3.

Salt, John, and Jane Millar, 2006, "Foreign Labour in the United Kingdom: Current Patterns and Trends", *Labour Market Trends*, ONS, October 2006, www.statistics.gov.uk/articles/labour_market_trends/foreign_labour.pdf

Sassen, Saski, 1988, *The Mobility of Labour and Capital: A Study in International Investment and Labour Flow* (Cambridge University).

Sinclair, Upton, 2006 [1906], *The Jungle* (Penguin).

Stalker, Peter, 1994, *The Work of Strangers: A Survey of International Migration*, International Labour Office.

Stobart, Luke, 2008, "The Case of Spain's 'Border of Death': A Critical Evaluation of the 'No Borders' Position", unpublished MA thesis.

Strikwerda, Carl, and Guerin-Gonzalez, Camille, 1993, "Labor, Migration and Politics", in Guerin-Gonzalez and Strikwerda, 1993.

Tinker, Hugh, 1974, *A New System of Slavery: The Export of Indian Labour Overseas, 1830-1920* (Oxford University).

Waldinger, Roger, Chris Erickson, Ruth Milkman, Daniel Mitchell, Abel Valenzuela, Kent Wong and Maurice Zeitlin, 1998, "Helots no More: A Case Study of the Justice for Janitors Campaign in Los Angeles", in Kate Bronfenbrenner, Sheldon Friedman, Richard Hurt, Rudolph Seeber (eds), *Organizing to Win: New Research on Trade Union Strategies* (Cornell University).

Wills, Jane, 2008, "Making Class Politics Possible: Organising Contract Cleaners in London", *International Journal of Urban and Regional Research*, volume 32, number 2.

Woolfson, Charles, and Jeff Sommers, 2006, "Labour Mobility in Construction: European Implications of the Laval un Partneri Dispute with Swedish Labour", *European Journal of Industrial Relations*, volume 12, number 1.

Zabin, Carol, 2000, "Organizing Latino Workers in the Los Angeles Manufacturing Sector: The Case of American Racing Equipment", in Milkman, 2000.

From bubble to black hole: the neoliberal implosion[1]

Neil Faulkner

"**R**evolutionary socialists today should not be...pontificating on the degree of damage that capitalism has done to itself, on whether we are in 1929, 1992 or whatever... We do not have a crystal ball...but we can see all too clearly what is happening now and what our responsibilities are." So argues Chris Harman in his article in the previous issue of this journal.[2]

Harman's caution reflects a concern lest we cry wolf. We risk undermining the credibility of Marxist arguments and confounding political expectations if we get it wrong. We have done this before. In the wake of the 1987 Stock Exchange crash we announced that "the omens point toward the start of a new recession. The shock to credit delivered by the crash will deepen that recession. It is clear that capitalism is not on course for a return to the bright days of the post-war boom".[3] We were wrong. For at this very time, in the dark places of global finance capital, the mechanisms of the neoliberal boom were being forged.

But sometimes there is a wolf. And if we are not prepared, we can be taken unawares. The political and business elite still argues that we face a

---

1:   Thanks are due for critical comments on the first draft of this article from Chris Bambery, Eddie Cimorelli and Peter Segal.
2:   Harman, 2009, p46.
3:   Lapavitsas, 1988, pp17-18.

recession of limited duration. Indeed, they are banking on it—banking on a new boom enabling them to pay off the cost of state bailouts, and banking on the short-term quiescence of workers. Millions of workers buy that argument. Amid the fear and anger there is also a sense that the recession is like a natural calamity that comes, passes, and is gone. This perception encourages resignation and passivity, and Harman's conclusion that "we do not have a crystal ball" does nothing to challenge the sense of powerlessness and paralysis that afflicts many workers, including many activists, in relation to the recession.

And the fear and anger remain. If the left does not direct them, other forces will. The slogan "British jobs for British workers" on recent protests is a warning. We need to see ahead, to be aware of what is coming, so that we can plan initiatives of appropriate form and scale. And we need to know why we fight. Knowing the stakes are high, we will fight harder, for longer, with greater determination. And the stakes are very high indeed.

This is the beginning of a new epoch of global slump. We need to understand that if we are to act with the speed, energy and decisiveness necessary to help direct history's course. We need to remember that the choice last time was socialism or barbarism.

A short history of the permanent debt economy

The main purpose of this article is prognosis: it is our perspective on future developments that is in dispute. But this must build on diagnosis, so let us first summarise what seems to be agreed about what Harman has aptly dubbed "the permanent debt economy".[4]

The long-term tendency for the rate of profit to fall has made late capitalism prone to under-investment, overproduction and sluggish, erratic, crisis-prone growth. Though profit rate comparisons are difficult, the evidence is compelling that a long-term tendency for the rate of profit to fall underlies the present crisis. Profit rates in key developed economies appear to have roughly halved between the 1960s and the 1990s.[5] This has discouraged productive investment and slowed down the rate of growth of the "real economy" (defined as that in which surplus-value is actually produced).

The last major crisis—that of the 1970s—gave rise to a distinctive ruling class response. Faced with falling profits, over-accumulation, chronic inflation and a militant working class, a section of the bourgeoisie, led by Margaret Thatcher in Britain and Ronald Reagan in the US, promoted an anti-consensual "neoliberal" free-market ideology.

4: Harman, 2008.
5: Harman, 2007, pp148-150; Harman, 2008, p20.

Its purpose was to legitimise a frontal assault on unions, wages and the welfare state in order to substantially redistribute wealth from labour to capital, that is, to restore the rate of profit at the expense of the working class. This project enjoyed some success. Welfare was cut. Wages stagnated. Profit rates improved. The rich got richer. US bosses earned around 30 times as much as their workers in 1970, and around 500 times as much by 2000.[6]

But the effects were limited and contradictory. Heavy damage was inflicted on the real economy, much of it in a deliberate effort to break working class resistance with mass unemployment. Profit rates recovered, but never to the levels of the great post-war boom.[7] And while individual capitalists want low wages in their own firms, they want high wages elsewhere so that workers can buy the goods and services they produce. So the neoliberal economy has faced the intrinsic danger of being derailed by growing income inequality and inadequate demand.

The problem of a real economy afflicted by low profits, under-investment and inadequate demand were resolved in the neoliberal era by a vast growth in finance capital. Market deregulation, low interest rates ("cheap money"), financial "innovation" and rising household debt stoked this into the biggest bubble in the history of the system.

Loans were secured against assets that were rising in value only because of the availability of loans: a classic, self-feeding, speculative frenzy. Workers in many parts of the developed world became heavily indebted because of stagnant incomes, easy credit and rising house prices. And workers buying on tick then became the base of a vast inverted pyramid of financial "derivatives", unsecured debts, and inflated asset values. Average US household debt more than doubled between the late 1970s and 2006. Total debt grew from about 1.5 times US national output in the early 1980s to nearly 3.5 in 2007. Consequently, the financial sector's share of US profits increased from about 15 percent in the early 1950s to almost 50 percent in 2001.[8]

Precision is impossible, but one recent estimate of the total size of the global asset bubble is $290 trillion—more than five times the annual output of the world economy, and a figure which completely dwarfs the $1.9 trillion of state bailouts since the crisis began.[9]

The boom has been limited, uneven and unstable. Neoliberalism has failed to restore profits, investment and growth to the levels achieved in the

6: Harvey, 2005, pp16-17.
7: Harman, 2007, pp148-150.
8: Harman, 2008, p22.
9: The *Guardian*, 30 January 2009.

immediate post-war period.[10] The global economy has been characterised by huge, destabilising "imbalances" and a succession of bubbles and crashes.

The so-called "emerging market economies" had turned a collective current account deficit in 1999 into a surplus of \$544 billion by 2006, accumulating some \$2.65 trillion of foreign currency reserves. At the same time the US deficit soared until it accounted for three quarters of the global total.[11] US dollars paid for Chinese goods were being recycled into US debts to pay for more Chinese goods.

Equally pathological was the recurring pattern of bubbles and crashes. Between 1945 and 1971 there were, on one estimate, 38 financial crises across the global economy; between 1973 and 1997 there were 139.[12] Each time, however, the policy of finance ministers and central bankers in the leading capitalist states, especially in the US, was to pump liquidity into the system.[13] The mega-bubble finally burst with devastating effect in September–October 2008.

The crash

The crash was preceded by a "credit crunch". The crisis began when mounting distress in the US subprime mortgage market reached breaking point. Subprime loans had been repackaged with better-quality loans and sold on in the form of "collateralised debt obligations" (CDOs). It looked like a good way to spread risk. A slowdown in consumer demand and an easing of house prices triggered a "panic" in relation to subprime mortgages. This quickly mutated into a "contagion" sweeping across global financial markets on fears about the degree to which the banking system as a whole was infected by the 'toxic' debt of CDOs and other financial derivatives.[14]

The credit crunch prevented debts being rolled over, and this, in September–October 2008, brought a series of giant financial institutions to the brink of bankruptcy as losses and write-downs were announced and share prices plunged. The panic trigger this time was the collapse of US investment bank Lehman Brothers. The danger of global financial meltdown prompted the biggest nationalisations and bailouts in the history of capitalism. This crash, unprecedented in scale, shattered the confidence of both capitalists and consumers—and tipped the real economy, already slowing, into freefall.

10: See Glyn, 2006, pp129-155, especially p148.
11: Wolf, 2009, pp57, 83.
12: Wolf, 2009, p31.
13: Foster, 2007.
14: Kindleberger, 2002, pp91-107, 109-137.

The contradiction between regulation and profiteering has characterised capitalist banking since the 17th century.[15] Each crash is followed by tighter regulation, gradual relaxation and then a fresh frenzy of speculation. The centralisation of capital means that crashes tend to get bigger. The first international crash, affecting both the US and Europe, did not come until 1857.[16] The first Wall Street crash was that of 1907.[17]

Three crashes have been of exceptional significance, marking the beginning of depressions or slumps. The 1873 crash tipped the world economy into the long, shallow depression of 1873-96, feeding an intensification of imperial rivalries and an arms race that culminated in the First World War. The 1929 crash inaugurated the Great Depression, leading to fascism, rearmament and the Second World War. The series of 1973-5 price shocks and crashes was followed by a protracted slump which dragged on for a decade. The crash of 2008 looks like the biggest ever. Two questions present themselves. Can the state take the strain? And can the state engineer recovery?

Bailing into a black hole

Black holes are regions of space in which gravitational forces prevent matter and radiation escaping. This is a good analogy for the third phase of the neoliberal implosion: after the credit crunch and the crash we now have the black hole.

Capitalism's leading finance ministers and central bankers have, since September-October 2008, prevented a global meltdown, but that is all they have done. Unprecedented amounts of state capital have been poured into the system: a global total of $1.9 trillion so far, two thirds of it direct spending, one third in the form of guarantees.[18] The funds have been shovelled into the banks in tranches amid a chorus of injunctions to start lending again.

In October 2008 chancellor Alistair Darling gave the British banks £37 billion of taxpayers' money. It vanished instantly with no apparent economic effect. So in January he gave them another £50 billion. This too seems to have vanished—amid a collapse in share prices. Breaking news is that Obama's new treasury secretary, Tim Geithner, is injecting $2 trillion more into the US banks, almost three times as much as the original bailout in October. The Dow Jones index plunged 381 points on the news.[19]

Equally ineffective have been attempts to reflate consumer spending

---

15: Galbraith, 1976.
16: Kindleberger, 1986.
17: Galbraith, 1976, p123.
18: The *Guardian*, 30 January 2009.
19: The *Guardian*, 13 February 2009.

by cuts in taxes and interest rates. Neither Darling's £12 billion cut in VAT nor the Bank of England's reduction in interest rates to 1 percent has had any appreciable impact. Instead the British economy is dropping like a stone, with 70,000 to 80,000 losing their jobs every month, and predictions of 3 million or more out of work by the end of 2009.

The attempts to revive lending are a comprehensive failure because the bubble has been transformed into a black hole. Busted banks do not lend money: they hoard it. Workers who fear they may lose their jobs do not spend: they pay off debts and save.

The state handouts are dwarfed by the scale of private debt, and as the real economy dives, the debt gets bigger. The Bank of England has estimated total losses to global finance capital so far at $2.8 trillion.[20] But Will Hutton has contrasted this with an estimated total of at least $55 trillion of financial derivatives held by the world's banks.[21] The shrinking real economy is feeding bad debt back into the banks. A gigantic negative feedback mechanism is swelling the black hole of bankrupt capital at the centre of the system.

Despite the scale of the financial disaster, Chris Harman has argued that there are two crucial differences between the present and 1929. First, the ruling class has moved exceptionally quickly to prevent a general banking collapse and, second, much higher levels of state spending constitute a "floor" limiting the depth of any downturn.[22]

How important are these factors? The 1929-33 Hoover administration's management of the crisis in the US was uncertain and incompetent, but it was not wholly deflationary. There were attempts to bolster the economy before Roosevelt's New Deal.[23] And during its famous "First Hundred Days", notwithstanding the limitations and contradictions, the new Roosevelt administration did take rapid and radical action.[24]

This, moreover, was in response to a financial crisis smaller in scale and slower to develop than that of 2008. No major banks collapsed in 1929,[25] and back then finance capital was less centralised and globalised. In 2008 the ruling class faced an immediate meltdown of the entire global financial system. They acted as they did because they had to.

It is undoubtedly of real economic significance that in 1929 federal government expenditure represented only 2.5 percent of GNP whereas

20: The *Guardian*, 1 January 2009, p14.
21: Hutton, 2008.
22: Harman, 2009, pp35-37.
23: Galbraith, 1976, pp194-207; Kindleberger, 1986, pp117-196.
24: Badger, 2008.
25: Galbraith, 1976, pp200-203, 209.

in 2007 it accounted for around 20 percent.[26] Because state investment is determined by political decisions, as opposed to profit calculations, government spending can hold up in a downturn. And the more of it there is, the higher the "floor". But this assumes the state itself is not bankrupted. The nationalisation of banking losses, debts and debt insurance comes at massive cost. The bailouts and guarantees have more than doubled Britain's national debt. Add in the liabilities of the crippled, state-controlled Royal Bank of Scotland, and the total financial obligation of the British state now stands at £3 trillion—two and a half times annual national income.[27]

State debt has to be funded like any other. Private investors could "lose faith" in Britain's ability to pay. There are already signs of that with a plummeting pound. In 1976 a combination of recession, inflation, a militant working class and high government spending triggered a sudden "loss of confidence" and a run on the pound. The subsequent International Monetary Fund (IMF) bailout came at massive cost—wages were cut, public services slashed and unemployment doubled.[28]

A string of states in Central and Eastern Europe are already at this point. The IMF has imposed austerity measures on Hungary and Ukraine as a condition of financial support, and collapsing economies are being further deflated by high interest rates and spending cuts.[29] At the same time, the credit ratings of Greece, Spain, and Portugal have been downgraded, there is growing concern that Iceland and Ireland might soon default, and plans have been put in place in the Eurozone for the reintroduction of national currencies if the weaker economies start quitting the euro.[30]

Brown and Darling's response hinges on things not getting worse and the recession ending soon. The state needs to bail itself out with rising tax revenues and public spending cuts. The neoliberal elite is betting everything on a short recession. But there are no good reasons for thinking it will be. It is not simply the damage already done by the bursting of the neoliberal bubble. It is what has replaced it: a gigantic black hole of busted banks and bad debt that is sucking capital and spending power out of the system, deflating the real economy, turning ever more debts bad. And it evolves: the monster is growing new heads.

With inflation close to zero, and tax and interest rate cuts apparently unable to reflate the economy, the system faces the danger of a "liquidity

26: Harman, 2009, p35.
27: The *Guardian*, 20 January 2009.
28: Whitehead, 1985, pp181-201.
29: Harman, 2009, p38.
30: Choonara, 2009, p16.

trap". Capitalists will borrow money to invest only if they think they can make a profit. If demand is falling, and in particular if prices are falling, the fear is that eventual returns will not cover the cost of investments—even when interest rates are close to zero. The best thing then is simply to hoard money: if prices are falling, a cache of savings will buy more in the future.

It is when a liquidity trap threatens that cutting interest rates can be like "pushing on a piece of string". This was a key feature of the Japanese crisis of the 1990s. Though interest rates were sometimes at zero and the Bank of Japan repeatedly pumped money into the system (the "quantitative easing" now much discussed), the economy stagnated. Capitalists and consumers continued to save rather than borrow and spend.[31]

Another growing problem is protectionism. After 1929 world trade fell by two thirds and global unemployment quadrupled, as protectionist barriers went up across the world.[32] The reason is simple: capitalism is a competitive system in which the long-term interests of the global system may clash with the short-term interests of blocs of capital. So protectionism increases in a crisis, and that makes the crisis worse.

It is happening already. China has long been charged with running a form of protectionism with an "undervalued" yuan making exports cheap and earning a huge balance of payments surplus. With the Chinese economy now in freefall and tens of millions facing unemployment, the yuan, if anything, is likely to be further devalued. A series of tit for tat competitive devaluations is one possible form of protectionism. Alternatively, there are state subsidies to ailing industries. Both the US and leading European states Germany, France, Italy and Britain have announced support packages for their respective car industries. Already, in different ways, capitalist states are attempting to shore up and protect their own industries

Faced with similar problems in the 1930s John Maynard Keynes put forward the case for fiscal stimulus: the government had to both make money available and spend it. This meant governments abandoning balanced budgets and going deeply into debt to fund programmes of public spending. If Marx is the spectre at neoliberalism's funerary feast, Keynes is the awkward guest. Keynesian economics cannot resolve the contradictions of capitalism. It is an attempt to manage them. But it is not true that it does not work in any sense. The problem, as Chris reminds us, is that Keynes was radical in theory but cautious in practice.[33] The full development of his policy prescriptions

---

31: Turner, 2008, pp135-187.
32: Harman, 1984, p62.
33: Harman, 2009, pp33-34.

ran up against a political barrier: the opposition of the capitalist class to state encroachment on the commanding heights of the economy.

This seems confirmed by three counter-examples. In Russia there was no depression at all, since state-direction of investment and labour maintained high levels of growth in what was, in effect, a siege economy insulated from the global market.[34] In Germany by the mid-1930s the depression was more or less over and virtually everyone was back at work. The Nazis smashed organised labour, restructured industry, imposed state direction and borrowed heavily to fund public investment.[35] And in the United States the end of the depression amounted to a bastardised form of Keynesianism: the full-employment war economy was created by levels of government borrowing and spending in the early 1940s that dwarfed those of the late 1930s.[36]

The inherent logic of Keynesianism is the transformation of private capitalism into state capitalism. Historically, state-directed investment on the scale necessary to terminate a slump has occurred in the context of social upheaval and political crisis—the Stalinist counter-revolution in Russia, the Nazi seizure of power in Germany, the US entry into the Second World War. It was "military Keynesianism" that ended the Great Depression.

What the ruling class fears, on the other hand, is a left wing variant powered by mass struggle from below. It is the job of socialists to make that fear a reality.

Struggle, socialist economics and transitional demands

We are witness to perhaps the greatest crisis in the history of the system. Yet the economic and political barriers to Keynesian-type programmes of state spending are immense. Barack Obama's $800 billion stimulus package has been derided on one side as nowhere near enough and attacked on the other as profligate and irresponsible. The ruling class is deeply split over what to do. The problem is not simply the cost. It is also a problem of politics.

The neoliberal elite remains in power across the globe. Defenders of the rich, big business and the rule of profit for 30 years, they are deeply committed to the interests of their class. Boom may have turned to bust, and increasingly panic-stricken measures to regenerate private investment and private consumption proved futile. But the alternative—a wholesale switch from monetary to fiscal policy, to direct state investment and a programme of public works—would, if on a sufficient scale to have a significant

---

34: Hobsbawm, 1994, pp96-97.
35: Galbraith, 1976, pp237-238.
36: Galbraith, 1976, pp253-255.

impact, involve a frontal attack on the power and profits of capital. It would also break the separation between economics and politics that is so central to bourgeois ideology. The idea that the "invisible hand" of market forces determines what happens in the workplace and the economy, that this most important realm of social life is beyond the reach of democratic decision making and rational planning, is a critical barrier to the development of revolutionary consciousness. The "reification" of the economy—the conception of it as an impersonal force outside human will—structures the "alienation" of workers under capitalism, their sense that they do not have, and cannot have, control over the world that shapes their lives.

Public works fuse economics and politics. If the state can build railways, hospitals and council houses—if, indeed, it can do this better without the chaos, waste and profiteering of private capitalism—then why not publicly controlled steel making, car production and supermarket chains? The risk to the ruling class is that a massive programme of public works designed to kickstart the economy would risk generating a political dynamic of change that could rapidly spin out of control.

So we are at an impasse. Bankers will not lend because their banks are bust and they do not think borrowers can repay. Industrialists will not invest because markets and profits are collapsing. Consumers will not spend because they are deeply in debt and fear for their jobs. The system is like Frankenstein's monster lifeless on the slab however many thousands of volts are pumped into it.

How should socialists intervene? It is not enough to argue that socialism would be a better system: to do that and nothing more would be abstract propaganda. It is necessary to agitate for action from below—for protests, strikes and occupations—against the jobs massacre and its consequences for the working class. But we also need to bridge the gap between propaganda and agitation, between the need for socialism and the class struggle of workers today. We need "transitional demands".

Tainted by the dogmatism of orthodox Trotskyists, in whose hands Trotsky's 1938 Programme fossilised into the Ten Commandments, transitional demands have in fact been central to revolutionary strategy in periods of acute crisis. The "Theses on Tactics" approved at the Third Comintern Congress in 1921 argued that "communist parties must put forward demands whose fulfilment is an immediate and urgent working class need, and they must fight for these demands in mass struggle, regardless of whether they are compatible with the profit economy of the capitalist class or not"[37].

37:   Hallas, 1985, p56.

Trotsky's "Programme of Action for France" of June 1934 is a classic example of a set of transitional demands to be raised by revolutionaries in the context of mass struggle.[38] The central demand of the Communist-led National Unemployed Workers Movement in Britain for "work at trade union rates or full maintenance" is a concrete instance of a transitional demand that mobilised hundreds of thousands of unemployed workers in militant protests during the 1920s and 1930s.[39]

When the system is broken and cannot satisfy basic needs, or when the system is challenged by an insurgent working class whose aspirations it cannot realise, it is appropriate to raise demands which unite workers in struggles for reforms which challenge the logic of capital and push beyond the limits of what the system can afford.

We should demand the right to work, not simply because all workers are entitled to a living, but because employment is reflationary, because labour is productive, and because there are social needs to be satisfied. We should demand a programme of council house building, not only to house the hundreds of thousands who are homeless, stuck in temporary accommodation, or paying extortionate rents to private landlords, but also because it would employ tens of thousands of construction workers. We should demand that benefits are doubled, restoring them to their 1970s level, not only because the poor are needy and innocent, but because those on low incomes have to spend virtually everything they get, so welfare is reflationary.

The neoliberal elite is panic stricken, divided and discredited. Its response to the crisis has failed and will continue to fail. Yet its class allegiance precludes wholesale state control and public works.

But for workers state control, public works and better welfare are common sense: if politicians have billions for war and the banks, why not billions for homes, health and the unemployed? On every front, on every issue, we have to counterpose the political economy of the working class to the political economy of capital. The role of transitional demands is to crystallise the difference, bridge the gap between propaganda and agitation, and marshal our side for struggle.

Tens of thousands of school, college and university students joined the Gaza protests this winter. The radicalism and militancy of the anti-capitalist and anti-war movements might feed a revival of class struggle. But transmission will not be automatic. Socialists have to fight to make it happen.

Many of those young people will be seeking work this summer.

38: Trotsky, 1934.
39: Hannington, 1967.

Many will not find it. A new Right to Work Campaign could infuse the class struggle with the spirit of young radical protest. It could also focus the demand for state action, challenge the logic of capital and encourage workers' resistance to the jobs massacre.

If we underestimate the scale of the crisis, we will underestimate the scale of response that is necessary. The wolf is upon us. We must arm.

References

Badger, Anthony, 2008, *FDR: the First Hundred Days* (Hill and Wang).

Choonara, Joseph, 2009, "The Crisis Deepens", *Socialist Review* (February 2009), www.socialistreview.org.uk/article.php?articlenumber=10709

Foster, John Bellamy, 2007, "The Financialisation of Capitalism", *Monthly Review 58* (April 2007), www.monthlyreview.org/0407jbf.htm

Galbraith, John Kenneth, 1976, *Money: Whence it Came, Where it Went* (Penguin).

Glyn, Andrew, 2006, *Capitalism Unleashed: Finance, Globalisation and Welfare* (Oxford University).

Hallas, Duncan, 1985, *The Comintern* (Bookmarks).

Hannington, Wal, 1967, *Never on our Knees* (Lawrence & Wishart).

Harman, Chris, 1984, *Explaining the Crisis: a Marxist Re-appraisal* (Bookmarks).

Harman, Chris, 2007, "The Rate of Profit and the World Today", *International Socialism 115* (summer 2007), www.isj.org.uk/?id=340

Harman, Chris, 2008, *Capitalism's New Crisis: What do Socialists say?* (Socialist Workers Party).

Harman, Chris, 2009, "The Slump of the 1930s and the Crisis Today", *International Socialism 121* (winter 2009), www.isj.org.uk/?id=506

Harvey, David, 2005, *A Brief History of Neoliberalism* (Oxford University).

Hobsbawm, Eric, 1994, *Age of Extremes: The Short History of the Twentieth Century, 1914-1991* (Michael Joseph).

Hutton, Will, 2008, "Without Real Leadership, We Face Disaster", *Observer*, 12 October 2008, www.guardian.co.uk/commentisfree/2008/oct/12/marketturmoil-creditcrunch

Kindleberger, Charles, 1986, *The World in Depression, 1929-1939* (University of California).

Kindleberger, Charles, 2002, *Manias, Panics, and Crashes: A History of Financial Crises* (Palgrave).

Lapavitsas, Costas, 1988, "Financial Crisis and the Stock Exchange Crash", in *International Socialism 38* (spring 1988).

Trotsky, Leon, 1934, "A Programme of Action for France", www.marxists.org/archive/trotsky/1934/06/paf.htm

Turner, Graham, 2008, *The Credit Crunch* (Pluto).

Whitehead, Philip, 1985, *The Writing on the Wall: Britain in the Seventies* (Michael Joseph).

Wolf, Martin, 2009, *Fixing Global Finance: How to Curb Financial Crises in the 21st Century* (Yale).

Take neoliberalism seriously

Eddie Cimorelli

The International Socialist tradition has made some remarkable intellectual breakthroughs, above all the theories of state capitalism, the permanent arms economy and deflected permanent revolution. A strength of our tradition has been the ability to look reality in the face, no matter how unpalatable. Our recognition of the post-war boom and the downturn in industrial struggle in the late 1970s are examples. In recent years, however, our theory has not played the same role in understanding the latest developments in capitalism, variously known as the Washington consensus or neoliberalism.

The key issue is the extent to which neoliberalism involved, if not a boom comparable to that of the post-war period, then at least significant growth of the system, without this leading to a rise in class confidence and combativity. We have successfully defended the centrality of the working class against those on the left who argue that under the neoliberal project it has ceased to be an agent of change. But what is missing from our analysis of neoliberalism is an understanding of the impact of the reorganisation of capital and an assessment of its success in its own terms. For example, the section of Chris Harman's recent article that asks "How effective is neoliberalism for capitalism?",[1] does not consider how successful it has been in raising profitability or in undermining working class organisation and consciousness.

Neoliberalism is a particular organisation of capitalism. Its most basic feature is the use of the state to protect capital, impose market imperatives

---

1: Harman, 2008, pp108-112.

on society and curb the power of labour. This strategy has shifted power and wealth away from the majority. The state remains paramount but its role has changed. Privatisation and deregulation have introduced greater flexibility and made workers more compliant. Instead of a demand management approach with government intervention, which was previously used to ease the worst excesses of the productive process, the lives of most people are now subordinated to the system.

Financialisation

Financialisation does not represent a "coup" by financial capital as some on the left claim; it represents a new dominance of finance primarily in the US and UK. Financial markets now play an important role in accelerating the restructuring of capitalism. Banking changed dramatically in the quarter of a century after the mid-1980s. Capital controls were removed to restore the unrestricted flow of finance. Features of financialisation include: asset-price bubble blowing; the drive to maximise leverage and expand balance sheets; the financialisation of much economic activity, with most significant manufacturers increasingly profiting from finance and banking profits increasingly made from individual customers; the rise of the shadow banking system, whose operations made the City of London a kind of economic Guantanamo Bay in which Wall Street could indulge in practices banned at home.

Readily available credit has meant that consumption for workers has continued to climb, despite falls in real take-home pay. The ratio of outstanding consumer debt to consumer disposable income more than doubled from 1975 to 2005 in the US. In the neoliberal context debt has two functions. One is to ensure that consumption and consequently realisation can still take place. The other is as a means of disciplining the working class. The pressure of debt repayment can force an extreme work discipline on people—long hours in multiple jobs, which are often less secure, casual, temporary and precarious.

What was different about the neoliberal boom?

The ruling class offensive that ran through the recessions in the 1970s and 1980s resulted in restructuring and generated a new wave of capitalist expansion. Previously growth and reducing unemployment were priorities for the system. Now these were replaced with fighting inflation. This slowed growth, weakening the ability of labour to fight back against capital's assault. Slow growth was combined with direct assaults on organised labour. For example, overseas production was increased. Consequently domestic unemployment rose, leading to downward pressure on wages and benefits. Sometimes the success of this strategy is overstated, as Bill Dunn has noted.[2] Often what was more important was its value as a threat against demands for wage increases or unionisation.

However, it is important to try to understand the actual impact of the neoliberal offensive. According to the UK Trade and Investment website:

> Hourly compensation costs for production workers in the UK are…lower than in many other European Union countries…social costs on wage bills are amongst the lowest in Western Europe… Compared to the European Union average of 41.8 hours, full-time employees in the UK work an average of 43.0 hours per week. UK law does not oblige employers to provide written employment contracts… The UK has a highly flexible labour market.[3]

Of course, this website is likely to overstate the flexibility of labour in Britain. Nevertheless it should be acknowledged that British capitalism has had a greater degree of success than most of its competitors in disciplining labour. In the aerospace industry production has remained in the UK but changed dramatically over the past two decades. The outsourcing and/or off-shoring of many components has led to significant reductions in numbers of employees and considerable changes to skill sets.

Dunn correctly points out that this is a double-edged process, which is usually associated with the introduction of more efficient production techniques, such as "just in time". Two years ago workers at the Rolls Royce plant in Derby struck for an hour against a below inflation pay deal. They won a significant rise, which had to be rolled out across the group. So the changes increase the potential power of workers where they are organised. However, changes imposed during the neoliberal era, with low levels of class conflict, have, on balance, been quite successful for the employers.

Recovery and boom

According to Fred Moseley there has been a substantial recovery of the rate of profit in the US, much of this attributed to a successful three-decade neoliberal wage squeeze. This underpinned expanded capitalist reproduction, by helping to produce new centres of accumulation, particularly in China.[4]

The growth of financial markets and profitability is tied to the neoliberal wage squeeze. The recovery after 1997 was built on exceptionally

---

2:   Dunn, 2009.
3:   www.uktradeinvest.gov.uk
4:   Moseley, 2008.

low US interest rates and a steady growth in consumer indebtedness, with a swelling US current account deficit, creating a kind of Keynesian global engine to drive the world economy.

Although the world economy has grown, levels of UK employment have not increased significantly. This is what could be termed a jobless boom and is characteristic of neoliberal growth. The reduced living standards of working class people contrast with concentrated wealth at the top of the economic ladder as workers have increasingly been forced to borrow. Half of all earners saw no growth at all and a third saw their real pay fall— mainly due to public sector pay and the minimum wage being held below inflation for several years. Moreover, working class confidence and organisation have not grown as they did in the long post-war boom. This is not to say that working class organisation has been defeated. However, a process of capitalist reorganisation has had an impact on working class organisation, and this impact has been extremely uneven.

The capitalist expansion enabled the finance industry to significantly increase its share of corporate profits through recycling surplus capital. As the first signs of over-accumulation set in, with the Asian Crisis in 1997, massive credit expansion, combined with a turn to blowing bubbles in the "new economy", real estate and commodities, postponed the slump. As financial markets seized up with the credit crunch in summer 2007, over-accumulation meant that financial meltdown triggered global slump in an accelerated and unprecedented fashion, the dynamics of which to date the left have yet to properly explain. Whatever happens next, there is unlikely to be much more scope for blowing bubbles. Problems of over-accumulation and the overproduction of goods that cannot profitably be sold can only be resolved in capitalist terms via bankruptcies, plants closing and mass layoffs. As world demand and sales fall, the effects of overcapacity, previously masked by credit, are already having a serious impact.

The current crisis is unlike all the others of the past decade. While previous financial shocks in the US were contained, this one has become a generalised economic crisis. Previous crises have been regionally confined. However, this is a globalising crisis at the heart of the system. We are now faced with a generalised global crisis of over-accumulation combined with a banking crisis that leaves neoliberal capitalism systemically shaken. It is impossible to predict exactly how this crisis will play out or how long the slump will last, though there is a strong possibility that it will be deep and protracted. The recession has revealed that Britain is not the successful and prosperous society purportedly created by the neoliberal turn. In fact, it is now widely recognised that UK PLC is the proverbial basket case of Western capitalism.

Social liberalism and its impact on the movement

As we enter the crisis it is important to understand the impact of neoliberalism on our movement. Many social democratic parties and national liberation movements have accepted the neoliberal agenda. One of the more extreme examples is of the African National Congress (ANC) in South Africa. Naomi Klein, in her very readable and detailed work on the neoliberal onslaught, *The Shock Doctrine*,[5] describes the disastrous transformation of the ANC as apartheid collapsed. The ANC dropped their "freedom charter" and adopted a full-blown neoliberal programme which had a tragic impact on those liberated from the apartheid regime. However, she spoils her argument by seeing this through the prism of her "shock doctrine", which runs like a conspiracy where, following a societal "shock" such as war, coup or disaster, the Chicago Boys are waiting in the wings to apply neoliberal medicine.

John Newsinger has described the fundamental transformation Brown and his supporters have engineered in the Labour Party.[6] Brown regularly boasted to business that New Labour made Britain "the most business friendly environment in Europe". To achieve this Brown admitted that making Britain a playground for business and the rich involved a break from 100 years of Labour history. These changes were fundamental. The Labour Party has haemorrhaged members and support. What has been the wider political impact on the labour movement? Previously Labour's stated commitment to reformism with genuine reforms was the ideological glue holding together a political cadre of activists in the unions. This ideology was combined with varying degrees of support for the Stalinist states, helping to provide this core of activists with something approaching a worldview.

The combination of the ideological assault of New Labour with the loss of the ideological ballast of Stalinism presents some unique problems. How does Brown's commitment to the neoliberal project impact upon the unions? When union leaders such as Derek Simpson, Tony Woodley and Dave Prentis claim that Brown represents "Old Labour" values, how does this affect the lower levels of the bureaucracy and layers of activists? When the neoliberal frenzy of experiments on British society is pushed both through and against our movement, the left needs to assess the impact. The corrosive combination of the decline of organised reformism, the demise of Stalinist politics, the neoliberal offensive and the importation of neoliberal ideology via New Labour and the union bureaucracy is a unique phenomenon. The dislocation of many workers from the official labour movement and its leadership

---

5:    Klein, 2007.
6:    Newsinger, 2007.

is but one consequence with potentially explosive connotations. We need to understand the impact on confidence, class consciousness and organisation as the movement approaches its greatest of political challenges.

Conclusion

The neoliberal global model has enabled the system's failures to spread throughout the world. The previously beneficial symptoms of this reorganisation of capital are now, with a neat dialectical twist, turning into their opposite and stoking up the problems of over-accumulation. The working class has experienced significant change at work in the recent decades of the neoliberal offensive. The revolutionary left must assess:

(1) The neoliberal framework that prioritises capital accumulation over all else.

(2) The dynamics of capital accumulation that preceded the crisis, which must be analysed in order to understand the likely trajectory of the Great Crash.

(3) New Labour's transition from reformism to neoliberalism and its impact on the labour movement, working class confidence, consciousness and organisation.

The problem is not that we have avoided the issue of neoliberalism; it is rather that we have focused almost exclusively on downplaying the economic changes it involves, while exaggerating its purely ideological aspect and completely ignoring the social implications. We must get to grips with the intersection of over-accumulation, declining profitability and financialisation with the changes the neoliberal project has had on society and our movement. The onus is on us as a tradition to prepare our class for the dangers and opportunities this historic period offers.

References

Dunn, Bill, 2009, "Myths of Globalisation and the New Economy", *International Socialism* 121 (winter 2009), www.isj.org.uk/?id=509

Harman, Chris, 2008, "Theorising Neoliberalism", *International Socialism* 117 (winter 2008), www.isj.org.uk/?id=399

Klein, Naomi, 2007, *The Shock Doctrine: The Rise of Disaster Capitalism* (Allen Lane).

Moseley, Fred, 2008, "Some Notes on the Crunch and the Crisis", *International Socialism* 119 (summer 2008), www.isj.org.uk/?id=463

Newsinger, John, 2007, "Brown's Journey from Reformism to Neoliberalism", *International Socialism* 115 (summer 2007), www.isj.org.uk/?id=334

Revolutionary paths: a reply to Panos Garganas and François Sabado

Alex Callinicos

The responses in the previous issue of *International Socialism* by Panos Garganas and by François Sabado to my article "Where is the Radical Left Going?" are very welcome.[1] As their articles bear witness, the condition of the radical left in Europe is quite diverse. Though I have disagreements with some of the things that both have to say, these differences are quite minor.

We in the Socialist Workers Party (SWP) are enthusiasts for the New Anticapitalist Party (Nouveau Parti Anticapitaliste, NPA) that Sabado and his comrades in the now dissolved Ligue Communiste Révolutionnaire (LCR) have played a key role in launching. I also recognise the significance of the realignment that is bringing together the Greek Socialist Workers Party (SEK) and the other far-left organisations allied in the Anti-Capitalist Front (Enantia) with the New Left Current (NAR), the most important recent breakaway from the Communist Party. I also express my disagreements in some humility: the disastrous recent experiences of the radical left in Britain do not exactly set up any of the participants in these catastrophes to preach to their comrades elsewhere in Europe. As will become clear, the debate, and the concrete development of the NPA have shifted my own position.

1:   Sabado, 2009; Garganas, 2009; responding to Callinicos, 2008.

A new model party?

The most important point to emerge from the discussion is that the general term "radical left formations" encapsulates two quite different types of organisation, even though they are both a product of the radicalisation of the past decade. There are those cases where the level of class struggle and the political traditions of the left make it possible for revolutionary Marxists to unite with others who regard themselves as revolutionaries in new, bigger formations. So far the only example where this has come to fruition is the NPA, whose founding principles, as we shall see below, are in a broad sense revolutionary. Then there are other cases in which the most important break is by forces that reject social liberalism but have not broken with overt reformism—Die Linke in Germany, the Partito della Rifondazione Comunista (PRC) in Italy under both its old and its new leadership, Synaspismos in Greece and some elements in the Left Bloc in Portugal.

Both Garganas and Sabado argue that radical left projects should follow the first model, basing themselves on a clearly anti-capitalist platform, rather than on an "anti-liberal" platform that targets neoliberalism and not the capitalist system itself. They justify this partly by pointing to the negative experiences of centre-left coalitions such as the plural left government in France in 1997-2001 and the Prodi government in Italy in 2006-8. Garganas also argues that significant sections of workers and young people are not attracted to "the traditional reformism of the past".[2]

What seems to me valid in these arguments arises from the different paths taken by the class struggle and by the workers' movement in various parts of Europe. France and Greece are the European states that have seen the most intense social struggles in recent decades. Indeed, in Greece these have been so sustained and so fierce (think of the huge wave of rioting by young people that swept the country in December 2008) as to create, in relative terms, the largest radical left in Europe. Moreover, these are both societies with strong Communist traditions where social democracy has only succeeded in establishing itself as the dominant force on the left in recent decades and on a fragile and contested basis. In these conditions, seeking to build parties of the radical left on an anti-capitalist programme makes perfect sense.

It remains the case, however, that these parties will still have to grapple with the problem of reformism. One of the main lessons of the history of the workers' movement is that the development of the class struggle, by drawing new layers of workers into class-conscious activity, will tend to expand the base of reformist politics, since seeking to change the

---

2:    Garganas, 2009, p154.

existing system seems, initially at least, an attractive halfway house between passive acquiescence in the status quo and outright revolution. Thus if we consider the great revolutionary experiences of the past century, the Russian working class, after the overthrow of Tsarism, gravitated first to the Mensheviks and Social Revolutionaries, not the Bolsheviks. In Germany, thanks to the ingrained experience of reformism and the relative weakness of the far left, it was the Social Democrats and the Independent Socialists who were the first main beneficiaries of the revolution of November 1918. Nor are these experiences confined to the imperialist countries. Consider how the Brazilian Workers Party, which Sabado's comrades in the Fourth International helped to build in the belief that it was a non-reformist organisation, has become, under the Lula presidency, a pillar of social liberalism.

The implication of these historical experiences is not the fatalistic conclusion that the mass of workers will never break with reformism: on the contrary, the Bolsheviks achieved, within the space of a few months, majority support in the Russian working class, and the German Communists were able to win over the bulk of the Independent Socialists and build a mass workers' party. Nevertheless, these cases show how reformism remains a strategic problem for revolutionary parties far bigger and better socially implanted than the NPA, SEK or the SWP.

A major driving force in the development of the new radical left parties is the experience of social liberalism. After Tony Blair, Lionel Jospin, Gerhard Schröder and Romano Prodi large numbers of workers and young people are looking beyond the "old house" of social democracy. But it doesn't follow that they have broken with reformism as such. Indeed, so tight has been the embrace between recent centre-left governments and neoliberalism that some tendencies on the far left (the Committee for a Workers' International, for example) argue that the British Labour Party, the German Social Democratic Party, the French Socialist Party and their like can no longer be regarded as reformist parties. I think this view is mistaken—apart from anything else it ignores the fact that large sections of the working class continue to vote for these parties, partly out of habit, partly for fear of the even harder neoliberal policies of the traditional bourgeois parties. But the sharp shift to the right by mainstream social democracy that gives this view whatever plausibility it possesses creates a large space to the left of these parties that is ideologically diverse and open to various political currents.[3]

3:   Garganas mentions one of these currents, autonomism, when he writes, "Young people may be more influenced by autonomists rather than 'left Labour' ideas"—Garganas, 2009, p154. This is plainly true in a number of European countries. But it is important to recognise

It should be added that the revolutionary Marxist tradition, which both the Fourth International and the International Socialist Tendency have tried to continue, is not exactly a mass force at this precise moment in time. Sabado says this is because it "is more than 30 years since the advanced capitalist countries experienced revolutionary or pre-revolutionary situations".[4] That's true. It is also true that, whatever achievements the LCR or the SWP can claim, we have not led mass workers' struggles of any kind, let alone (as the Bolsheviks did) a successful socialist revolution. Moreover, we have to struggle with the incubus of Stalinism. None of this is a reason for liquidating the revolutionary Marxist tradition, but it does imply that we cannot hope in the short term to regroup the radical left on a platform that simply reproduces the strategic conceptions developed by revolutionary Marxists. That does not mean that these conceptions are simply irrelevant—a point that I return to below.

What does this mean concretely? The situation in France has allowed Sabado and his comrades to launch a party three times the size of the LCR whose programme, while in some respects remaining strategically open, nevertheless explicitly calls for a revolutionary break with capitalism. Conditions differ elsewhere. Thus in Britain and Germany we confront workers' movements in which social democracy has been deeply entrenched to the extent that it is often assumed that the two are identical. This is why the emergence of Die Linke in Germany is such a historic development. Sabado acknowledges that it is "a step forward for the workers' movement" in Germany,[5] but this recognition is rather grudging and he prefers to accentuate the negative, stressing the "left reformist" character of the project, the weight within Die Linke of the ex-Stalinist PDS and so on.

All of this is true enough, but it ignores the fundamental fact that, for the first time in decades, the decay of social democracy has produced a serious breakaway to the left. Of course, Die Linke's politics is left reformist: what else could it be given the balance of forces in Germany? Elsewhere the process of decomposition is so far advanced that such major splits are unlikely. As I noted in my original article, this is the problem that we are grappling with in Britain. The chronic, historic weakness of the Labour left would not matter so much

---

that, precisely because of the autonomists' evasion of the problem of political power, their ideas can often fit quite well with versions of reformism. This is shown by, for example, the collusion between autonomists and the right wing of the altermondialiste movement at the London and Athens European Social Forums, and the use of autonomist rhetoric by the PRC leader Fausto Bertinotti to conceal his shift to the right. See, for detailed discussion of this issue, Callinicos, 2004.

4:    Sabado, 2009, p149.
5:    Sabado, 2009, p144.

if their ideas were not still supported by millions of people (as is indicated by the immense popularity Tony Benn enjoys well into his eighties).

The continuing influence of reformism constrains us in different ways. Respect was doomed ultimately by its failure to bring about a major split in the Labour Party. But, even so, Labourism continued to make itself felt. If the SWP had, in the negotiations that led to the formation of Respect in 2003-4, insisted on the kind of anti-capitalist platform championed by Garganas and Sabado, the project would have been stillborn (or would have gone ahead without us). As it was, it was hard enough to have the word "socialism" included in the coalition's title (via the acronym forming the name "Respect"). Were we wrong to have gone ahead on a weaker platform of opposition to neoliberalism, racism and war? Absolutely not: despite the ultimate outcome, it was right to have tried. But human beings make history not in circumstances of their own choosing, and an explicitly anti-capitalist party was not on the agenda in Britain then.

Similarly it is not on the agenda in Germany today. Does that mean that our comrades in *Marx21* are wrong to throw themselves enthusiastically into building Die Linke? Again, absolutely not. They are right to seek to try to develop Die Linke in the most militant and dynamic way possible. Sabado takes a cheap shot at *Marx21*, accusing it of "a relativisation of the critique of the policies of the leadership of Die Linke on the question of participation in governments with the SPD".[6] Fortunately, this misrepresents the real situation. Our comrades take a principled position of opposition to participation in centre-left governments. But what they refused to do, before the formation of Die Linke, was to allow the wrong policy of the PDS in participating in social-liberal state governments in Berlin and elsewhere to be used as a pretext, as it was, for example, by the local Committee for a Workers' International group, for attempting to prevent the creation of the new party. Were they wrong about that? Would it have been better if what Sabado recognises as "a step forward" hadn't taken place? Once again the question answers itself.

Even where circumstances permit the formation of a party on a stronger programmatic basis, this does not mean the problem of reformism goes away. Sabado mentions the case of Jean-Luc Mélenchon, a leader of the French Socialist Party (PS) left and a key figure in the campaign against the European Constitutional Treaty in the 2005 referendum, who has now broken away from the PS with the aim of creating a "French Die Linke". Sabado asks, 'Should we support him and join with him in his proposals and projects for alliances with the French Communist Party, which maintains the perspective

---

6:    Sabado, 2009, p146.

of governing tomorrow—with the PS?"[7] Of course not. The balance of forces in France allows the anti-capitalist left to relate to Mélenchon from a position of relative strength. But nevertheless his break with the PS is a significant one, which exposes the disarray of the reformist left in France in the face of Nicolas Sarkozy's victory in the 2007 presidential elections and the attractive power of the NPA embodied in the person of Olivier Besancenot.

The development of the NPA may generate more breaks, not just in the PS but in the Communist Party as well. The NPA will have to know how to relate to such openings in a way that involves more than just offering the choice of joining the party or engaging in "classic" united fronts on specific issues. For all the excitement it has generated, the NPA will be quite a small force (albeit significantly larger than the LCR) on the French political scene and in the workers' movement. This will limit its capacity to lead in any real upsurge of social struggles. Realising the NPA's very great potential will require a willingness to intervene in the broader political field and sometimes to make alliances with other political forces, some of which, in the nature of things, will be reformist. Having said that, I think the NPA's founding congress was probably right to have rejected an electoral pact with Mélenchon in the European parliamentary elections in June 2009. The NPA is the stronger force and it is important that it demonstrates and builds up its independent electoral force as quickly as possible.

There is nevertheless a danger implicit in Sabado's argument and sometimes explicit in what other comrades in the ex-LCR and in Fourth International sections when they say that the NPA should serve as a general model. This is encouraged by Sabado's dismissive attitude towards what the forces immediately to his right do. Thus he pours cold water on the defeat of the forces allied to Fausto Bertinotti, the former general secretary of the PRC and architect of its disastrous participation in the Prodi government, at the last party congress. I wonder if this is helpful to Sinistra Critica, the left breakaway from the PRC that is led by Fourth International members. It might be if the correct perspective for Sinistra Critica were to build a hard revolutionary propaganda group that needed to inoculate itself against pressure from bigger, more right wing forces. But if Sinistra Critica is to act as a catalyst to the development of a stronger radical left in Italy, it needs to attend carefully and relate to what is going on inside the PRC. It is surprising that Sabado barely mentions the Left Bloc in Portugal, which (despite the prominence of Fourth International members in its leadership) is plainly pursuing a different approach from that of the NPA, as is reflected

7:    Sabado, 2009, pp145-146.

in its membership of the European Left Party, founded by Bertinotti and now dominated by Die Linke.

The variety of circumstances we face in Europe make it a mistake to treat any party as a general model. It was a mistake for the leadership of the Scottish Socialist Party to offer themselves as a model and a mistake to the extent that we offered Respect as an alternative model. The NPA has, I believe, a much more promising future ahead of it, but it would be a mistake to make it a general model either. In stressing the importance of the specific circumstances I am not relapsing into a kind of national pragmatism. No, we operate in the context of a common field of problems that allows us to draw comparisons and learn from each other. Moreover, we share the aim of building large revolutionary parties. But it is still necessary to engage in a concrete analysis of the concrete situation in different countries.

Revolutionaries and the radical left

This brings us to the famous formula, coined by John Rees, that radical left parties should be seen as "united fronts of a particular kind". Sabado attacks the formula at length, and it became clear in the debates that the SWP has had about the lessons of the Respect debacle that quite a lot of SWP members do not like it either. The formula is in fact an analogy, which involves comparing things that are different yet involve important similarities. A radical left party is unlike a "classic" united front in that it is based on a broad programme rather than a specific issue. The Stop the War Coalition is directed against the war on terrorism, not wars in general, let alone the capitalist system that generates them. Respect, by contrast, sought to connect that war with a range of other issues and to win electoral support on the basis of a political programme that sought to address them all.

But a radical left party is like a united front of the classical kind in that it brings together politically heterogeneous forces. This is partly a consequence of the relatively open character of such parties' programmes, which generally finesse the alternatives of reform or revolution (though this not true of the NPA). More profoundly, however, it reflects the character of a period in which it is possible to draw people from a reformist background into parties of the radical left where revolutionaries play an important role. The programmatic openness (what Sabado would call the "incomplete strategic delimitation") of these parties reflects the recognition that it would be a mistake to make membership conditional on breaking with reformism. This stance is correct, but the price is a degree of political heterogeneity.

Before considering the implications of this reality, let me say a couple of things about Sabado's specific objections to the formula. He asks, "Didn't this conception of 'a united front of a particular kind around a minimum programme' contribute to disarming the leadership of the SWP in its relationship with George Galloway, for whom Respect had to sustain 'alliances with Muslim notables who could deliver votes'?"[8] In the first place, "around a minimum programme" is Sabado's own addition, presumably to highlight the contrast with the NPA. But in fact the degree of strategic delimitation (to put it more simply, of political hardness) in a party's programme is a relatively open question. Whether or not it is anti-liberal, anti-capitalist, or indeed full-bloodedly revolutionary depends on the basis on which it is possible to unite real forces in an alliance that is both principled and sustainable.

Did the fact that the SWP leadership saw Respect as a united front disarm us in dealing with Galloway? Not at all. Sabado's suggestion doesn't make much sense, since the united front conception is likely to make one attentive (over-attentive, he says elsewhere) to the tensions within the party. Moreover, as a matter of simple historical fact, growing tensions developed between the SWP and Galloway as early as the summer of 2005. The mistakes we made were arguably to compromise too much and certainly to conceal the seriousness of the conflict from all but a small minority of immediately affected comrades till much too late. But we were quite right not to follow the Scottish Socialist Party model of a unitary broad socialist party and liquidate the SWP. Had we done that it would have been much harder to salvage anything from the train wreck. To some degree, avoiding that catastrophic mistake was a consequence of using the united front formula, since a united front requires the existence of an organised revolutionary pole of attraction.

Sabado also elaborates on a suggestion in his earlier piece that to "consider an anti-capitalist party in a united front framework can also lead to sectarian deviations. If the united front is realised, even in a particular form, might we not be tempted to make everything go through the channel of the party, precisely underestimating the real battles for unity of action?"[9] Once again this suggestion does not make very obvious sense. Why should we imagine we are engaging in one united front at a given time? In the past decade the SWP has been engaged simultaneously in a range of united fronts—Respect, Stop the War, Unite against Fascism, Defend Council Housing, and Globalise Resistance. In the majority of these we work alongside people from a Labourist background.

Having defended the formula of a united front of a particular kind, I

8:   Sabado, 2009, p146.
9:   Sabado, 2009, pp146-147.

must concede that it does not fit the NPA very well. The party's founding principles declare, "It isn't possible to put the state and its current institutions in the service of a social and political transformation. These institutions, geared to the defence of the interests of the bourgeoisie, must be overthrown to found new institutions at the service and under the control of the workers and the population." The principles add:

> The logic of the system invalidates the pretensions to moralise, regulate or reform it, to humanise it, whether they are sincere or hypocritical. At the same time, the logic of the system helps to create the conditions of its overthrow, of a revolutionary transformation of society, by showing daily the extent to which it is true that wellbeing, democracy, and peace are incompatible with private ownership of the major means of production.[10]

So Sabado is right when he says that the NPA is a revolutionary party, in the broad sense of seeking the overthrow of capitalism from below, although he acknowledges that "this definition is more general than the strategic, even politico-military, hypotheses that provided the framework for the debates of the 1970s, which were at that time illuminated by the revolutionary crises of the 20th century".[11] In other words, the NPA has "a strategic programme and delimitations but these are not completed".[12] Sabado justifies this in the following terms: "The examples we can use are based on the revolutions of the past. But, once again, we do not know what the revolutions of the 21st century will be like. The new generations will learn much from experience and many questions remain open".[13]

Now, of course, there is an important debate to be had about how much of the strategic inheritance of the revolutionary Marxist tradition remains relevant today.[14] And it is also true that revolutions always comprise a decisive element of the unexpected and the novel. In that very general sense "we do not know what the revolutions of the 21st century will be like". But it does not follow from this that we start at what Daniel Bensaïd has called a "strategic degree zero".[15] The "revolutionary crises of the 20th century" contain certain strategic lessons. They confirm that the overthrow

10: "Principles Fondateurs du Nouveau Parti Anticapitaliste", February 2009, http://tinyurl.com/NPA2009
11: Sabado, 2009, p148.
12: Sabado, 2009, p148.
13: Sabado, 2009, p149.
14: For two contributions to this debate, see Callinicos, 2006, and Callinicos, 2007.
15: Bensaïd, 2004, p463.

of capitalism requires the forcible overthrow of the capitalist state, that this process presupposes the development of organs of workers' and popular power into a challenge to the state, and that a revolutionary party must seek to win the majority of the workers and oppressed to this objective. Not simply do Sabado and his comrades agree about this, but much of its substance is affirmed in the NPA's founding principles.

There are also other subsidiary lessons that are important, for example, those developed particularly by Lenin in *Left-Wing Communism*, namely that the conquest of the majority requires revolutionaries to be active in the mass organisations of the working class, even though these are normally under (at best) reformist leadership, and in fights around partial demands, which require, among other things, pursuit of the united front tactic. And there is the complex set of issues related to the struggle against imperialism and national oppression to which the first four congresses of the Communist International devoted much valuable discussion.

Then there are the lessons of the experience of Stalinism. These do not simply reaffirm the fundamental truth that socialist revolution can only succeed if it is based on a more advanced form of democracy than that offered by liberal capitalism. They also imply the rejection of what Leon Trotsky called "substitutionism"—in other words, strategies that seek to bypass the task of conquering the majority by, for example, relying on a guerrilla vanguard to seize power (here there may be a disagreement with Sabado and with Olivier Besancenot given the latter's espousal of a 21st century Guevarism). And then, less a matter of strategy than of its analytical presuppositions, there is Marxist political economy, the whole body of analysis of the development of capitalism, its specific class structures and its interlacing with imperialism that is essential if we are to begin to comprehend what a socialist revolution means in the 21st century.

It would be the worst kind of dogmatism to imagine that this body of strategic lessons and analyses begins to define exhaustively the nature of revolution today. Many questions do indeed remain open. Nevertheless, the strategic heritage of revolutionary Marxism remains in my view an indispensable reference point today. Sabado and I are agreed that it should not define the programmatic basis of the NPA and parties like it. But I think that, in reality, we also agree that this heritage should be available to the members of the NPA and should help shape their debates on its future strategy and tactics.

The real problem is how practically to achieve this. In my original article I argued that it is necessary for revolutionary Marxists to form an organised current or to retain their own autonomous party organisation within radical left formations. Sabado agrees that this is sometimes the correct option but argues that it would be wrong in the case of the NPA for two reasons. First, "there is the anti-capitalist and revolutionary character of the NPA, in the broad sense, and the general identity of views between the positions of the LCR and those of the NPA".[16] Second, "in the present relation of forces, the separate organisation of the ex-LCR in the NPA would block the process of building the new party. It would install a system of Russian dolls which would only create distrust and dysfunction".[17]

These are good arguments in the concrete context of the formation of the NPA. It is at once a qualitative expansion and transformation of the old LCR, and one that retains a substantial continuity at the level of both politics and leadership with the new organisation. Moreover, the relative weight of the ex-LCR within the new party means that if its members were constantly caucusing separately this could create a dangerous "them and us" climate. The problem of being a big fish in a small pond is something that the SWP grappled with inside Respect, and, though it was absolutely correct to maintain our independent organisation, this evidently was not a recipe that guaranteed success. Sabado is also probably right, at least in the short term, that "it is not very probable, with the present political delimitations of the NPA, that bureaucratic reformist currents will join or crystallise".[18]

Nevertheless, the problems I set out in my original article remain. The more successful the NPA is, the more liable it will become to reformist pressures from within and without. Negotiating these pressures will often be difficult and will require a demanding combination of political clarity and tactical flexibility. More broadly, the whole experience of revolutionaries in the face of mass struggles since at least 1848 is that these can pull militants in different directions. Old arguments about ultra-leftism, the temptations of centrism, syndicalism and abstentionist purism of the Bordiga sort, the problems arising from the relationship between exploitation and oppression (for us the key issue in the debate about the veil), are bound to arise.

This means that those who come from a revolutionary Marxist background have to be putting their own arguments within any anti-capitalist party. As Antonio Gramsci pointed out, spontaneity always involves diverse elements of leadership: the question for the new party is how these diverse elements will determine the party's response as urgent strategic and tactical decisions have to be made. Of course, revolutionary Marxists have to avoid imposing their ideas in a top-down manner on others or turning every

16: Sabado, 2009, p152.
17: Sabado, 2009, p152.
18: Sabado, 2009, p151.

meeting of the NPA into a sectarian row. But they also have to find ways of organising themselves so as to articulate their arguments in a way that can win others in the new party to them.

Hence Panos is right that "it is necessary to maintain revolutionary organisation as a source of education and political initiatives that pushes the rest of the left forward".[19] The complication is that the NPA has carried over much of the revolutionary substance of the old LCR. Nevertheless, at the very least, there is a pressing need for political education that makes available, in an open and critical way, to the non-LCR members of the NPA the theoretical and strategic heritage of revolutionary Marxism. The very welcome merger of the excellent Marxist theoretical journal *Contre Temps* with the LCR's journal *Critique Communiste* is a recognition of this necessity, but a good journal cannot substitute for the much broader process of education and debate that is required.[20]

These reservations are secondary to my recognition of the importance of the venture on which Sabado and his comrades have embarked. We wish them good luck. Their success will be ours as well. Grappling with the same set of problems and discussing and working together, we can learn from each other. I regard these exchanges as a contribution to this process.

References

Bensaïd, Daniel, 2004, *Une Lente Impatience* (Stock).

Callinicos, Alex, 2004, "The Future of the Anti-Capitalist Movement", in Hannah Dee (ed), *Anti-Capitalism: Where Now?* (Bookmarks).

Callinicos, Alex, 2006, "What Does Revolutionary Strategy Mean Today?", *IST International Discussion Bulletin 7*, January 2006, www.istendency.net/pdf/ISTbulletin7.pdf

Callinicos, Alex, 2007, "'Dual Power' In Our Hands", *Socialist Worker*, 6 January 2007, www.socialistworker.co.uk/art.php?id=10387.

Callinicos, Alex, 2008, "Where is the Radical Left Going", *International Socialism* 120 (autumn 2008), www.isj.org.uk/?id=484

Garganas, Panos, 2009, "The Radical Left: A Richer Mix", *International Socialism* 121 (winter 2009), www.isj.org.uk/?id=513

Sabado, François, 2009, "Building the New Anticapitalist Party", *International Socialism* 121 (winter 2009), www.isj.org.uk/?id=512

19: Garganas, 2009, p155.

20: One implication is that the review *Que faire?*, initiated by IST supporters inside the LCR, which emerged as a valuable venue for discussion in the lead-up to the launch of the NPA, can still play a useful role in the new party, provided that it continues to conceive itself as a catalyst for wider debate open to militants of all and no tendency.

Book reviews

Sociology of the suicide bomber

Richard Seymour

Alan B Krueger, **What Makes a Terrorist: Economics and the Roots of Terrorism** (*Princeton University, 2007*), £17.95

Explaining terrorism is a difficult and controversial business. Witness George Bush's perplexed response to the 9/11 attacks: "I'm amazed that there's such misunderstanding of what our country is about that people would hate us. I am—like most Americans, I just can't believe it because I know how good we are."

Such mock innocence notwithstanding, a sort of folk wisdom has formed around the topic of terrorism, shared by both Bush and Tony Blair, which is that it results from poverty and ignorance. Thus Blair pledged (apparently without conviction) to deliver "the slums of Gaza" from statelessness and poverty. In the US media the explanation was more usually expressed as a particularly crass "politics of envy" argument, in which the terrorists were said to be "jealous" of American wealth and freedom. For the duration of the "war on terror" Alan Krueger has been disputing such explanations.*

* See, for example, Alan B Krueger and Jitka Maleckova, "Does Poverty Cause Terrorism? The Economics and the Education of Suicide Bombers", *New Republic*, 24 June 2002.

As he argues in this book, based on a series of lectures, these claims are unsustainable in the light of overwhelming empirical evidence to the contrary. He seeks to discern the relevant factors generating the "supply of" and "demand for" terrorists. In his view, the "supply" is quite elastic as any number of socio-economic conditions can produce a terrorist. Krueger believes it is the "demand" for terrorists, produced by terrorist organisations and by the lack of alternative political outlets, that needs to be reduced—by attacking terrorist organisations and protecting civil liberties.

Krueger's first substantial case study is that of Palestinian terrorism. He looks at surveys of public opinion on the question of violence against "Israeli targets" and "Israeli civilians", carried out during and after the al-Aqsa Intifada. He finds that there is little correlation between lower incomes or poor education and a propensity to support such attacks. Majorities among Palestinians at all educational levels believed that such attacks stood a better chance of success than negotiations. Krueger also draws on data suggesting that those who carry out the attacks are themselves much less likely to be impoverished than the general population. More than 60 percent of them, he finds, have more than a high school qualification, compared to 15 percent in the general population (pp26-35).

These findings are supported, to some extent, by other analysts. For example, Robert Pape's study of suicide attacks found that as a rule such attackers are not

"egoistic" but tend to act "altruistically".*
Luca Ricolfi's study of Palestinian suicide
missions found that those who actually carry
out the attacks tend to have higher incomes
and education than the reference population, in part because those who carry them
out need to be resourceful and capable
of carrying out sophisticated operations.
Nonetheless, Ricolfi does acknowledge
that material deprivation, alongside repression, has a significant role in generating the
sense of humiliation and rage that prepares
people to commit suicide missions.†

Krueger does not discuss these dimensions at all. Indeed, the fact that patterns
of support for, and implementation of,
Palestinian suicide attacks have been closely
correlated to the rhythm of diplomacy—in
the case of the al-Aqsa Intifada, the failure
of the Oslo negotiations—falls below
his radar. The lack of any discussion of
Israeli oppression or of the closing down
of options for peace is curious, especially
given his finding that the lack of liberty is
the single greatest determinant of terrorism
(pp75-79).

Another important case study is that
of "foreign insurgents" in Iraq. Here a
problem of definition clearly emerges.
"Terrorism" is a notoriously difficult
term to pin down. Krueger suggests
it may be understood as premeditated
political violence intended to influence
audiences beyond the immediate victims.
He also believes that terrorism belongs to
a category of "randomly targeted acts of
violence" (pp14-15).

However, the vast majority of attacks by
insurgents in Iraq are clearly not random

but directed against occupation troops or
Iraqi security forces deputised by the occu-
piers. Thus, at the height of the insurgency
in 2006, a report to Congress by the US
Department of Defence suggested that 68
percent of all attacks were directed specifically against coalition troops.

Nonetheless, Krueger proceeds to dissect
the nationality of captured foreign
insurgents—who he acknowledges have
been a minority—and finds that statisti-
cally the most significant factors are a high
Muslim population and a lack of liberty
in their country of origin. Although the
support of Muslims has been important to
the Iraqi insurgency, Krueger rejects the
Islamophobic narrative of the hard right
that castigates Muslims in particular as being
inclined to terrorism. He finds "no significant differences across major religions"
in terms of whether affiliation is likely to
produce terrorism (pp80-81).

Another factor discussed is the level of
"economic freedom" in the country of
origin of the foreign insurgents, as defined
by the World Bank, the *Wall Street Journal*,
and the Heritage Foundation. Those
countries producing the insurgents tended
to rank higher on the indices for economic
freedom. The author seems to conclude
that this rules out any underlying economic motivation, but there may well be
some significance in the findings that he
misses. After all, the Index of Economic
Freedom considers a large state, restrictions on "property rights" and curtailments
of financial and trading freedoms to be
harmful to overall "economic freedom".
An "absolute minimum of expenditure"
is considered a boon.‡ But the degrada-
tion of social welfare systems, the freeing
up of financial markets and the reduction

---

* Robert Pape, *Dying to Win: The Strategic Logic of
Suicide Terrorism* (Random House, 2005).
† Luca Ricolfi, "Palestinians 1981-2003", in
Diego Gambetta (ed), *Making Sense of Suicide Missions*
(Oxford University, 2005).

‡ See www.heritage.org/research/features/index/
chapters/pdf/Index2008_Chap4.pdf

of trade barriers produce immense social misery. Krueger relies on rightist orthodoxy as if it was self-evident. This is true elsewhere. For data on civil liberties, for example, he cites the right wing US foundation Freedom House, which has the dubious honour of having praised the 1979 elections in Rhodesia staged by Ian Smith as well as the 1982 elections in El Salvador, which took place in a context of massive state terror.*

The problem of defining his subject plagues Krueger's findings throughout. In his haste to write off poverty as a significant factor in the generation of terrorism he relies on some unsustainable distinctions. For example, dealing with evidence showing that it was generally the poorest of the Catholic working class who supported the IRA in Northern Ireland, he speculates that this could be an example of something closer to guerrilla warfare than "the activities of a small terrorist organisation". But this could equally be said of many other examples that he does accept as terrorism. As Robert Pape has pointed out, suicide attacks are generally carried out by "broad based national liberation movements" and are seen as a "last resort" where other tactics have failed. There is no sense in which Hamas, for example, is simply "a small terrorist organisation".

There are certain elite terrorist groups that *do* fit Krueger's definition which are not discussed. Readers will search in vain for a mention of the United Self-Defence Forces of Colombia, which was certainly one of the most indiscriminately murderous groups in the world before its apparent demobilisation in 2006. In the first ten months of 2000 alone it was held to have carried out 75 separate massacres. For a book that takes

such pride in its handling of empirical data and conceptual clarity, the absence of any discussion of counterinsurgency terrorism is a curious weakness.

Krueger concedes in the "Q & A" section that if he were to rewrite the book, he would avoid the word "terrorism" altogether. But he goes on to insist that what he is studying remains "politically motivated violence carried out by sub-state actors with the goal of spreading fear within the population" (pp145-146). It would be more appropriate to say that he is studying a particular form of insurgency and that his book is intended as a guide for counterinsurgency.

As the introduction explains, he had intended to call the book "Enlisting Social Science in the War on Terrorism". Krueger is broadly a supporter of what he sees as the attempt to create democracy in Iraq. Having divined that the lack of civil liberty is the main determinant of terrorism, he does not ask why those repressed by their own state should choose to attack the US army or its embassies. This would involve discussing imperialism and placing it, as Pape does, among the foremost causes of terrorism.

For all the wealth of data contained in this book, there is no convincing case made as to what a terrorist is, never mind what makes a terrorist. Krueger acknowledges that it might have been better entitled "What Doesn't Make a Terrorist" (p171). But even when he is undermining glib myths about terrorists being largely poor and ignorant, he is insufficiently attentive to the relevant social and political backgrounds and far too apt to reach for glib formulae himself. The book is also encumbered by superfluous statistical jargon that gets in the way of the information and undermines the author's otherwise breezy and discursive manner.

* For a summary, see Noam Chomsky and Edward Herman, *Manufacturing Consent: The Political Economy of the Mass Media* (Bodley Head, 2008).

Putting "culture" into context

Penny Howard

Kate Crehan, **Gramsci, Culture and Anthropology** *(Pluto, 2002), £18.99*

Gramsci, Culture, and Anthropology is a welcome contribution to the revival of interest in the work of Antonio Gramsci. Kate Crehan's clear and succinct book begins with a brief biographical summary, emphasising Gramsci's engagement with revolutionary politics in Turin and his later imprisonment by Benito Mussolini. Refreshingly, Crehan emphasises that "to understand Gramsci's project in the *Prison Notebooks*, it is important not to lose sight of either the political engagement out of which they emerged or the circumstances in which they were composed. They were above all an intervention, of the only kind possible for Gramsci in his prison cell, in what he saw as the fundamental struggle between the interests of capital and the interests of those oppressed by the dominant capitalist order" (p18).

She quotes extensively from the *Notebooks* to encourage the reader to engage directly with Gramsci's writings, but she also emphasises their fragmentary nature by referring to them throughout as quotes from a "note" on particular subjects.

Crehan then turns to a critique of the anthropological use of the term "culture", a usage which also underpins the popular understanding of "cultural differences" or "culture clash". She criticises the assumption that cultures are "patterned" or "bounded" wholes with their own logics, and that there exists "a basic opposition between tradition and modernity" (p66). She shows that these assumptions continue even among writers who claim to criticise the concept themselves.

Crehan emphasises that Gramsci's interest in culture stemmed from his interest in revolutionary change, because "how people see their world and how they live in it necessarily shapes their ability to imagine how it might be changed, and whether they see such changes as feasible or desirable" (p71).

Instead of seeing culture as a bounded whole explaining the behaviour of its individual members, Gramsci saw it as the continuously changing ways of living that are in "organic" relationship to economic and historical processes, especially class relations. This section contains useful and interesting discussions with extensive quotes from Gramsci on the relationship between culture and economic relations, hegemony, "subaltern" cultures, common sense and good sense, and the role of intellectuals. Crehan argues with conviction that there is much in Gramsci that should be of value to anthropologists.

The final section of the book traces and criticises the use of Gramsci within anthropology today, especially the concept of hegemony, which has been distorted in academic circles into what Crehan describes as "hegemony lite". She traces most citations of Gramsci in anthropology to the interpretations by cultural historian Raymond Williams and the anthropologists John and Jean Comaroff. Unfortunately, in these cases Gramsci's concept of hegemony was interpreted to be virtually synonymous with that of ideology. But Gramsci himself understood hegemony as the complex and practical ways in which power is exercised by the state and its various institutions in Western bourgeois democracies.

He also used it as a term to describe the process by which revolutionary parties could practically interact with working class movements to link struggles, generalise lessons learned, gain their confidence, and eventually provide the credible leadership necessary to transform society. For Gramsci, hegemony involves a complex mixture of social relations, practical activity, consent, force and ideas. Crehan then applies this critique to three well known anthropological works that draw on Gramsci, demonstrating the contribution a more rounded understanding could bring.

The book is indicative of the present tentative shift within the discipline of anthropology to go beyond its introspective "writing culture" phase, and return to a more materialist and political approach. For example, Gaston Gordillo's *Landscapes of Devils: Tensions of Place and Memory in the Argentine Chaco* explicitly draws on Gramsci and Georg Lukács to understand the effects of class exploitation and state violence on the lives of the indigenous Toba now living in Argentina. Gordillo's book won a "first book award" from the influential American Ethnological Society.

The 2008 annual meeting of the American Anthropological Association (AAA), attended by over 6,000 people from all over the world, featured several packed meetings about the occupation of Iraq and the ethics of anthropological engagement with the US military. The AAA has now voted in favour of a change in its ethics code that specifically draws a line between legitimate anthropological research and spying for the military.

These debates are having a wider impact on the discipline. As anthropologist David Price argued to an AAA session debating the use of anthropology by the US Air Force and Marine Corps, "Anthropology is embedded in political economy whether it likes it or not. The postmodern rejection of meta-narratives that has been dominant in anthropology leaves us ill-equipped to understand what is happening in anthropology and the world today."

Those at the AAA meetings who sought to justify the participation of anthropologists in US imperial projects emphasised the power of "cultural understanding" to save lives. Yet if there is one thing that we can take from Crehan's reading of Gramsci, it is that, far from being a progressive force, a world understood in terms of discrete cultures can blinker us to much more important dynamics of class, history and power.

The history of capital
Ken Muller

Francisco Boldizzoni, **Means and Ends: The Idea of Capital in the West, 1500-1970** *(Palgrave, 2008), £45*

Francesco Boldizzoni sets out in this short book (169 pages plus notes) to write the history of capital or rather "the evolution of the idea of capital" over a period of five centuries: from an end in itself to a means of producing additional wealth. However successful or otherwise he has been in this project, I have to say, unfortunately, that Boldizzoni's book is unlikely to be widely read outside the upper reaches of academia.

Ways and Means is very expensive, especially given its size, and readers no better educated than me will need several good dictionaries to make sense of much of the book, especially its early chapters, not least because it contains a number of untranslated quotations in Latin, Italian and French, along with section headings such as "The Maieutics of Production" and "The Form of Capital: A Phylogenetic Approach". This is a pity because, despite a number of reservations about some of the book's arguments and conclusions, I learnt a considerable amount of interest by reading it.

My 1987 edition of the more accessible (if nothing else) *Pocket Economist* defines capital as "stuff used to produce things", the third factor of production, along with labour and land. According to the neoclassical theory found in most standard A level and undergraduate textbooks, the providers of each of these factors are paid a "fair price" for their contribution to the productive process, as determined by the laws of supply and demand operating in a free market. Just as wages are a reward to workers for forgoing leisure, so profits are the reward for abstinence on the part of the capitalist.

Notwithstanding the problem most of us must have finding examples of abstaining capitalists in the boardrooms of Lehman Brothers, Goldman Sachs, the Royal Bank of Scotland, General Motors or BP, we are supposed to believe that such ideological claptrap is, in fact, a scientific analysis based on timeless assumptions about human nature.

But as Boldizzoni shows, it took a long time for this "neoclassical" conception of capital to emerge, a time of "profound changes of social processes" and of "rivalry between cultures and visions, as nations rose and declined". And when it did in late 19th century Britain—most notably in the work of Alfred Marshall—it was, to some extent, a response to Karl Marx's devastating exposure of the exploitation that lies beneath the appearances of free market capitalism and the impact it was making among the victims of that exploitation, the industrial working class, even if the earliest

formulations of marginalism predated Marx's mature economic writing.

Boldizzoni tells us that the term "capital" derives from the Latin *caput*, meaning, among other things, "stock", the outcome of which is its "yield". It was, at first, a purely monetary and financial phenomenon, an "end in itself", the proceeds of trade and speculation. As Marx noted in volume one of *Capital*, capital first takes the form of money, as "moneyed wealth, as the capital of the merchant and usurer". But while capital can take the form of money, not all money is capital. It only becomes so when labour power itself becomes a commodity and for this to happen the worker has to be deprived of all control over the means of production so she or he has no choice but to work for someone else: a capitalist.

In the case of Britain, the first capitalist country, this "primitive accumulation of capital" was largely achieved by successive waves of land enclosure, beginning in the 15th century and culminating with the parliamentary enclosures carried out between 1760 and 1830, which robbed millions of peasants of their means of subsistence. Marx (again in *Capital*, volume one) commented that "the history of this, their expropriation, is written in the annals of mankind in letters of blood and fire".

For Marx, as Boldizzoni explains, capital is not a thing, not a means or an end, but a social relation between accumulated dead labour, personified by the capitalist class, and the living labour of the workers who are paid less than the value of what they produce. To suggest that the worker and the capitalist face one another as equals in the marketplace, each being paid a fair price for his or her contribution to the making of the finished product, is a "deception" which covers up the exploitation that is taking place.

The first half of the book takes us via the Franciscan, Dominican and Jesuit orders of Renaissance Italy, the physiocrats of France, and the classical economists Adam Smith, Thomas Malthus and David Ricardo, of industrialising Britain, to a chapter entitled "The Revolt of 1867" (when *Capital* was first published). The second half is largely devoted to describing and explaining the neoclassical backlash in Britain, the US and Europe, and later theoretical debates in the workers' movement.

But even if Marx's critique of political economy is the hinge on which Boldizzoni's history of the "idea of capital" turns, I doubt very much that Boldizzoni himself would claim to be a Marxist. After brazenly referring to "the obscurities of Marx's often vertiginous prose", Boldizzoni goes on to identify what he considers to be a number of errors and ambiguities in his account. These include Marx's analysis of the process by which the primitive accumulation of capital occurred, including his dating of the emergence of the proletariat to the period of manufacturing, and his obsession with the "three phantoms of the late 19th century—high capital intensity, colonial imperialism and finance—which he projects backwards into history" (pp96-98). These alleged ambiguities, Boldizzoni claims, are responsible for the competing interpretations of the origins of capitalism by 20th century Marxist historians and sociologists.*

If he has reservations about Marx's historical account of the rise of capitalism, Boldizzoni rejects altogether any suggestion that Marx has anything relevant to say concerning what he calls, following Daniel Bell, post-industrial society. "The

decline of the world of the factory and manual labour, the diminishing contraposition between wages and profits, and the fact that the very concept of 'social class' continues, still today, to lose its connotations," he claims, "have brought the period which began with Ricardo and Marx to an end"—even if the history of capital continues as it transforms itself into human, social or institutional capital (p5).

Such a perspective, once fashionable among certain intellectuals who had little personal experience of being exploited in an alienating and oppressive working environment, suddenly seems dated. Try telling the white collar workers in the banking and finance industry—who are losing their jobs and maybe their homes while their fat cat bosses continue give themselves astronomical salaries, bonuses and severance packages—that social class no longer counts.

To be fair to Boldizzoni, he was not a great fan of the status quo, even before the boom turned to bust. Bewailing the fact that "Keynesian voices" had been "sidelined practically everywhere", there is, he laments, "no effective counterbalance to the prevailing order as it now stands". "For the future," Boldizzoni predicts, "a certain degree of pessimism thus seems to be justified" (p169). At the time of writing, with neoliberalism thoroughly discredited and the injustices of capitalism itself increasingly being questioned by striking workers and students in France, Greece, Ireland and elsewhere, on the contrary, a certain amount of optimism can be justified, just so long as the left can rise to the challenge.

Like André Gorz in France, a few months before the events of May 1968, Boldizzoni has had the misfortune to foretell a future of continued economic growth and relative social peace just as the world was about to be turned upside down. The root of his poor predictive abilities is his

---

* For a review of the debates about the origins of capitalism, see Chris Harman, "From Feudalism to Capitalism", *International Socialism* 45 (winter 1989), www.isj.org.uk/?id=21

dismissal of Marx's argument that the inevitably rising "organic composition of capital" (loosely, the amount of money spent on machinery, etc, compared to that spent on labour power) would eventually lead to a falling rate of profit and thus to a crisis—which is, as Chris Harman and others have shown, exactly what has happened with the current global slump.

For all that is interesting and novel in the history of capital recounted in *Means and Ends*, Boldizzoni fails to recognise what Marx understood when he wrote volume three of *Capital*: that "the real barrier to capitalist production is capital itself".

Imperialism that runs clear
Jonathan Maunder

Mark Zeitoun, **Power and Water in the Middle East: The Hidden Politics of the Palestinian-Israeli Water Conflict** *(IB Tauris, 2008), £47.50*

Water is one of the most obvious symbols of the injustice of Israel's oppression of the Palestinians. In Israeli settlements water is used for swimming pools and garden sprinklers, while Palestinians largely make do with supplies for basic consumption. The recent Israeli onslaught on the Gaza Strip left 500,000 people without access to clean water.

Mark Zeitoun is a water engineer with wide experience in the Middle East and Africa, and in *Power and Water in the Middle East* he attempts to explain how Israel secures its dominance in the struggle over water resources and what drives it. On

a day to day basis the Palestinian water authorities have to cooperate with the Israeli authorities over the supply of water, and yet as Zeitoun argues (quoting Noam Chomsky), "the outcome of cooperation between an elephant and a fly is not difficult to predict" (p7).

He starts with a striking image, the indoor water fountain at a new Tel Aviv airport: "The water appears from outlets arranged in a wide circle falling from the ceiling of the large open hall, as rain from the sky. The mood and rain gets heavier, with a loud, soft swoosh as it falls onto the lake underneath, around which people with luggage sip coffee at tables" (p1).

Zeitoun contrasts this with life in the Gaza Strip. In Gaza families north of Beit Lahia had to set up home on the banks of a lake of sewage as it was the only free space they could find. The children suffer from water-borne infectious diseases and in summer 2006 Oxfam warned that Israeli shelling of the area increased the risk of the banks bursting. This did indeed happen in April 2007 when five Palestinians, ranging in age from 70 years old to 11 months, drowned in the ensuing torrent (p6).

The fact that such a sewage lake existed, and families had to live next to it, is a product of Israel's longstanding disruption of Palestinian control over their own resources. This was seen most recently by the imposition of the economic blockade on Gaza following the election of the Hamas government in 2006 (compounded by the withdrawal of aid from the US, which stopped the building of a water desalination plant).

Zeitoun traces the shift in the Israeli approach to Palestinian water resources, moving from the direct "domination-occupation years" (p82), to a more subtle form of control instituted after the 1995 Oslo Accords. These accords recognised

Palestinian water needs (but not rights) and created forums of negotiation in which representatives from both Palestinian and Israeli water authorities would work out how to allocate resources. Zeitoun argues, however, that this formal equality obscured continued Israeli dominance. In reality the negotiating forums became places where Israel bullied and threatened the Palestinians in order to allocate water to the settlements and for Israel's internal use.

What makes this book interesting is that Zeitoun attempts to give his account a theoretical underpinning, mainly through a concept of hegemony that he derives from the Italian Marxist Antonio Gramsci. Zeitoun writes, "It is when the existing 'order of things' is taken as the natural order of things that we know hegemony is active. One cannot go far in understanding power relations between parties that are formally equal yet evidently not equally strong, without referring to the concept of hegemony" (p30).

He argues that Palestinian water authorities have conformed to Israeli hegemony by internalising their own weakness, no longer demanding Palestinian water rights but meekly accepting the fact of Israeli domination and trying to obtain a few crumbs (or droplets) from the table. This is seen by Zeitoun as emblematic of a shift from "imperial" type rule based on force and formally unequal relations, to "hegemonic" rule, where power disparities and the use of force are concealed behind a veil of formal equality and cooperation.

This certainly adds some depth to our understanding of the situation, but there is also a lack of clarity in Zeitoun's use of the term hegemony. For Gramsci and the Marxist tradition, the concept helps explain how the ruling class maintains its rule most of the time without having to resort to violence. Capitalist hegemony operates both in the fact of the ruling classes' influence over the media and other sources of ideology (such as the education system), and in the nature of wage labour. Workers are compelled to sell their labour power to the capitalist in order to survive, and yet the exploitative nature of this relationship is not immediately apparent because it is hidden behind the wage relation. Therefore the concept of hegemony is rooted materially. It is not just about certain ideas attaining dominance because they are particularly well articulated or forcefully argued.

At times Zeitoun suggests that Israel's water hegemony over the Palestinians is in some way connected to the process of capital accumulation: "The situation may be compared to the ever hungry and predatory nature of the capitalist system...new opportunities to make profits must constantly be made available, through continually opening up access to wider markets...and/or reserves of cheap labour" (p83).

However, he ultimately rejects the idea that Israeli water hegemony is driven by a search for new profits, concluding rather that this is a feature of "a general Israeli strategy of maintaining disparity with the Palestinian side at the broader political and economic level" (p83). This seems to make sense if we consider that Israel is propped up ultimately not by profits gained through exploitation of the Palestinians, but by US dollars which it gets in return for fulfilling its role as "the cop on the beat"* for US imperialism in the oil rich and strategically important Middle East.

Therefore Israel's policy towards the Palestinians is informed mainly by a fusion of imperialist motives and ideological motives (Zionism), rather than a simple

---

* The term used by Noam Chomsky in *Fateful Triangle: The United States, Israel and the Palestinians* (Pluto, 1999).

desire to accumulate capital through use of Palestinian resources and labour.

However, Zeitoun seems to miss the imperialist and ideological factors, and their implication for how Israel behaves. In rejecting the reductionist economic argument he seems to argue that water domination is just the result of a mistaken policy, or "discourse", unconnected to Israel's material interests. He writes that a change in Israeli water policy in relation to the Palestinians will only occur "if the discursive identification of water with security is shattered". He argues that inequality in the water sector is not "a necessary condition for Israeli state security" or of "the wider Israeli strategy of asymmetrically containing the Palestinian population" (p84).

But there seem to be three reasons why this conclusion is mistaken, all of which are implicit in Zeitoun's own analysis. First, Israel does benefit substantially from Palestinian water. The settlements in the West Bank around the western, eastern and north eastern aquifers provide Israel with a third of its water supply (p84).

Second, the fragility of Palestinian water infrastructure can make it hard to disentangle Israel's overall dominance from its water dominance. One example comes from Israel's invasion of Jenin in 2002. The water pipes in Jenin are either above ground or buried just below the surface. When Israeli tanks rolled into the city to occupy it they immediately destroyed much of the water system (p92).

Third, control of water is a very important strategic tool in maintaining control over the Palestinians through "collective punishment" of the population. Israel can shut off or reduce supplies to Palestinian cities when it wants to increase pressure at specific times, as it did during the invasion of Jenin.

There is a broader point to be made here about how we understand imperialism and how it expresses the interaction between capital accumulation and the territorial logic of states. The Marxist David Harvey has argued, "The relation between these two logics should be seen...as problematic and often contradictory (that is, dialectical) rather than being functional or one-sided...the difficulty for concrete analysis of actual situations is to keep the two sides of this dialectic simultaneously in motion and not to lapse into either a solely political or a predominantly economic mode of argumentation".*

In relation to Israel this means not only accurately weighing the importance of economic and political factors and how they interact but also looking at how Israel operates according to its own specific imperialist logic, which is shaped by it being a smaller ally of a major imperialism, driven by a powerful Zionist ideology and with a level of economic security provided by the "floor" of US dollars.

Ultimately Israeli "security" depends upon being engaged in an ongoing conflict, varying in intensity and form but always present, with the Palestinians and the wider region. It can be no other way for a state founded on ethnic cleansing, which does not believe that Arabs and Jews in the Middle East can live and work together as equals, and which is armed to the teeth

* David Harvey, *The New Imperialism* (Oxford University, 2005). There is a debate over whether this implies the existence of a logic of states separate from that of the logic of capital. For an excellent argument that the logic of states emerges from, and is profoundly shaped by, the logic of capital see Colin Barker, "The State as Capital", *International Socialism 1* (summer 1978), www.marxists.de/theory/barker/stateascap.htm See also Alex Callinicos and Sam Ashman, "Capital Accumulation and the State System: assessing David Harvey's *The New Imperialism*", *Historical Materialism*, volume 14, number 4.

with the latest and most deadly weapons supplied by the US.

This book is written by a technical specialist angered by the oppression of the Palestinians who wants a theoretical explanation to help understand the situation. That makes it both useful and interesting. But for a broader and deeper theoretical understanding of the connections between imperialism, Israel and the oppression of the Palestinians it is necessary to return to some classic Marxist writings on the topic, such as Tony Cliff's "The Palestine Question",* in order to start to work out how Palestine can be free today.

In the shadow of orthodox Trotskyism
Joseph Choonara

Emanuele Saccarelli, **Gramsci and Trotsky in the Shadow of Stalinism** *(Routledge, 2008), £60*

Books culled from doctoral theses are rarely page-turners but this work by unashamed Trotskyist Emanuele Saccarelli is better than most. Saccarelli attempts to rescue Antonio Gramsci and Leon Trotsky from the slander, misappropriation, distortion and, especially in Trotsky's case, silencing that academia has subjected them to. The chapters that focus on this task will contain few surprises to longstanding readers of this journal—with one exception that I will return to—but they form a

---

* In Tony Cliff, *International Struggle and the Marxist tradition: Selected Writings, Volume One* (Bookmarks, 2001).

useful survey and are written in a pugilistic style with plenty of wit.

The author's second aim is to assess the two revolutionaries' relationships to, and analyses of, Stalinism. Saccarelli argues that from the mid-1920s Gramsci occupied a position somewhere between that of the majority in the Communist Party, led by Joseph Stalin and Nikolai Bukharin, and that of the opposition led by Trotsky, Grigory Zinoviev and Lev Kamenev. While Gramsci "formally supported the political line of the Stalinist majority, he rather systematically infused its slogans and policies with a distinct political content that alarmed and angered" the Stalin-Bukharin grouping.

Drawing on recent work by scholars such as Giuseppe Vacca, Francesco Benvenuti and Silvio Pons, Saccarelli shows how this ambiguity shaped both Gramsci's political stances and his famous *Prison Notebooks*. The latter contain, among much else, a spirited defence of the united front in the face of Stalinism's break with this approach. But, confusingly, the passages in which Gramsci develops this argument also explicitly attack Trotsky, who, alongside Lenin, was the main protagonist for the adoption of the united front.

Saccarelli quite convincingly argues that Trotsky's name is used as a "lightning rod" to mount a coded attack on Stalinism. The cryptic style in the notebooks was not simply to evade the prison censor but also to avoid an open break with Stalinism. Even if Gramsci had resolved the ambiguity in his political position, an attack on Stalin would have broken the one lifeline securing his contact with the workers' movement beyond the prison walls and would have been exploited by his fascist jailors.

It was Trotsky, rather than Gramsci,

who most clearly identified Stalinism as a novel political phenomena. This book details Trotsky's pathbreaking analysis of the degeneration of the Soviet Union. However, it is here that the limitations of Saccarelli's own particular brand of orthodox Trotskyism are most evident.

The author sees 1923 as a key turning point. That year saw Lenin's effective withdrawal from political life and his replacement by "a semi-secret ruling 'triumvirate'...of Stalin, Kamenev and Zinoviev". It was the year of the consolidation of the New Economic Policy. This policy allowed some capitalist mechanisms to function under the tight control of the workers' state in order to gain time for revolution to spread beyond Russia. But it also laid the basis for Stalin to break with Kamenev and Zinoviev and temporarily ally himself with Bukharin's right wing of the Communist Party, which now argued for a transition to socialism at a "snail's pace" and called on peasants to "enrich themselves".

Finally, 1923 saw the defeat of the German Revolution, paving the way for Stalin's later doctrine of "socialism in one country" rather than international revolution. These events each strengthened the bureaucracy around Stalin, which increasingly dominated the state machinery and the Communist Party, but this did not yet mark a complete break with the legacy of the 1917 Revolution.

Saccarelli fails to recognise the significance of a second turning point in 1928-9. He notes a series of political manoeuvres that ultimately saw Trotsky exiled and political opposition to Stalin broken. But this period also saw the bureaucracy forge itself into a social class through the forced collectivisation it imposed on the peasantry and the first Five Year Plan through which it established its control over industry.

Now the bureaucracy was not simply a "caste" controlling "the mechanisms of economic distribution" as Trotsky believed. It had established itself as a new ruling class presiding over the economic exploitation of the mass of workers. It subordinated the consumption of the masses to the accumulation of capital as it sought to compete with the Western powers. In short, a system of "bureaucratic state capitalism" was born. This system eradicated the last vestiges of workers' control. The fact that capitalist property was nationalised does not alter the facts; it is the ruling class's control over the means of production, rather than its legal ownership of them, that is crucial.

A transition to socialism would now have required a new social revolution, not simply the political revolution that Trotsky advocated. Trotsky's prognoses, for instance, that the Stalinist regime was inherently unstable or that it was not an imperialist power, were dramatically disproved in the aftermath of the Second World War. Not only was Stalinism stable but it also established its grip over a number of Eastern European regimes.

At one point Saccarelli quotes Trotsky's assessment of the distortion of "Leninism" by the Stalinists: "the transformation of Leninism from a method demanding for its application initiative, critical thinking and ideological courage into a canon which demands nothing more than interpreters appointed for good and aye". The same could be said of Saccarelli's brand of Trotskyism.

So in the chapter devoted to rescuing Trotsky from the academics Saccarelli also seeks to rescue him from more sympathetic theorists—including Tony Cliff, who the author recognises as "the most prominent contemporary theorist of 'state capitalism'." But the kind of cheap academic sleight of hand Saccarelli deploys here would send a shiver down his spine if it were applied to Gramsci or Trotsky. For instance, he lumps together "CLR James, Raya Dunayevskaya, James Burnham, Tony Cliff, Alex Callinicos, Anton Ciliga, Milovan Djilas, Robert Brenner, Sidney Hook, Cornelius Castoriadis and Max Eastman" in a single tendency—hinting that some of this group "openly sided with Western imperialism".

Rather than engaging with Cliff's argument, Saccarelli simply asserts Trotsky's position—that the Soviet Union remained a degenerated workers' state and that it should be defended against the Western imperialist powers. This is doctrinarism of the worst kind. Trotsky's provisional and evolving account of Stalinism was brilliant. But by the end of the Second World War it was clear to some that the analysis had been pushed to breaking point. For instance, if "workers' states" almost identical to the Soviet Union could be established in Eastern Europe by military means, what was the point of workers' revolution?

Cliff's theory was an attempt to defend the notion of revolution as a process that took place from the bottom up, creating new organs of workers' democracy. Its goal was not to undermine Trotsky, but to defend and extend his life's guiding principle—that the emancipation of the proletariat must be the act of the proletariat itself. Saccarelli's failure to take this seriously mars what would otherwise be a useful book.

Exploring the peasant crusaders
Elaine Graham-Leigh

Conor Kostick, **The Social Structure of the First Crusade** *(Brill, 2008),* £93.99

In 1095 Pope Urban II called on the faithful to retake the Holy Land for Christianity. This unleashed a crusading movement which saw hundreds of thousands of Europeans flock to the Middle East, capture Jerusalem and establish a crusader kingdom in Palestine which persisted for almost 200 years.

The wars in Iraq and Afghanistan have given the concept of crusading a particular contemporary resonance for both critics and cheerleaders of Western imperialism. George Bush's first phrase for the war on terror was a "crusade against terrorism". However, despite the relevance of crusade history, the domination of the field by a right wing view of crusading as religious, noble and an all round "good thing" has meant that materialist analysis of the Crusades has been limited.

This book is a welcome attempt to address this deficiency in Crusade studies, although it is obviously aimed at an academic rather than a general socialist audience. The liberal use of untranslated Latin terms and lack of a narrative description of the course of the First Crusade would make it a difficult introduction to the subject. However, there is much here that is valuable for anyone interested in a Marxist view of crusading.

Kostick concentrates on the experience of the poorest crusaders, analysing the Crusade from below by reinterpreting the contemporary narrative accounts. The usual assumption is that large numbers of poor peasants, including serfs, attempted to join the First Crusade, particularly those mobilised by Peter the Hermit and others in the People's Crusade of late 1095-6 but that only very few of these actually managed to reach the Middle East.

Kostick argues that, on the contrary, large numbers of poor non-combatants remained alongside the armies right up to the capture of Jerusalem in 1099. They were not simply a burden on the armies, requiring food and protection, but were sometimes able to determine the course of the Crusade. When, for example, the princely leaders of the Crusade wanted to stop and consolidate their conquests, Kostick suggests that it was the pressure of the poorest crusaders that forced them to keep on to Jerusalem.

These are important arguments but they could have been further developed to draw out their significance, not just for the history of the First Crusade but also for our understanding of class struggles in medieval society.

I am not entirely convinced by Kostick's portrayal of large-scale peasant and serf participation in the Crusade, as there are counter-arguments to which he gives perhaps too little weight. It is possible that the People's Crusade's reputation as a popular, rather than an elite, movement may not reflect its actual social composition. It was these crusade armies which perpetrated the massacres of Jewish communities in many Rhineland towns, and it may be that description by the authors of the contemporary accounts of the People's Crusade as a mob of poor peasants was designed not to reflect reality but to deny elite participation in these atrocities. It would not be the only example of elite writers blaming the poor for the crimes of the ruling class.

However, if Kostick is correct about the substantial enthusiasm among the poorest in medieval society for joining the First Crusade, the important question is why this should have been. Kostick's reassessment of the social composition of the First Crusade does not change the nature of the Crusades as a ruling class project, part of an emerging relationship between the nobility and the church that enabled the peasantry to be increasingly exploited.

The church was a significant factor in the feudalisation of Western Europe. In the 10th and 11th centuries increasing church involvement at village level, from the prescription of working hours to control over the personal lives of peasants, meant that production could be much more closely controlled than it had been before. This spread from lands owned by the church to those of the secular nobility but was accompanied by the increasing expectation that those nobles should accept the church's authority and, most importantly, abandon their habit of attacking church personnel and possessions.

The Peace of God movement in France in the early 11th century showed the power of the church to mobilise sections of the peasantry on its behalf against noble violence, although this was not without its problems, as the peasant movements showed a distressing tendency to get out of the church's control. The Gregorian Reform, from the mid-11th century, was a wide ranging, top down programme to rid the church of secular influence and establish it as independent of noble control.

The Crusades can be seen as part of these processes as the church, having set down rules to control secular violence against itself within Europe, then provided a religiously sanctioned outlet for it in conquest in the Middle East. If Kostick is correct and the church was also able to mobilise the peasantry for crusading, this demonstrates a remarkable enthusiasm from the peasantry for a project that was helping to drive forward their own exploitation—extending not only to risking (and mostly losing) their own lives for it but also massacring large numbers of Jews and Muslims in its cause.

Kostick is clear that different classes would have crusaded for different reasons, and the reader is left with the impression that, in comparison to the material concerns of the nobles, peasant participation was driven by religious conviction. This opposition of religious and material motivation reflects one of the major debates in Crusade history. But it serves to separate religious concerns from economic and social realities in a way which precludes dialectical analysis.

At various points in the book Kostick demonstrates a view of medieval religion as a factor with which the historian has to dispense in order to reach the material issues to be studied. So, for example, when discussing the value of the contemporary Crusade historian Albert of Aachen, Kostick comments that he is particularly useful as a source because he does not "organise his material to suit theological themes", by implication rendering it easier to get at the reality beneath the theological veneer.

This approach effectively separates base and superstructure in medieval society, whereas the church should be seen as both the product and the producer of social relations. The church in medieval Europe was an integral part of the ruling class—both a major landowner in its own right and a significant force for feudalisation. Religion provided both the language of oppression and the language of dissent in medieval Europe, and as such it cannot be excluded from a materialist analysis of medieval society.

Large-scale peasant participation in the First Crusade, even participation arising from sincerely held religious convictions, would have been a social, not just a religious, phenomenon. As such, it could shed much light on class relations in the 11th and 12th centuries. It is possible, for example, that the apparent lack of major peasant rebellions against feudalisation in the 12th century could be explained by a large proportion of the peasantry in the late 11th century being already so under elite control that they were prepared to flock to an elite project such as crusading.

Kostick's work will be a useful contribution to the academic debates about the First Crusade and a valuable corrective to much of the recent Crusade scholarship. However, a more dialectical view of the relations between the church and secular society as revealed by crusading would have raised this from a work of academic importance to an advance in the socialist history of the medieval past.

You say goodbye, I say hello
John Cooper

Antonio Negri, **Goodbye Mr Socialism: Radical Politics in the 21st Century** *(Serpent's Tail, 2008), £8.99*

This collection of interviews with Antonio Negri provides some insights into one of the most important thinkers on the anti-capitalist left. Negri is the co-author, with Michael Hardt, of *Empire* and the subsequent *Multitude*, two texts which explicitly linked themselves to the rising anti-capitalist movement at the turn of the century and aimed to provide philosophical under-pinning to the political aspirations of the activists involved.

As the title *Goodbye Mr Socialism* indicates, however, a key plank of Negri's project has been to argue that socialist politics belong to a bygone age, and he has instead associated himself with autonomist currents in the movement. Thus he maintains in the first interview that "the history of socialism, of real socialism in particular…is not a monster; it is a product above all of our weakness, of our capacity to hurt ourselves. It was indeed a failure but a very special failure."

He wants to reclaim the idea of communism in the 21st century, understood as the "common capacity to reproduce the social in freedom", as opposed to the apparently statist tradition of what he calls "real socialism". For Negri, communism is the "only alternative to postmodernism and [is] the beginning of a new great cycle of civilisation".

If this is rather vague, further into the collection we get a better insight into his thinking when it comes to envisaging a new society coming into being. The 1999 Seattle anti-capitalist demonstrations were "the affirmation that capitalism is not necessary and that there exist other ways of living, political-economic alternatives to capitalism. Seattle represented that consciousness… 'Another world is possible'."

Moreover, the anti-capitalist movement itself could only take place because of real changes in society since the fall of the Berlin Wall. According to Negri, the "information revolution" led to a change in the nature of work, with "immaterial labour" coming to predominate. For the "new working classes and the movements that follow", labour "escapes capitalist measure", giving rise to a recognition by

that "I am productive outside of my relations with capital", something which no longer has "anything to do with capital as a physical structure in the hands of bosses".

The multitude, as Negri calls this new collectivity, simply has to assert itself through its cognitive labour power, which is itself already "characterised by autonomy, independence, and cooperative capacity". This is quite different, he claims, from the traditional left which "manages to imagine only a seizure of power, that is, putting itself in the place of the capitalists in order to manage the reality of economic development".

But he is never really clear about the multitude and how it is to assert its power, sometimes simply referring to the desire for "exodus" and the world being on the verge of something new. At best, he puts his faith in the myriad movements for "another globalisation" and celebrates their resistance. At worst, as his boosterism about the immaterial labour of the "information economy" implies, he appears to suggest that work today has a liberating potential, with "precarity that liberates and precarity that limits the horizons of life". However, as well as being somewhat incoherent conceptually, the notion of immaterial labour just does not fit the reality of work today.

Aside from this main theme, there are also some interesting reflections on Iraq and the "war on terror". While he maintains that the US-led invasion "constituted the definitive point of a project of a monarchical approach to global order", he also holds that, although "the Leninist conception of imperialism and of inter-capitalist contradictions was pertinent in his time, today it appears to be superannuated". Thus it may still be possible to talk about inter-capitalist contradictions, but these are "secondary in the construction of global power"—a notion which he calls "Empire".

However, here Negri simply repeats the rhetoric of neoliberal globalisation in claiming that a new global order is being constructed beyond the contradictions of inter-state and inter-capitalist conflict. And, as with the concept of the multitude, the notion of a "monarchical" project is ambiguous, allowing him to claim that the invasion of Iraq was an exceptional form of unilateralism, as opposed to the standard "police actions" in Afghanistan and previous wars which enjoyed greater support within Empire.

It would seem to be difficult to claim, as he does, that "within Empire the tendency is therefore toward the formation of continental and subcontinental potentates" (ie regional blocs of power) without some understanding of imperialism, but this is exactly his approach. Perhaps this conceptual confusion can explain his position on the European Union, which he contemplates becoming "the new democratic mediator within this new global constitution". Bizarrely, he even claims that the French "no" vote on the proposed EU constitution "had the nationalist socialist stamp of the left", as only a "united Europe can construct a space in which the proposition of a truly revolutionary project makes sense".

Similar problems come to the fore in his discussion of contemporary Iran, where he proclaims that "probably the only chance at freedom for the Iranian people is that of struggling, together, against the clerical regime and for globalisation"—but what he means by "globalisation" here is not at all clear.

There are some positive aspects to this collection, particularly Negri's often vivid and poetic descriptions of the broad range of social struggles that have erupted over the past decade. For example, he points out the "extreme importance, culturally unifying and politically militant, of the expressions of hip hop" in the movement in France during 2006, which were "characterised by a persistent rap that was anything but monotonous... Rap is the soundtrack of the revolt of the hybrid multitude".

However, in order to change the world you have to understand it as well. This collection reveals that Negri falls far short on this point.

"We can always shoot them later"
John Baxter

Ethan Pollock, **Stalin and the Soviet Science Wars** *(Princeton, 2009),* £17.95

The post-war period was a time of rapid reconstruction and modernisation in the Soviet Union, and science and technology were expected to play a huge part in the process. As such, the rewards and prestige for those working in Soviet science were particularly high. But the risks were great too. Whole academic disciplines could find themselves out of favour—academics might be arrested or killed if their ideas were deemed unpatriotic or "anti-Soviet".

Ethan Pollock has studied the Soviet archives to give an unprecedented insight into the post-war (1945-53) machinations of Joseph Stalin and the bureaucracy in six academic areas: philosophy, biology, physics, linguistics, physiology and political economy. In each area the party planned huge set-piece debates at which they hoped to demonstrate the superiority of Soviet ideas. Some of these areas have been extensively analysed in the past (biology, physics and physiology) and in these cases his work arguably does not add to the general picture we already have. However, in every case Pollock's painstaking work means that we now have a level of detail we have never had before, particularly on the personal role of Stalin.

Take, for example, the story of the decline of Soviet genetics and the rise of the pseudo-scientist Trofim Lysenko. This is a tale which has been told many times before, most often in an attempt to demonstrate how awful it is when politicians intervene in science. Lysenko was an agricultural scientist, who rejected the science of genetics and promoted his own theories, which included the inheritance of acquired characteristics. The Stalinist apparatchiks particularly liked Lysenko as he promised huge increases in crop yields (though these never actually materialised). Lysenko had already flourished in the 1930s, promoting his supposedly "proletarian" biology against the "bourgeois" science of genetics. In 1943 the leading Russian geneticist Nikolai Vavilov was sentenced to death and died in prison.

A huge conference on agricultural science was planned to take place in July 1948. Lysenko, his scientific supporters and his backers in the bureaucracy planned to use this conference to confirm the dominance of his ideas and to smash genetics. The conference would also serve to demonstrate the superiority of Soviet science to that in the bourgeois West. Beforehand Lysenko presented a draft of his proposed conference report to Stalin for comment. The archives show that Stalin was not convinced by all of Lysenko's claims and was not happy that Lysenko planned to use the stamp of approval of the Communist Party's central committee to establish his scientific validity. Stalin produced an extensive hand-written commentary on the draft of the speech. When Lysenko claimed that all science was class based and that all conflict in science was based on class conflict, Stalin wrote, "Ha ha! And what about mathematics? And Darwinism?"

Stalin removed whole sections which dismissed all science in bourgeois society and which claimed Stalin's *Anarchy or Socialism* was the correct guide for biologists to consider when thinking about species formation. Pollock, following other recent historians, argues that this shows that Stalin wanted to emphasise the "universal, scientific scope of Lysenko's claims".

So instead of emphasising the class nature of their "science", Lysenko and his supporters emphasised its practical utility and Russian pedigree, opposing this to the supposed abstractions of the Western influenced "Weismann-Morganism" (genetics) of their opponents. They claimed that Lysenko's theories were a direct continuation of the ideas of the highly influential Russian plant breeder Ivan Vladimirovich Michurin, who had died in the mid-1930s.

Many of Lysenko's opponents were not convinced that he had the full backing of the central committee and defended genetics vigorously. Towards the end of the conference Lysenko was able to trump his opponents: "The question is asked in one of the notes handed to me: 'What is the attitude of the central committee of the party to my report?' I answer: the central committee of the party examined my report and approved it."

According to the records, the conference rose to give a standing ovation and ended as, one by one, Lysenko's opponent recanted and promised to emancipate themselves from their "Weismann-Morganist views".

Despite Stalin's desire that Lysenko should be able to win on the merits of his science, in the end Lysenko's victory only came when he was able to claim unequivocal central committee support.

Stalin and the party intervened in the other subject areas with largely the same objective in mind: to demonstrate their ideological and practical superiority over the West. But in each area the story played out differently. For example, in the other five cases explored here the party was less inclined to predetermine the outcome. I do not have the space here to develop all the stories, but let us contrast the tale of Lysenko with those of physics and political economy.

After the "success" of the 1948 Agricultural Science Conference, plans were made for an All-Union Conference of the Physicists to overcome the ideological problems in Soviet physics. During the war divisions had grown between the physicists of the academies and those of the teaching universities. Broadly speaking, the academies tended to recruit the more talented and often older physicists, who became involved in highly funded and prestigious war-related research, not least the project to build an atomic bomb. The teaching universities tended to employ those left behind—often younger physicists more integrated into the party. This division helped to foster an ideological rift in physics, which the conference was supposed to resolve.

Taking their lead from the biologists, university physicists accused many of the academy physicists of kow-towing to bourgeois, idealist Western physics, in particular regarding their adoption of quantum mechanics and relativity. They attacked as anti-materialist the notion, proposed by the German physicist Werner Heisenberg, that it is not possible to know precisely both the momentum and position of sub-atomic particles. They pro-posed the elimination of these so-called "Machist" tendencies from Soviet physics. (Ernst Mach was a philosopher and physicist who had been criticised by Lenin in his *Materialism and Empiriocriticism*.) They attacked the often Jewish physicists of the academy for their alleged lack of patriotism and their "cosmopolitanism" (widespread official anti-Semitism at this time was dressed up as "anti-cosmopolitanism").

A series of detailed planning meetings were held to prepare for the conference, where many of the committee members assumed the supporters of quantum mechanics and relativity would be routed. But the date for the conference was constantly put back. The planning committee could not agree on the structure of the conference or what it could be expected to achieve. It became increasingly apparent that many of those around Stalin felt that the conference was not in their interest. The conference was eventually cancelled.

The exact reasons for the cancellation are not explicit in the records that Pollock has studied, but it is pretty apparent why the decision was made. Without quantum physics there could be no hope of a Soviet nuclear weapons project—something which the Stalinists were not prepared to contemplate. David Holloway, the historian of the Russian bomb project, has argued that Stalin and his henchman Lavrentiy Beria were perfectly aware, from sources in their spy network, that Western physics was not useless, idealistic nonsense. It had been used to build the American atomic bomb, after all. Stalin allegedly agreed to cancel the conference, saying, "Leave them in peace. We can always shoot them later."

Political economy was the subject of the last central committee sponsored scholarly discussion in Stalin's lifetime. The party needed Soviet political economists to demonstrate the superiority of the Soviet system over the capitalist West; as such they planned an official Soviet text-book on political economy. They hoped to mirror the success of the *History of the Communist Party of the Soviet Union: Short Course*, published in 1938, which had rewritten the history of the 1917 Revolution in order to maximise Stalin's role (and his closeness to Lenin) and minimise or eliminate the role of his opponents.

But rewriting history proved to be easier than rewriting political economy. The first plans for the book were made in 1937—there were endless drafts and re-drafts as Stalin and other leading apparatchiks criticised and rewrote sections. The economists were placed in an impossible position. They were expected to blindly praise all of Stalin's decisions and at the same time provide an objective scientific analysis of the Soviet economic system.

The tensions between science and propaganda made it impossible to produce a book which satisfied Stalin, not least because the changing needs of the system meant that what was important in one period could be denounced in the next. One draft of the book praised the role of Soviet planning, suggesting that it allowed the USSR to "surmount the Law of Value" and eliminate the anarchy of capitalist production methods. Stalin criticised the draft, saying, "This is all schoolyard nonsense, some sort of schoolyard bumbling!... The main task of planning is to ensure the independence of the socialist economy from capitalist encirclement."

Stalin went on to argue that planning allowed the country to invest in heavy industry for the country's defence, irrespective of its profitability. In private at least, there was little pretence of planning for socialism—it was very clear that planning was a tool to allow more effective competition with the West.

Pollock provides a fascinating and detailed account of the attempts to produce the textbook, including the debates over whether the law of value applied in the Soviet Union (Stalin insisted it did) and Stalin's insistence that Karl Marx was not a starting point for understanding the Soviet system. It took nine years to produce, in 1946, what was considered to be a final draft of *Political Economy: A Short Course*. But the book was still not good enough for Stalin. There were still a huge number of problems, including the fact that it did not do enough to stress the achievement of the Russian nation through the ages.

By 1951 yet another draft had been prepared, and this time it was circulated more widely. A discussion was planned to debate the merits of the book and how it could be improved. In this case the session was to be held in private, as the tensions over the interpretation of Soviet political economy were too sensitive to be made immediately public without suitable vetting. Over 250 economists and leading party members met in continuous session for over five weeks, with 110 speeches, but it didn't help—the problems were insurmountable, not least because it was hard to know what Stalin wanted to hear on a given subject. The book was eventually published in 1954, a year and a half after Stalin's death and 17 years after it had first been proposed.

Pollock has written a fascinating book. Its focus on the arguments in and around the sciences should not deflect from the fact that it throws a great deal of light on the nature of the Soviet Union at the height of the Cold War. The book is not without its problems. The author seems to shy away from theorising about the nature of the Soviet system or from making judgements and drawing conclusions about the interrelation of science and politics. There is much here that will come as no surprise to readers of this journal, and the private behaviour of Stalin only serves to reinforce the idea that the Soviet regime at this time had nothing in common with socialism or communism, but instead was a highly centralised state capitalist regime locked in competition with the West.

As Pollock makes clear, Stalin's interventions in the academic fields came at times when his attention might easily have been focused elsewhere. At the height of the Berlin crisis in 1948 he was actively engaged in the campaign to rid Soviet science of Mendelian genetics. In early 1950 he was busy shaping the new Sino-Soviet pact and planning the invasion of South Korea, yet he found time to write an extensive article on linguistics, to "orchestrate a coup" in physiology and to hold three extensive meetings to discuss the new book on political economy. For Stalin it is clear that these ideological battles were an important part of the Cold War.

Liberal apologists autopsied
John Newsinger

Richard Seymour, **The Liberal Defence of Murder** *(Verso, 2008),* £16.99

As I write this review, Gaza lies in ruins after the Israeli government's most recent exercise in collective punishment. This latest atrocity has excited massive opposition in Britain (not least the widespread student occupations). But the concern of the "liberal establishment" remains, quite incredibly, how to protect Israel from further Hamas attacks and so prevent the need for any more embarrassing Israeli reprisals. We have even seen Gordon

Brown offer British warships to help maintain the naval blockade of Gaza, but, we are assured, only in the interests of the Palestinians! Without any doubt, defending Zionism is going to become increasingly difficult.

At the same time, however, liberal apologists have been offered some relief. The election of Barack Obama as US president has undoubtedly bolstered the ideological standing of American imperialism. A veneer of liberalism will be painted over the US Empire as it attempts to recover from the disaster that was the Bush-Cheney presidency. Whatever Obama's rhetoric (overrated in my opinion anyway), the American state will continue to defend the interests of US imperialism by whatever means necessary.

For the liberal apologists of empire, Obama must surely be a welcome relief, however. Swallowing Bush-Cheney must have been an unpleasant experience, with at least some of them having to fight down a continual urge to throw up. It is one thing to ignore or cover up the use of torture, but Bush-Cheney actually required that their liberal apologists actively condone it. Thankfully for the apologists, those days are over, though there are still likely to be some embarrassing revelations, not least regarding the complicity of the New Labour government in general and David Miliband in particular. What is astonishing, of course, is how much these people were able to swallow while still continuing to identify themselves as liberals, as radicals, as part of the left.

All is made clear in Richard Seymour's excellent *The Liberal Defence of Murder*. Here he provides us with a relentless forensic account of the sophistries of the "pro-war left", of that "loose coalition of liberals, former radicals and ex-socialists" who have rallied to American imperialism in its hour of need. Immensely enjoyable though this is, even more important is his excavation of "the origins of these liberal apologists of empire", his careful tracking of "their development over the course of three centuries, on both sides of the Atlantic". As Seymour points out, the same John Locke who "devised the principles that would underpin the British polity and property relations…also formulated the principles justifying the British Empire". Locke, the intellectual fountainhead of British liberalism, not only defended colonial slavery, but also personally profited from it.

There have always been liberals, radicals and reformist socialists who have embraced empire as a progressive cause. They have condemned the abuses committed by other people's empires but extolled the virtues of their own. For these people the imperial project brought progress, good government and economic development to the colonies. Seymour draws together a remarkable amount of material that leaves these apologists naked in the storm.

In India, for example, in the period from 1876 to 1900, "the pinnacle of colonial good governance", famine deaths when averaged out probably totalled at least one million a year. This would constitute a crime of some enormity in the history of any other empire. It would absolutely discredit the regime that presided over such slaughter. But not in the history of Britain's liberal Empire. Indeed, Seymour could have brought the discussion more up to date with a consideration of the 1942 Bengal Famine. This horror took place while there was a Conservative-Labour coalition government in power in London and the Labour leader, Clement Attlee, was deputy prime minister. It is a huge embarrassment for liberal apologists and accordingly either disappears from the history books altogether or, at best, gets cursory treatment.

Among many other good things, Seymour also provides a very useful account of the development of Karl Marx's thinking on empire and imperialism, a discussion that he cuts too short for my money. He provides a history of liberal apologetics for US imperialism: the First World War saw an intrepid band of renegade American socialists embrace the slaughter on the Western Front and the repression of their former comrades.

Eugene Debs, the Socialist Party leader, was sentenced to ten years in prison for his opposition to the war—and he was not alone. Seymour identifies John Spargo, one of the leaders of the Socialist Party, as providing a sort of template for betrayal at this time. It is worth noticing that Debs had Spargo's measure as early as 1912. Seymour is also outstanding in his discussion of Bernard Henri Levy's apologies for the Contra counter-revolutionaries in Nicaragua and his account of the pro-war left's performance during the recent Balkan Wars is required reading. Altogether an outstanding book. My only criticism is that there are so many areas where you wish he had written more.

Pick of the quarter

The best thing to appear in recent issues of *New Left Review* is the article "Obama At Manassas", which was in issue 56 (March–April). In it Mike Davis gives an analysis of the outcome of the US presidential election. This includes a detailed breakdown of what the voting meant and strong warnings about the make-up of Barack Obama's new administration.[*]

Also of considerable interest is a long interview of Giovanni Arrighi by David Harvey, which appears in the same issue. In it Arrighi explains his own intellectual trajectory and his distinctive ideas on the origins and development of capitalism.

The best piece in the latest *Historical Materialism* (volume 17, number 1) is Henry Heller's article on the development of French capitalism during the three centuries before the 1789 Revolution. He provides a mass of empirical material to refute the claim, made by revisionist mainstream historians and by Marxists such as Ellen Meiksins Wood and George Cominel, that the bourgeoisie was too weak for it to have been a bourgeois revolution.

Recent issues of the *London Review of Books* have contained a lengthy two-part article on Italy by Perry Anderson. The first part, "An Entire Order Converted int[...] [...] very readable diatribe.[†]

The second part is much less satisfactory.[‡] It is scathing on the record of what it calls "The Invertebrate Left", from the old Italian Communist Party's helping hand to the Christian Democrats at the end of the Second World War through to the failure of its present day successor, the Democratic Party (previously the Democratic Left) to challenge prime minister Silvio Berlusconi.

But it attacks the left from a perspective that misses out the dynamics of the mass struggle. It endorses the notion that a struggle for socialism was not possible at the end of the Second World War ("an insurrection was not on the agenda"). It underestimates the extent of the struggles of the late 1960s and early 1970s. And it provides a very distorted view of the wave of struggles against the second Berlusconi government, claiming that this started "a year after" it took office as the result of an initiative from a group of intellectuals.

In fact, the struggle began within four months of the huge demonstrations at the Genoa G8 summit and in protest at the murder of Carlo Giuliani. The leading role in these protests was played by the radical left, including Rifondazione Comunista—which made its later

* www.newleftreview.org/?page=article&view=2769

† www.lrb.co.uk/v31/n04/ande01_.html
‡ www.lrb.co.uk/v31/n05/ande01_.html

economist Doug Henwood in New York. The audio from the talk is available online.[§]

Readers who want to take a break from economic debates can read a useful article on Richard Wright, the important black American writer of the 1930s, by Alan Wald in *Against the Current*'s January-February issue.[¶]

JC and *CH*

he repeats … … … … in Britain" won "workers away from their traditional allegiance to the left", even though Anthony Heath, Roger Jowell and John Curtice disproved this in their study, *How Britain Votes*, nearly a quarter of a century ago.[*]

New on the Marxists Internet Archive is Mike Kidron's mistaken, but illuminating, 1971 article "Memories of Development", which ruled out economic development in the Global South.[†]

There are a growing number of pieces by Marxist economists putting their own particular stances on the economic crisis. Robert Brenner spells out his ideas in a long interview with a Korean journalist, reprinted in the March-April issue of *Against the Current*.[‡] Most of his immediate conclusions are close to those expressed in this journal, although his starting point is rather different, with a theory of the "law of the tendency of the rate of profit to fall" rather different from that developed by Karl Marx.

Anwar Shaikh also presents an account of the crisis that is in many ways similar to ours in a talk he gave with the left wing

---

* For a resumé of their conclusions, see Alex Callinicos's "The 'New Middle Class' and Socialists" and Chris Harman's, "The Working Class After the Recession", available from www.isj.org.uk/?s=resources#classarticles
† www.marxists.org/archive/kidron/works/1971/03/memories.html
‡ www.solidarity-us.org/node/2071

§ http://nyusociology.org/blogs/radical/2008/12/08/the-deepening-economic-disaster
¶ www.solidarity-us.org/node/2031